To Mr. and Mrs. Edwin L. Kennedy

of New Vernon, New Jersey

That light
Burns bright
From afar.

CONTENTS

PREFACE

The first Part of this book is the most recent in origin, resulting as it did from an attack that appeared only yesterday on Henry James and those who read and write about him. The stature of the chief personal targets of that attack and of one of the journals that lent its pages to such abuse seemed to me to call for a reply. Although the journal in question was not receptive to my proposal that a reply be printed, I wrote one, anyway. It appears in a few (chiefly, the last few) pages of this Part. It is preceded by a review of the episodes of the battle thus violently reopened, a sampling of the evidence that others have been submitting for the greater part of the exactly one hundred years since Henry James first invited it by appearing in print. Voluminous though it be, my compilation is obviously only a fragment of the possible whole. In the arrangement of its materials by theme, my review roughly approximates

Mr. Philip Rahv's essay, "Attitudes Toward Henry James" (1943), at the same time as it extends those necessarily brief materials in both directions of time and magnifies (as well as duplicates) some of what Mr. Rahv brought together.* His essay can be found reprinted in Professor F. W. Dupee's *The Question of Henry James* (1945), which contains other substantial portions or the entirety of the dicta it anthologizes in a chronological arrangement. My materials thus are like, but considerably longer than, Mr. Rahv's, and unlike and considerably shorter than Mr. Dupee's; but they are in debt to both, not to speak of Mr. Simon Nowell-Smith's *The Legend of the Master* (1948). Particularly valuable are the bibliographies contained in this and Mr. Dupee's anthologies (Mr. Dupee in turn reprinting Mr. Lyon Richardson's of 1941). And of course more recently all scholars and critics of Henry James have been debtors of Professor Robert E. Spiller for the vast ingathering of his bibliographical chapter in *Eight American Authors* (1956). My own presentation I have tried to make impartial, caring not whether James is praised or dispraised (he occupying far fewer of my waking moments than his Vereker does those of the madly enchanted group in "The Figure in the Carpet") but whether enough of the facts bearing on his case are submitted for justice to be done. If I have not succeeded, it is not so much because, like Hamlet, I am indifferent honest as because I am indifferent thorough.

Just as Part Two, here and there, incorporates numerous judgments on Henry James that may be added to those systematically offered in Part One, so nothing in Part One is not useful to a reading of the second. Nevertheless, Part Two does constitute a whole by itself and has, I hope, a symmetry of its own. Its introductory chapter is a study of James's first novel in its first form; and its last, of a novel that James did not live to complete; and although (as well as because) the two novels are forty-five years and two poles apart, I hope that I have indicated at least one or more character-

---

* Professor Leon Edel has provided a valuable review and extension of the Rahv "Attitudes" in his Introduction to *Henry James: A Collection of Critical Essays*, New York, 1963.

istics that they share, not only with each other but with the most widely-acclaimed novel of James's maturity, interpreted at some length in the first half of the central chapter of this Part. Within this symmetry I have attempted yet another. Chapter III studies novels of an American, a European, and an English novelist in the light of the fiction that they (at least in part) may have influenced James to write; whereas the two modern American writers in Chapter V are studied, in turn, as students of James himself. The materials in the middle of the book (Chapter IV) also consist of two parts, each an examination of one fairly separate aspect of James's complex art. The first explores the lengths to which he would go on occasion to make himself understood. The second is an exposition of that art from still another point of view, its pervasive fabulousness.

Paull F. Baum, James B. Duke Professor Emeritus of English at Duke University, a kind and exacting man, watched over me as I took my first steps in James-land: under his direction I wrote those pieces (possibly as much as a fourth) of Part Two that have already appeared in *The Boston Public Library Quarterly, Modern Fiction Studies, The Philological Quarterly,* and *The University of Kansas City Review.* Although all of them have undergone thorough (at times, radical) revision, I am grateful to the editors of these periodicals for permission to make use of them again, in whatever form. To Professor Oscar Cargill I owe many more insights than those which the following pages make it possible for me to acknowledge. And there are considerable local debts. The Research Committee of Ohio University awarded to me a grant in 1962 that transformed the period of study necessary for a good part of the making of this book from a weariness of the flesh to an invitation to the soul. For a light on the endless road from lucubration to letterpress I am indebted to Mr. Mark McCloskey and Mrs. Carol Harvey of the Ohio University Press and to its editor-in-chief, Mr. Cecil Hemley. What good fortune for me that he is also a man of letters.

EDWARD STONE
Athens, Ohio

PART ONE:

THE BATTLE

Enter the 1960's, and Mr. Maxwell Geismar's book,[1] the new decade's first prominent summation by the prosecution in an endlessly arguable case. For the international court hearing that case has been in session even from before Henry James's first success in fiction, in 1878, when he caused talk on both sides of the Atlantic because of his subtlety, until the time of his death, in 1916, when he had become in legend a literary mandarin, making a profession of preciosity and obfuscation—all in all, a literary life span that, as E. P. Whipple described Hawthorne's Marble Faun, begins in mystery and ends in mist. Since then, too, for a half-century now, he has confronted us, like the new Russia—born almost the year he died —continually a puzzle and a major issue. Surely, with both, the abuse and adulation they have incurred over the years are indisputable evidence of the inescapability of the problem, whether political or artistic, which they pose.*

This last statement, because of the implication of its analogy, will merely add another instance to the many that Mr. Geismar cites of attempts to claim stature for Henry James's works by investing them with borrowed attributes. One can easily expose Mr. Geismar's inaccuracies and deplore the level of his charges without denying, of course, that James leaves much to be desired, whether as a man or as a writer. In fact, one can easily substitute real limitations for the "cluster" of alleged ones that Mr. Geismar has marshalled for the occasion. Indeed, whether or not it is truly "an instinctive act" for certain spirits in the "epoch of the Cold War, of McCarthyism" to cling to a man who symbolized "safety, propriety and gentlemanly behavior" or not, over the years Henry James has frequently been thought of in those terms. Has the association been a just one? If that pejorative trinity of qualities is a truth, is it a whole truth?

---

* At times, literally inescapable. For just as Ezra Pound tells us in a poem how Walt Whitman has at long last forced him to accept him, so James's most prominent attacker, recalling the time, after his attack, when he suffered a mental breakdown, confesses that "I was pursued especially with nightmares in which Henry James turned great luminous menacing eyes upon me. I was half aware, in connection with him, of the division within myself, and with all the bad conscience of a criminal I felt I had viewed him with something of Plato's 'hard little eye of detraction.' " (Van Wyck Brooks, *Days of the Phoenix*, New York, 1957, p. 187.) Unlike Pound, however, Brooks never made his peace with the enemy. (*Ibid.*, Chapter XII, "My Books.")

I.

A. THE MAN

Certainly Henry James was, from the first, what he himself called a far inferior artist, "the novelist of literary people." This "great and talkative man," [2] with his inveterate concern for the "fine measurements," lived with and in and for his art. He read all of and personally knew, a large number of his literary contemporaries who are now our literary history, and from the many letters and memoirs available we can assemble its pages: in this country, Henry Adams, Stephen Crane, Harold Frederic, Mary Wilkins Freeman, Hamlin Garland, William Dean Howells, Charles Eliot Norton, George Santayana, Edith Wharton, and Constance Fenimore Woolson, in England, George Du Maurier, George Eliot, Rudyard Kipling, R. L. Stevenson, and H. G. Wells; and on the continent, Balzac, Daudet, Dumas, Flaubert, Gautier, Maupassant, Mérimée, Sand, Stendhal, Turgenev, and Zola. His literary career extended from the

Civil War (he reviewed Whitman's *Drum Taps*) [3] to the First World War (when he admitted to having "trifled with the exordia" of D. H. Lawrence); [4] and it is probable that during the intervening half-century there was little literary activity that escaped his notice. Or few other artistic activities, for that matter. As readers of *The Tragic Muse* or of Allan Wade's *The Scenic Art* can readily attest, he had a passionate interest in the theatre; his *Roderick Hudson, Little Tour in France,* and biography of William Wetmore Story testify to his interest in sculpture; and *Italian Hours,* as well as "The Liar," *The Sense of the Past,* and *The Tragic Muse* (to which add his non-fiction) are eloquent proof of his familiarity with painting.

But this devotion to and absorption in the culture of his day was made possible only by a deafness to the many other voices of human endeavor, and of these there are too many uncomfortably important examples. Behind the contemporary civilization that made possible the arts so dear to him, as James was well aware, was "an immense and complicated machinery—the machinery of government, of police, . . . the professions, the trades." And for all that "Balzac moved easily and joyously" [5] among them, his avowed disciple did not. In fields of endeavor outside the arts, in fact, James had little interest. "What he saw he possessed; what he understood he criticized, but he never reckoned it to be any part of his business to sit in judgment on the deeds of men working in alien material for inartistic ends. . . ." [6] Unlike his younger contemporaries Shaw and Wells, he lived within the world of the arts and dedicated himself to the formal perfection of his own with an unremitting faithfulness. As his friend Ford Madox Ford recalled, "The Old Man knew consummately one form of life; to that he restricted himself." The middle and lower classes—characteristic source book of his favorite authors Balzac, Eliot, Maupassant, and Turgenev—he actually knew little about; and his attempts to incorporate people from these classes into stories like "Brooksmith," *In the Cage,* and *The Princess Casamassima* bear witness more to his imagination and sympathy than to his actual acquaintance with the materials he was using. Ford Madox Ford continues that James could talk "with extreme exactness and insight" of the poor farmers, but not of industrialism. Of the world of trade, he was admittedly ignorant." [7] "[M]y brother-in-law . . . has thirty 'business ideas' a day, while I shall never have had the thirtieth fraction of one in my whole life," the narrator of his "The Married Son" confesses; [8] and although in "The Jolly Corner" we are told that Spencer Brydon's return to America after a lifetime of expatriation coincides with a happy (and profitable) affinity for the facts of the new metropolitan architectural problems, we do not believe it: more convincing is the remark about White-Mason, a Brydon coeval in an equally late story ("Crapy Cornelia"), that to him "the angular facts of current finance were as harsh and metallic and bewildering as some stacked 'exhibit' of ugly patented inventions, things his medieval mind forbade his taking in." Most of these are honest admissions; when James attempted to characterize people from the business world in his novels (as his friend Howells was doing), he invariably failed.* Christopher Newman of *The American* has had to work for a living from boyhood on and has run the gamut of American trades by the time he has acquired wealth; yet he quite holds his own in repartee at the home of the aristocratic de Cintré family. Adam Verver of *The Golden Bowl* has a moral tone, Matthiessen finds, "far more like that of a benevolent Swedenborgian than it is like that of either John D. Rockefeller or Jay Gould." [9] And James's characterization of two aged businessmen in the unfinished *Ivory Tower* is, as Yvor Winters has noted, "never supported by exact knowledge." [10]

Looking back at the days (the 1880's) that his father-in-law's letters and papers opened to him, Van Wyck Brooks recently spoke of them as a "great age of isms . . . , the days when . . . Utopia seemed close at hand and benevolent motives governed every thinker. For that was the time not only of Tolstoy in Russia but of Edward Bellamy and Henry George at home." [11] Yet James's actual

---

* For an important dissenting opinion, see Edmund Wilson's (below).

familiarity with any of those isms was as lacking as his knowledge of industry or finance.*

"Writing in the time of Gladstone and Bernard Shaw, James seems hardly to have given a thought to the political destinies of men or to the practical consequences and bearings of personal conduct," [12] Beach notes; and Stuart P. Sherman refers to Captain Sholto of *The Princess Casamassima* as "almost unique among his characters in uttering a political thought." [13] Certainly one learns no more about the emphasized political enthusiasm of Lord Warburton in *The Portrait of a Lady* or of Nick Dormer in *The Tragic Muse* than one does of the deliberately concealed identity of the product manufactured in Woollett in *The Ambassadors;* and in other, less conspicuous, but significant contexts, the same lack of interest is manifested. A bomb-throwing incident in a little French town occasioned the frank admission from James that "I wondered, as I looked through [the newspapers], whether I was losing all my radicalism; and then I wondered whether, after all, I had any to lose"; [14] the ferrymen on the Grand Canal prompted a sarcastic remark on Nihilism ("a faith consistent happily with a good stroke of business"); [15] and the overthrow of papal supremacy in 1870 in one of the most momentous periods of Italian history evoked from James only an annoyed comment:

. . . something momentous had happened . . . to the elements of picture and colour and "style." . . . [T]en minutes after my [return to Rome] I found myself face to face with a newspaper stand. The impossibility in the other days of having anything . . . but the Osservatore Romano and the Voce della Verità used to seem . . . connected with the extraordinary leisure of thought and stillness of mind to which [Rome] admitted you. But now the slender piping of the Voice of Truth is stifled by the raucous note of eventide vendors of the Capitale, the Libertà and the Fanfulla; and Rome reading unexpurgated news is another Rome indeed. For

---

* But see Alma Louise Lowe (ed.), Henry James, *English Hours*, New York, 1960, xxv–xxvii.

every subscriber to the Libertà *there may well be an antique masker
and reveller less.*[16]

Corresponding to this unawareness of or aloofness from the
social history of his own day was James's even more grievous lack of
interest in the study of the mind itself. His notebooks, for example,
are as barren of references to ideas—philosophically speaking—as
they are full of suggestions gathered for their literary usefulness; and
his letters add little. Science, no longer slowly creeping on from
point to point, as in Tennyson's poem, but a force confronting his
fellow novelists with increasing frequency, is a topic James almost
never mentions. We do find him as a young reviewer approving the
speculation arising from Darwin's hypothesis;[17] and in his late
sixties, briefly opposing science and "the laboratory brain";[18] and he
has Hyacinth Robinson of *The Princess Casamassima* (1886) view
with apprehension certain possible effects on the Princess of her
unkind treatment at the hands of the aristocratic Casamassimas:
he fears "that the force of reaction and revenge might carry her far,
make her modern and democratic and heretical *à outrance*—lead
her to swear by Darwin and Spencer and all the scientific icono-
clasts as well as by the revolutionary spirit" *—an interesting and
early coupling of forces that had made for Karl Marx, as it
happens. But even these are truly rare occurrences: "He could let
Huxley and Gladstone, the combatant champions of Darwinism
and orthodox theology, enrich the pages of a single letter without
any reference to their respective beliefs," Bosanquet tells us.[19] The
sacred fount of the philosophers was a mystery which none of the
passionately curious observers in his novels ever explores; James's

---

* In his own person, James had already rejected Hippolyte Taine's scientific
theory about the origin of art (as explainable in terms of *race, moment, and
milieu* alone—that is, to be interpreted as one interprets an unknown in an
organic chemistry laboratory) in favor of Sainte-Beuve's more spiritual one:
"The truth for M. Taine lies stored up . . . in great lumps and blocks . . . ;
while for Sainte-Beuve it was a diffused and imponderable essence . . . and
we cannot but think his frank provisional empiricism more truly scientific
than M. Taine's premature philosophy." (Review of the Van Laun translation, *Atlantic Monthly*, XXIX [April, 1872], 469–472.)

review of T. W. Higginson's—God save the mark!—edition of
Epictetus apparently was his one nonfictional venture into the field
of philosophy.[20] Plato, Locke, Kant—there is no mention of these
names or of their thought in James's writings. Even with contemporary thinkers it was much the same. One is surprised to come
upon a brief reference to Auguste Comte, who had influenced a
James favorite, George Eliot, and whom James's friend Henry
Adams considered one of the seminal minds of the century; then
one notes that the judgment it passes is essentially an esthetic one:

> Balzac's "Comedie Humaine" is on the imaginative line very
> much what Comte's "Positive Philosophy" is on the scientific.
> These great enterprises are equally characteristic of the French pas-
> sion for symmetry, for making a system as neat as an epigram—of its
> intolerance of the indefinite, the unformulated.[21]

Moreover, if Henry James had ever heard about Henri Bergson from
so fervent an admirer and friend as James's own brother William,
there is no record of the fact.

> Henry was hardly more of a philosopher than he was a theo-
> logian, even though he was concerned, particularly in the cases of
> Isabel Archer and of Strether, with what Strether called "the illu-
> sion of freedom." But even though he continued to read his
> brother's works "with rapture," . . . he had scarcely the trace
> of a system. [He] was a spectator rather than either doer or
> thinker. . . .[22]

One discovers, from a brief allusion, that he had at least a hearsay
knowledge of Strauss and Renan in those disturbing times of the
New Criticism.[23] Yet he felt quite outside the Swedenborgian world
his father dwelt in, writing after the latter's death to William to
compliment him on his edition of their father's writings: the ex-
tracts were "beautiful and extraordinarily individual" and his
"whole system" was "intensely original and personal," but, he con-

fessed, "I can't enter into it (much) myself. . . . But I can enjoy greatly the spirit, the feeling. . . ." * As for Henry's professed interest in William's books, we may attribute it to his fraternal devotion, to the fact of William's philosophical adventures, rather than to the adventures themselves. As Ralph Barton Perry concludes, in reviewing their correspondence:

It is evident . . . that Henry let William do his philosophizing for him. There is no indication, even in these passages, of the ideas which the writer so greatly esteems—no exposition of them, still less a criticism. In Henry James's other correspondence there is no philosophy at all. . . . [H]is mind was quite naive on that side, and . . . his profession of pragmatism was an extension of that admiring pride with which he had from childhood viewed all of William's superior qualities. The relation was not symmetrical.[24]

The prospect of having to share William's company with that of the leading philosophers of the day seems only to have annoyed James during his first visit to the United States in twenty years.[25] In general, James's recorded attitude toward the thinkers of his day

---

* Letters of Henry James, I, pp. 111–112. In Notes of a Son and Brother, recalling his teens, James spoke fully of his consistent "detachment" from his father's passion for Swedenborg: "I freely confess that, so far from the taking any of it all 'straight' went, my lips rarely adventured. . . ." Also: "I feel almost ashamed of my incurious conduct," and began to feel aware "of something graceless . . . in the anything but heroic impunity of my inattention." (F. W. Dupee [ed.], Henry James: Autobiography, New York, 1956, pp. 331, 332–333.)

Similarly, in his commentary on the Brook Farm colonists, he confesses that he "envies" their "convictions and interests—the moral passion" (and then, somewhat surprisingly, states that there was in Transcendentalism "a certain noble credulity and faith in the perfectibility of man, which it would have been easier to find in Boston in the year 1840, than in London five-and-thirty years later"). (Hawthorne, Ch. IV.)

On the other hand, Professor Richard Chase thinks that Professor Quentin Anderson's argument, in the latter's The American Henry James, that The Ambassadors, The Wings of the Dove, and The Golden Bowl constitute "in their cumulative significance 'a divine novel' allegorically presenting James's version of his father's Swedenborgian theology is an important discovery." (The American Novel and Its Tradition, New York, 1957, p. 136.)

was one of immense separation and humility. "*Le prestige de son frère William, l'emulè de Bergson, il s'en disait heureux, approuvait que 'la gloire d'un aussi profond esprit' obnubilât 'la fragile figure d'un conteur d'historiettes,' "* [26] one of his painters recalled; and when asked to come to luncheon to meet Santayana, " 'Come!' Henry James cried, raising his hands to Heaven, 'I would walk across London with bare feet on the snow to meet George Santayana.' " [27] At their shrine James was frankly a distant, unquestioning worshipper. Balzac, he noted, "has an opinion on everything in heaven and on earth." [28] And James? Openly admitting his limitations, he wrote to his nephew in 1899: "Thank God . . . I've no opinions—not even on the Dreyfus case. I'm more and more only aware of things as a more or less mad panorama, phantasmagoria and dime museum." [29]

Although it is unfortunate that this utterly candid and intimate confession proved most injurious to his reputation, as we shall see, when it and others were exposed to public gaze after his death, it was not merely a rare outburst stemming from the weariness of middle age. Rather it was an attitude toward any kind of theoretical thinking (except concerning the theory of writing and the arts) that he took quite early and never departed from. In 1865, at the age of twenty-two, reporting with pleasurable irony the untruth of the common assertion that Louisa May Alcott's *Moods* dealt with the "doctrine of affinities," he writes that "we are inclined to think that our author has been somewhat maligned. Her book . . . is innocent of any doctrine whatever." It is significant that in his 1879 book on his early master, James found Hawthorne's diaries almost free from "convictions or theories of any kind" and that he spoke of them as "the exhibition of an unperplexed intellect"; and in an 1889 essay he spoke admiringly of Guy de Maupassant as giving "the impression of the active, independent observer who is ashamed of none of his faculties, describes what he sees, renders, with a rare reproduction of tone, what he hears, and is more anxious to see and to hear than to make sure, in advance, of propping up some particular theory of things." [30] Statements such as these convince us of the discernment of T. S. Eliot's ironic remark that James "had a mind so fine that no idea could violate it." *

B. THE ART

From limitations of his own person so severe, what art could result? Certainly not one that students of an age identified with "The Rise of Realism" could not be uneasy about. And their uneasiness would merely be a reflection of James's own, for he objected artistically not only to the R. L. Stevenson kind of "adventure" of the obvious romances of his day but also to the realistic kind of fiction that some of the most important writers of the day professed. Of particular interest in this regard are his various statements of literary position during the 1870's, when he was beginning to produce the first ambitious fiction of his own. Extricate them from their original, obscure contexts, put them on display, and you have both an indication of the direction that fiction would take and the terms

---

* "In Memory," *The Little Review*, August, 1918. (Reprinted in Edmund Wilson, *The Shock of Recognition*, New York, 1943.) Similarly, F. O. Matthiessen, while noting with surprise that James should have "felt the impenetrable mystery of whiteness" of *Arthur Gordon Pym* (whose final symbolic image figures prominently in the opening chapter of *The Golden Bowl*), also notes that James failed to catch "the horror of its unrelieved light" such as we also find in Melville's use of symbolic whiteness, and concludes that "in such a brief passage you can observe the greatly different treatment of symbols in the hands of Melville and of James. Whereas Melville's take his reader ever farther into the multitudinous seas of speculation, James's are more essentially those of a novelist, and are designed, like every other detail in his book, to illustrate character." (*American Renaissance*, New York, 1941, pp. 301–304.)

of the detraction and even abuse that both he and his admirers would experience for half a century after his death. To read his description of Rebecca Harding Davis's *Margaret Howth* as "dreary" [31] in its realism is not to be surprised; but to find him referring to one of the supreme achievements of fiction in the nineteenth century—Flaubert's *Madame Bovary*—as "dingy realism" [32] is almost to be shocked; yet only in the light of such contempt for the actual, the details of daily living observed close up, can one understand the otherwise cynical—and supercilious—sounding defense of his own kind of fiction. Questioned as to "where on earth" he had "found" such central figures for the stories in one of his collections, having it put to him that they were worthless unless he could find their counterparts in real life, "I was reduced to confessing I couldn't"; that he could claim only the great justification of "operative irony":

If the life about us . . . refuses warrant for these examples, then so much the worse for that life. . . . How can one consent to make a picture of the preponderant futilities and vulgarities of life without the impulse to exhibit as well from time to time, in its place, some fine examples of the reaction, the opposition or the escape? [33]

In so insisting, he was making the same point as he had made long years before when, in his review of Zola's *Nana*, he had questioned the current definition of *realism*, pointing out that the *real* need not be merely the *ugly* or the disgusting:

On what authority does [Zola] represent foulness rather than fairness as the sign that we are to know [nature] by? On the authority of his predilections alone. . . . Nothing tends more to compromise [reality] than to represent it as necessarily allied to the impure. . . . The real has not a shade more affinity with an unclean vessel than with a clean one. . . . [34]

The reaction from the vulgar and miserable aspects of life, the

escape from them into fiction, into romance, into the poetry of art
—this credo is enunciated again and again in James.* In his early
twenties he complimented Louisa May Alcott on the imaginative
truth of the characterizations in her *Moods*: "For, in the absence
of knowledge, our authoress has derived her figures . . . from the
depths of her moral consciousness. If they are on this account the
less real, they are also on this account the more unmistakably instinct with a certain beauty and grace." [35] He returns to the topic ten
years later in another piece of journeyman reviewing. This time we
are given Hippolyte Taine's appraisal of George Sand's novels.
James quotes approvingly Taine's judgment that if Sand's novels
"have not the solid realism of those of Balzac, their species is a
higher one," then goes on to quote from Taine himself:

> *Only, to relish them, you must put yourself at a certain point of
> view, interest yourself in the portrayal of a finer and better human-
> ity. That of Madame Sand's novels is two or three degrees superior
> to ours; the men have more talent and genius, the women more
> heart and devotion, than among ourselves; they all talk better and
> more eloquently than we; they are framed in a finer scenery, sur-
> rounded by landscapes and apartments that have been artistically
> arranged; it is an ideal world, and to keep up our illusion the writer
> tones some things down, suppresses others, and often, instead of
> painting an individual figure, sketches a general outline.*[36]

With how little alteration might this not pass for a contemporary

---

* Hear William Carlos Williams telling audiences at the University of Washington: "You do not get the novel until you begin to hide the cruel nudity;
until you get clothes. . . . Can you possibly imagine Henry James without
an accompaniment of corsets and Prince Alberts with striped trousers? I
can't. . . . [T]he novel is most at home and occupies its greatest esteem
when nothing but the clothes remain, which, when stripped off, reveal—a
cipher. The iconoclast at work. It should, as did Henry James's work, usher
in the classic age, the poem." (*The Autobiography of William Carlos Williams*, New York, 1951, p. 369.)
   And in the preface to his *Types of Prose Fiction* (New York, 1964),
George P. Elliott speaks of "the subtle, manicured shire of Jamesianism. . . ."

appraisal of Henry James's own kind of art! * As a reviewer only
five years later would observe:

Notwithstanding his realism, Mr. James does not dare to make
these commonplace types truly real. They talk and act after a superior fashion. . . . [M]ost, and perhaps all of his novels . . . [seem]
to have been worked up with extraordinary care and skill—and come
to nothing. We do not care two straws for the fate of the actors; we
are merely concerned with the evident cleverness of the author.[37]

When Stuart P. Sherman spoke of the invaluable "aesthetic sense"
of the man, he identified both the grounds of James's uniqueness
and of the general reading public's distaste for him:

To it he owes the splendid distinction that when half the novelists
of Europe, carried off their feet by the naturalistic drift of the age,
began to go a-slumming in the muck and mire of civilization, to ex-
plore man's simian relationship, . . . to prove the ineluctability of
flesh and fate and instinct and environment—he, with aristocratic
contempt of them . . . withdrew farther and farther from them,
drew proudly out of the drift of the age, and set his imagination the
task of presenting the fairest specimens of humanity in a choice
sifted society tremendously disciplined by its own ideals but generally liberated from all other compelling forces.

Sherman speaks of

an endless process of observation, comparison, discrimination, selection, and appreciation—a process which for this highly civilized,
highly sensitized young spirit, became all-absorbing, and made of
him a fastidious connoisseur of experience, an artistic celibate to
whose finer sense promiscuous mixing in the gross welter of the
world was wearisome.[38]

---

* The "finer scenery, surrounded by landscapes and apartments that have been
artistically arranged" finds its echo in Thomas Beer's cruel capsule: "This
master of groomed circumstance had found out a sunny garden where poisons
blew as perfumes too heavy for a refined sense and crimes were shadows, not
clouds, that swept across his shaved and watered turf." (*Stephen Crane*, New
York, 1923, p. 173.)

"Aesthetic sense." . . . "A choice sifted society" . . . "fastidious connoisseur" . . . "the finely assorted." . . . As opposed to the fiction of "naturalistic drift" in whose time (if not wake) James wrote most of his fiction. . . . To what lengths he himself would go in his art to tone down and suppress the "gross welter of the world" we know well. Of *The Golden Bowl,* one of the three novels of his last period of productivity, a friend (Edith Wharton) asked James the embarrassing question: "What was your idea in suspending the four principal characters . . . in the void? What sort of life did they lead when they were not watching each other, and fencing with each other? Why have you stripped them of all the *human fringes* we necessarily trail after us through life?" *

Of intellectuality, however, he would never strip them, even sympathetic critics complained. John Macy noted that the symbolism of James's titles "is intellectual, not poetic. They are like his metaphors, . . . analogies contrived by the mind, not the immediately sensational metaphors of the poet's vision. . . ." [39] In almost the same terms this is the verdict of André Gide. James's characters, he points out, "never live except in relation to each other. . . . [T]hey are desperately mundane. . . . [T]here is nothing of the divine in them, and . . . intelligence always explains what makes them act or vibrate." [40] And Stuart P. Sherman speaks of the society of *The Awkward Age* as one which "lives for 'the finer things,' . . . and so perfectly masters its instincts . . ."; and of the atmosphere of *The Golden Bowl* as "ineffably rich, still, golden, and, in the long run, stifling. . . ." [41]

For it is possible, as other responsible critics have also demonstrated, to concede James successful on his own terms and yet to find him wanting. The sanctity of the "experience of the individual

* * *

* *A Backward Glance,* p. 191. Matthiessen: "In concentrating so excessively on the personal relations of his quadrangle, [James] imagined for the Prince no further role than that of arranging his rare books and balloting once at his club. His height of 'sacrifice' is giving up on one occasion the opportunity of dressing for dinner." (*Henry James: The Major Phase,* p. 96.)

And E. M. Forster comments that James's characters "can land in Europe and look at works of art and at each other, but that is all." (*Aspects of the Novel,* New York, 1927, p. 230.)

practitioner" was one thing; the limitation of that experience might be entirely another. Thus, Edmund Wilson insists, one serious fault with *The Tragic Muse* is that James "does not get inside Miriam Rooth; and if he fails even to try to do so, it is because, in his experience of the world and his insight into human beings, he is inferior to a man like Tolstoy." [42] To Leon Edel,

Henry James was a solipsist: he believed . . . that each human consciousness carries its own "reality," and that this is what is captured and preserved in art. For the rest, he would try to compensate —by technical ingenuity, skill of form, grandeur of style—for elements which he lacked in his own experience. This was at times to make him the historian of the rarefied and the particular. . . .*

Was it just this artistry of the beautiful that distinguishes James's fiction? Perhaps no one has insisted so more emphatically than Stuart P. Sherman:

The thing which he as the high priest solemnly ministering before the high altar implored some one to observe and to declare and to explain is that he adored beauty and absolutely nothing else in the world. . . . What he offers us, as he repeatedly suggests, is a thousandfold better than life; it is an escape from life. It is an escape from the undesigned into the designed, from chaos into order, from the undiscriminated into the finely assorted. . . .[43]

Similarly, to another James partisan (and friend), Joseph Conrad, "Mr. James is the historian of fine consciences. . . . And, indeed, ugliness has but little place in this world of his creation." † And in

---

* *Henry James: The Conquest of London, 1870–1881,* Philadelphia and New York, 1962, pp. 168–169. (Professor Edel goes on: "but it would also enable him to render the delicate and the exquisite in the human mind.")
  "The material seems missing: it is the *im*material we find in his books. . . . His passion was his craft, but out of craft one cannot conjure up *the* grand passion." (Wright Morris, *The Territory Ahead,* New York, 1963, p. 95.)
† Joseph Conrad, "Henry James: An Appreciation (1905)," in *Notes on Life and Letters,* New York, 1924, pp. 17–18. (Reprinted in Leon Edel [ed.], *Henry James: A Collection of Essays,* New York, 1963.) But Conrad goes on to say about ugliness and James's fiction that "it is there, it surrounds the scene, it presses close upon it," as does Edmund Wilson (below).

our own time Glenway Wescott has recalled that as an adolescent
he and a sister read books by Henry James and wept. To them the
romance of his books was an antidote against "obviousness . . .
and the common. . . ."

So wherever we were or went, . . . we were in a sort of junk-shop,
as in The Golden Bowl, whose every bowl might have been an exalted grail, if not a shameful pot; whose every second-hand handker-
chief might have been the one the hunted Isolde waved, . . . or
the one Salome dried the Lord's sweat with on the way to the cruci-
fixion . . . —history and . . . symbolism, soft and mixed, in place
of the facts.[44]

To return to Sherman: "To the religious consciousness all things
are ultimately holy or unholy; to the moral consciousness, . . .
good or evil; to the scientific . . . true or not true; to Henry James
all things are ultimately beautiful or ugly." [45] If this was indeed the
principle of his art, was it a principle that Americans could consent
to? Perhaps the critical reaction to his fellow-expatriate (and admirer) Ezra Pound can shed some light. In a way, the two men
presented the same problems to Americans, for in a way their problems are complementary. Both are charged with distortion of reality, Pound for the intrusion of the ugly and James for its suppression
in his art. Thus, concerning Pound, William Barrett asked: "How
far is it possible, in a lyric poem, for technical embellishments to
transform vicious and ugly matter into beautiful poetry?" [46] And
Karl Shapiro: "Through his experience with vicious and ugly ideas,
what poetic insights into our world has this poet given us?" [47] Both
questions must elicit negative answers. Yet to both James and
Pound question and answer alike would be beside the point. For
when questioned as to his "view of life and literature," he wrote to
Wells that he had none "other than that our form of the latter in
especial is admirable exactly by its range and variety, its plasticity
and liberality, its fairly living on the sincere and shifting experience
of the individual practitioner." [48] For this reason the reader of
James's scenario of The Ambassadors for Harper's Magazine was

right in rejecting it on the grounds that the "moral" of the story was merely that Chad was better off in the captivity of Paris than in the freedom of Woollett and would have been even righter had he read the completed novel: here, James wrote much later in his Preface, he had been at his best because of his setting himself to and succeeding in mastering a challenging *technical* problem, namely that of a central observer who was "a man of imagination." * For James the problem, then, would appear to have been always an *artistic*, rather than a moral one. Thus his style, particularly the later one to which even some admiring readers object † has been considered an indispensable adjunct to this purpose. Speaking of his "long and intricate" sentences, Sherman writes that "they usually imprison and precisely render some intricate and rewarding beauty of a moment of consciousness luxuriously full." [49] (Two classic examples are those in *The Portrait of a Lady* cited by James himself in his Preface. Here the "intricate and rewarding beauty of a moment of consciousness luxuriously full" is James's sole intention, he would have us believe.) Thus, too, Owen Wister, the novelist, explains James's "bewildering style" to a fellow novelist as follows:

[H]e is attempting the impossible with it—a certain very particular form of the impossible, namely to produce upon the reader, as a painting produces upon the gazer, a number of superimposed, simultaneous impressions. He would like to put several sentences on top of each other so that you could read them all at once instead of getting them consecutively as the mechanical nature of his medium compels. [50]

* See F. O. Matthiessen and Kenneth B. Murdock (eds.), *The Notebooks of Henry James*, New York, 1947, p. 372. As they point out, in this reader's report there was "no indication that Strether, whose central consciousness marks James's final perfection of his method, even figures in the novel." (*Ibid.*)

† "That style of his in those later books! I began to hate it. Not layers of extra subtleness—just evasion from the task of knowing exactly what to say. Always the fancied fastidiousness of sensibility. Bright and sharp as he had been in the earlier books, the fact was that James had got vulgar—like a woman who was always calling attention to her fastidiousness." (Morley Callaghan, *That Summer in Paris*, New York, 1963, Ch. 27.)

This analogy between James's art and the art of painting is, it happens, one that he insisted on in his widely read "Art of Fiction" (1884). In this he claimed for both arts an immunity from morality. What do you mean, he asked, by "your morality and your moral purpose"? A novel is, after all, a picture, and how can a picture be either moral or unmoral?

If what James was doing was following in the footsteps of Poe (though not only of Poe, of course), in his insistence on fidelity, not to morality, but to the "sincere and shifting experience" of his individual powers of observation, he was on a path of art little traveled in this or any other country.* For the approach to that shore is guarded by its own triple-toothed Cerberus, whose inevitably exacted due is the drugged sop of morality. "The Heresy of the Didactic"? The history of fiction in the nineteenth century is the history of morality in literature, as the prefaces to so many of its novels attest. Hawthorne effectively illustrates the force of this requirement as much by his compliance with it in the preface to *The House of the Seven Gables* as by his brief mockery of it there: "Most writers lay very great stress upon some definite moral purpose, at which they profess to aim their works. Not to be deficient in this particular, [I have] provided [myself] with a moral. . . . In good faith, however, [I am] not sufficiently imaginative to flatter [myself] with the slightest hope of this kind."

On the other hand, no less inveterate a student and analytical a reader of Henry James than Edmund Wilson has insisted that James was fundamentally nothing less than a moralist. Chiding Van Wyck Brooks's reference to "the constant abrogation of James's moral judgment" in his later works, Mr. Wilson retorts that "on the contrary, James, in his later works, is just as much concerned with moral problems"; now more than ever he is concerned with the conflict of interest "between people who enjoy themselves without inhibitions . . . and people who are curbed

---

* For his awareness of the fact that "the reduction of all experience to the "aesthetic level" was "a hazardous adventure," see Sherman, *On Contemporary Literature*, pp. 238ff.

by scruples of aesthetic taste as well as of morality from following all their impulses . . . —between the worldly, the selfish, the 'splendid,' and the dutiful, the sensitive, the humble":

> This humility, this moral rectitude takes on in Henry James the aspect of a moral beauty which he opposes, as it were, to the worldly kind; both kinds of beauty attract him, he understands the points of view of the devotees of both, but it is one of his deepest convictions that you cannot have both at the same time. . . . So, in The Golden Bowl, the brilliant figures of Charlotte and the Prince are contrasted with the unselfishness and the comparative dreariness of Maggie Verver and her father. Almost all Henry James's later novels, in one way or another, illustrate this theme. Surely in this . . . tendency to oppose the idea of a good conscience to the idea of doing what one likes . . . there is evidently a Puritan survival. . . .[51]

Professor F. R. Leavis goes even further in this direction (when he is not also retreating from it). With him "intense moral preoccupation" is requisite for great fiction, and he categorically includes Henry James among the four "great English novelists"; yet in assenting to Yvor Winters's opinions concerning the strain of the moralist in James he points out the difficulty inherent in placing James in this tradition:

> Mr. Winters discusses him as a product of the New England ethos in its last phase, when a habit of moral strenuousness remained after dogmatic Puritanism had evaporated and the vestigial moral code was evaporating too. This throws a good deal of light on the elusiveness that attends James's peculiar ethical sensibility. We have, characteristically, in reading him, a sense that important choices are in question and that our finest discrimination is being challenged, while at the same time we can't easily produce for discussion any issues that have moral substance to correspond.[52]

Although this is not a position often taken about James's works, it is typical of the merits that these have begun to disclose in the pendulum swing of reader reaction during the past twenty years now referred to as the James Revival. There has arisen, Philip Rahv has noticed, an attitude of adoration of James's art as damaging to his cause as disparagement of it: "For it seems that the long-standing prejudice against him has now given way to an uncritical adulation which, in a different way, is perhaps quite as retarding to a sound appraisal of his achievement." In particular, he reminds us that "As against the sundry moralizers and nationalists who belittle James, there are the cultists who go to the other extreme in presenting him as a kind of culture-hero, an ideal master whose perfection is equaled by his moral insight and staunch allegiance to 'tradition.' " [53]

For all that he is far from a cultist, Professor Randall Stewart has recently gone to greater lengths in looking upon Henry James as a religious teacher than we would have expected before the Revival. He cites the Pritchett article "Two Great American Puritans," noting with interest that the two are Henry James and T. S. Eliot, then goes on to class James with Hawthorne and Melville as moralists: they are "counter-romantics" because they "recognize Original Sin, because they show the conflict of good and evil, because they show man's struggle toward redemption, because they dramatize the necessary role of suffering in the purification of the self." Stewart concludes with the observation that "It is an interesting sidelight on the moral temper of our time that [these] three writers . . . are regarded today . . . as the greatest American writers of the nineteenth century." [54] To Allen Tate, James is a greater novelist than either Flaubert or Stendahl.[55] Austin Warren asks us to grant to James—for all that he lacks "ideas"—a place beside Proust, Dostoyevsky, and Mann.[56] And Grattan also thinks of James in terms of Proust, in regard to James's "pursuit of the ultimate implications and overtones of each and every situation in his stories," *

---

* "He had emerged as an impassioned geometer—or . . . some vast arachnid of art, pouncing upon the tiny air-blown particle and wrapping it round and round." (Van Wyck Brooks, *The Pilgrimage of Henry James*, p. 130.)

or James Joyce, toward whom Grattan sees James as moving in his
"insistent development, to the point of fearing that he had over-
treated them, of each individual moment"; [57] yet Yvor Winters
warns that "It is only a step, in the matter of style, from *The
Golden Bowl* to Dorothy Richardson and Proust, from them to the
iridescent trifling of Mrs. Woolf, and from her to the latest
Joyce. . . ." [58] There is, therefore, more than coincidence in the
fact that both *The Ambassadors* and *A La Recherche du Temps
Perdu* were originally rejected on the grounds that their subject
matter was too attenuated for popular taste; and that Joyce's con-
flicting replies to the question of reader application required for an
understanding of *Ulysses* (at one time, very little, he said; at another, a lifetime) put the modern reader in mind of the subtitle
of Nietzsche's own *Also Sprach Zarathustra:* "A Book for All
and None."

Witness, too, the debate among critics in recent years about a
new modernity, a strength in James's fiction rooted in sociological
or even anthropological implications. Clifton Fadiman tells us that
"Faust . . . is Western Man, . . . the hero of experience," and
that James's John Marcher in "The Beast in the Jungle" stands for
no less than "un-Faust, for man the coward, not the hero, of experience." [59] According to Allen Tate's reading, in "The Beast in
the Jungle" "we have the embodiment of the great contemporary subject: the isolation and the frustration of personality. . . ." [60] To David Kerner the story is "a parable. . . . The
Law illustrated is: 'It is not good for man to live alone.' . . . By
isolating ingrownness, James wishes to terrify the reader out of
wasting his humanity." [61] Following Tate, Robert Rogers sees in
"the John Marchers, Spencer Brydons, and Lambert Strethers . . .
incarnations of the passive, powerless Futile Man—the antithesis
of Prometheus," and places "the Jamesian anti-heroes" in the
company of "Shakespeare's Hamlet, Dostoyevsky's Underground
Man, and Kafka's Gregor Samsa." [62] Edmund Wilson's "The Am-
biguities of Henry James," linking "The Turn of the Screw" with

Freudian symbolism, is an essay that has been widely circulated.* And Dr. Frederic Wertham's psychiatric headnote to the reprinting of James's "Beast in the Jungle" in an anthology of "Fiction Il- luminating Neuroses of Our Time" also contributed to the tend- ency to see James's fictional situations according to present-day interpretations of human conduct. Back in 1927, Demarest of Con- rad Aiken's *Blue Voyage* had asked, "Why is it that I seem always, in trying to say simple things, to embroil myself in complications" and to end by producing "not so much a unitary work of art as a melancholy *cauchemar* of ghosts and voices, a phantasmagoric world . . . perceptible only in terms of the prolix and fragmen- tary"; only to answer himself that "I have deliberately aimed at this effect, in the belief that the old unities and simplicities will no longer serve . . . if one is trying to translate, in any form of literary art, the consciousness of modern man." So, now Dr. Wertham re- minds us, in recent years James's fiction

has been more and more read, especially by prose writers who have come to demand of themselves the fusion of form and content that our complex age had achieved till then mostly in poetry. James's effort "really to see and really to represent" is best expended on character like himself, situations unhappily similar to his own. This is particularly true of "The Beast in the Jungle," the story of a man who is almost the archetype of the neurotic.[63]

* In a James Thurber drollery various people at a cocktail party are discussing Eliot's play of the same name. One named Charles Endless, who "is forever repeating the critical judgment of his psychiatrist, Dr. Karl Wix," is holding forth with this thesis: " 'There is no such thing as the power of conscious selection in the creative writer. . . . I should say that the psychic inspiration of "The Cocktail Party" was the consequence of something Eliot had done, whereas "The Turn of the Screw"—or "The Innocents," if you prefer to call it that—is clear proof of Henry James's conscious unawareness of something he had *not* done. . . . Observe the size of the symbols these two writers have been impelled to select from the stockpile of literary devices and prop- erties: the holy cross and the dark tower.' " But his auditor is " 'not interested in what Dr. Wix thinks was the matter with Henry James.' " (James Thurber, "*What* Cocktail Party?" *The New Yorker*, XXVI [April 1, 1950]. Re- printed in *Thurber Country*, New York, 1953.)

In opposition to which there is Matthiessen with his reminder that unlike later writers, James

> had naturally not felt the impact of more recent anthropology. He sought for his universals in the well-lighted drawing rooms of his time. When he groped his way back to "the sense of the past," it was only . . . for the sake of a contrast with later social manners. He was not to become aware of the obsessive presence of all times, of the repetition of primitive patterns in civilized life, as Eliot tried to express it through his anthropological symbol of "the waste land." [64]

But when one has said this, one has said far from all, there being so many rooms in the house of fiction. And, in any event, to say it is in no way to account for the extremes of critical expression that James's fiction has evoked almost from the start. How, indeed, to account for them?

C. THE REPUTATION

> In Heaven there'll be no algebra,
> No learning dates or names,
> But only playing golden harps
> And reading Henry James.

From the start—indeed, many years before the rarefaction of atmosphere that alienated so many readers became characteristic of his art—his countrymen and Henry James were not at home with each other: we can now read the private history of his first unsuccessful attempt to conform to the requirements of the *New York Tribune* subscribers' taste, to write "the poorest I can." [65] But what needs no scholarly exhumation is the harm he did to native complacency by one of the few truly popular successes he ever had, "Daisy Miller" (1878). Reject it though the alert *Lippincott's* editorial reader might as "a slur on American womanhood," when it eventually appeared in the English *Cornhill*, American readers of the late 1870's were not likely to overlook observations so "amused and aloof" as it (and other early James stories) contained—not even when, as Professor Edel also points out, he aimed his arrows with equal accuracy at English society:

In his strictly "international" stories he is a chiding critic of American egalitarianism and "newspaperism"; he describes the spittoons carefully arranged—as in parade formation—in the Capitol rotunda and the noisy aspect of American hotels, where the children roller-skate in the corridors or lie fast asleep late in the evening in the big lobby armchairs, wholly unparented. On the subject of maternal laxity, the glorification of the child in America, he is as eloquent as any child-psychologist of to-day.[66]

As early as 1881 a reviewer was complaining that James (like his own Winterbourne of *Daisy Miller*, in effect) had lived too long abroad:

The view of New York City [in Washington Square] is more like that of a foreigner who has lived a good portion of his life in America than that of a person American-born. . . . An exact analogy to this curious fact in Mr. James's novels may be seen in the kindred touch on the canvases of our young painters who have studios in Europe.[67]

This charge was to pursue James throughout his career. As Austin Warren put the case in 1943, "The general view of him, until fifteen years ago, simply scaled him down to a caricature of his

'humanism,'—namely, snobbery and aestheticism and Anglophilism, though equal evidence can be collected for his disapproval of
'high society,' for his Americanism and his moralism." [68]

During the present century, of course, we may assume that
James's reputation rested, to begin with (and still rests, even if
much less), on the facts of his personality, for he was known personally by many people, particularly literary, whose published
opinions helped to detract from or add to the unrelated fact of his
vast literary production.[69] It was possible, for example, to be extremely fond of the author as a man. The aged T. S. Perry who
pleaded for literary justice to his departed friend, insisting on
James's inveterate kindness was, of course, a lifelong friend; but
Ezra Pound recorded that James "had this curious power of founding affection in those who had scarcely seen him and even in many
who had not, but who knew him at second hand." [70] Stephen
Crane defended him vigorously for the same reason: " 'I agree with
you that Mr. James has ridiculous traits and lately I have seen him
make a holy show of himself in a situation that . . . would have
been simple to an ordinary man. But it seems impossible to dislike
him. He is so kind to everybody. . . .' " [71] And Professor William
Lyon Phelps (whose personal reputation was as impeccable during
the 1920's as Stephen Crane's was scandalous) wrote that he had
found James "an affectionate, lovable man," that one could not talk
with him without being "tremendously impressed both by his
genius and by the winsome lovableness of his character and disposition. He had a beautiful nature, as unspoiled as a child's." [72]

As frequently, however, the recollections were given to detraction, often unwilling and even unconscious. Ellen Glasgow, meeting James as a young author meets a master, in England in 1914,
conceded that "he was a great artist; and . . . no doubt . . . at
heart . . . he was a simple man," but his manner and way of life
went against her manifestly democratic grain:

Whenever we happened to meet him he was, invariably, imposing,
urbane, and delightful; but . . . we saw him only in crowds, and

we were always pushed on and swept away by gathering streams of people, before he had found the exact right beginning, middle, and end of the involved sentences he was laboring to utter. He was, I felt, a kindly soul, but, even in those too brief meetings . . . I felt also that there was a hollow ring somewhere. In looking back, I recall that I had seen him only in the houses of my wealthiest or my most important acquaintances. He had, I suspected, little use for the lowly; and when one industriously sifted his moral problems, there was little left but the smooth sands of decorum. . . . Placed beside Hardy or Conrad, Henry James would have appeared, in spite of his size and his dignity, slightly foppish in manner. Some years later, when his letters were published, I searched in vain for an intimate note addressed either to the obscure in station or to the impecunious in circumstances.[73]

Nor was this unflattering (and posthumously published) recollection greatly at variance with the reaction to James in the last ten years of his life, the years of his celebrity. Compare with it this portrait by an English journalist in 1905:

It is scarcely too much to affirm that "our Mr. James," as "The Society of American Women" loves to call him, is par excellence the foremost literary lion of each successive London season. His peers, George Meredith and Thomas Hardy, are domesticated countrymen, seldom to be seen at town functions, while Mr. Swinburne, also famous, and a bachelor, is a recluse and out of the running. Then among the younger men, which include J. M. Barrie, Kipling, Hewlett and others, the family life plays a prominent part, and they are all somewhat disposed to take society by the way. Mr. James, on the other hand, renders Caesar his full ceremonious due. In the springtime, as well as the early winter, he journeys up from Rye, establishes himself in Chambers or at the Athenaeum Club, and in a dignified, but none the less thoroughgoing fashion, enters upon a social campaign. Each day of his stay in town he has at least a dozen agreeable invitations to choose from, and even hostesses like Mrs. Humphrey Ward, Lucas Melet and the Duchess of Sutherland, struggle frankly to secure his presence at their parties.* Nor is it a difficult matter to follow Mr. James's movements during these semi-annual sojourns. So sought after is he that any man or woman who has entertained or been entertained by him is safe to let the fact leak out in conversation for months to come.[74]

Just how "sought after" he had become by 1905 might seem hard to believe to someone who happened to read only certain pages of the Lubbock edition of his letters in 1920, which inevitably provoked attack in this country. There, open to the eye, were at least two letters that proved almost ruinous to James's reputation. One contained a brilliantly merciless description of his art by his own brother which seems to have achieved wide circulation in the 1920's. Even a friend of the late master, William Lyon Phelps, quotes it, commenting that "The spectacle of a professional metaphysician on his knees to a novelist, begging him to write intelligently, has a humour all its own"; † and, as we shall see, a few years later Van Wyck Brooks would quote it to document his own thesis about James. The other letter contained James's own unfortunate expression of pleasure at his social acceptance in London one winter. For this last may be said to have spread far and wide in this country the equally unfortunate public image of "the Henry James who speaks of dining out a hundred and seven times in a winter, who is to be 'imaged' in the ritual garments,—the silk topper, the morning coat, the fawn-colored waistcoat, the gloves folded in hand. . . ." [75] As Ernest Boyd angrily pointed out, "Had his friends been cautious enough to withhold his correspondence, we might still be arguing about the significance of his method and the

---

* Compare Harold Frederic's version of a few years earlier, as reported by Thomas Beer: " 'Henry James is an effeminate old donkey who lives with a herd of other donkeys around him and insists on being treated as if he were the Pope. He has licked the dust from the floor of every third-rate hostess in England. . . .' " (Stephen Crane, pp. 151–152.)

† Howells, James, etc., New York, 1924, p. 150. The humour is doubled when we come to the disclosure that William James seems to have read every story of the hundreds that O. Henry wrote. (F. L. Pattee, Sidelights on American Literature, New York, 1922, p. 10.)

beauties of his style. But only eyes beglamored by excessive reverence can be deceived by this paraphernalia of words, behind which a timid, frustrated *déraciné* sheltered his poverty of ideas and experience." * Unfortunate, indeed, for that image crowded out one of the Henry James who was a lifelong votary of the "sullen art," as Dylan Thomas would term the literary life—who would counsel a struggling young writer in 1905: " 'My young friend, . . . there is one thing that, if you really intend to follow the course [authorship] you indicate, I cannot too emphatically insist on. There is one word—let me impress upon you—which you must inscribe upon your banner, and that,' he added after an impressive pause, 'that word is *Loneliness*.' " [76]

Doubtless the *Notebooks*, published in 1947, have since helped to right the wrongs done to James by the 1920 edition of his letters. Yet even they, displaying as they do James's inveterate hoarding of anecdotes and oddments of London gossip for future use in his fiction, apparently also rendered him vulnerable to invidious censure, at least from such readers as did not take the trouble to discover how he transformed every hint into a product unrecognizably different. Only a few years after the appearance of the *Notebooks*, James Thurber created one such reader in the form of a successful writer with the appropriate (and Jamesian) name of George Lockhorn, who, drunk and argumentative, does James the various disservices of identifying him as "the greatest master of them all" (yet misquoting him) and of insisting that " 'Henry James had the soul of an eavesdropper. . . . Everything he got, he got from what he overheard somebody say. No visual sense, and if you haven't got visual sense, what have you got?' " [77]

James the dandy, the lionized literary man, the sought-after bachelor of London and country-house society, with scarcely a trace of or appeal to the transatlantic society from which he sprang. . . . By 1905 he had become so much a part of England that the announce-

---

* *Literary Blasphemies*, New York, 1927, p. 225. Certainly not only such eyes failed to notice for half a century that all American editions of James's own favorite work *The Ambassadors* had printed two chapters in reversed order.

ment of his trip to the United States came to his English friends "as a surprise, not to say shock":

For years they had heard the distinguished American author out-line and project visits to his native land, but as a quarter of a cen-tury slipped by without any effort at fulfilling these threats, their skepticism was natural. He seemed, like Punch and Westminster Abbey, to have become an integral part of the national life, while all his early Yankee affiliations were forgotten. Even Great Britain, which assimilates foreigners with such ease, has found few strangers fit so snugly into her environment, until it almost seemed as though a special niche in the old world had been made and warmed in advance for the gentleman from Boston. And, truth to tell, with such ardor did England take him to her bosom, that to-day there is a decided dash of jealousy in the curiosity she expresses about the success of this present American visit.[78]

Around this time, too, he appeared in a volume of "imitations" of novelists of whom all were English except Henry James and "Mr. Dooley," beside which engaging and dialectic Chicago Irishman the James of *The Sacred Fount* (which was being imitated) must have seemed more English than the twenty other Englishmen se-lected for the occasion.[79]

As it turned out, this lifelong expatriation was most unfortunate to his posthumous reputation in this country. Doubtless his widely commented-upon naturalization as a British subject only months before his death in 1916 took on dramatic proportions in an Amer-ica still committed officially to detachment and neutrality, and thus heroic-seeming enough to occasion some self-reproach in his native land. But hardly for much longer than the twenty months that intervened before American entry into the war.* For it was actually this event that marked a turning point in America's own

---

* Even if a quarter of a century later the American writer Katherine Anne Porter remarked: "Of late, when America has somewhat reluctantly decided to claim Henry James as its own, in spite of his having renounced so serious an obligation as his citizenship. . . ." ("The Days Before," *Kenyon Review,* V [Summer, 1943], 481.)

reputation, with a contingent one upon Henry James's. To have lived the final forty years of his life in England during an era when America stood for all that was uncongenial to the artistic spirit and, more important, when it was still struggling for political and economic recognition by the haughty nations overseas *—this was, if not an act toward which America could feel kind, at least not one for which it could reprobate him. For if Paris was, as the quip had it, the place where good Americans went when they died (like Jane Rimmle of " 'Europe' "), from the very first Europe had also been the place where many of their creative spirits had gone when they were most alive—it being, in fact, the only place that—they claimed or demonstrated—could *give* them *life*:

Irving had escaped. . . . Twenty-one years he spent in Europe. Cooper . . . also escaped to the Continent where he resided for seven years. . . . Aside from Whittier and Thoreau and Whitman, every one of our major writers went abroad for long periods, escaping at the earliest possible moment. . . . Even one as redolent of America as Mark Twain was no exception. After his "arrival" with "The Innocents Abroad" in 1869, he spent one third of his remaining life in foreign lands.[80]

And the reviewer of *Washington Square* (1881), cited earlier, in referring to "our young painters who have studios in Europe" was calling attention to a trend even then long established.† But by the 1920's this country felt a pride in its importance which it knew it had demonstrated to the world's satisfaction: as probably more than one critic has pointed out, when the Swedish Academy awarded the Nobel Prize to Sinclair Lewis in 1930, it was not so

---

* Americans, James wrote in 1879, "are conscious of being the youngest of the great nations, of not being of the European family, of being placed on the circumference of the circle of civilisation rather than at the centre. . . . The sense of this relativity . . . replaces that quiet and comfortable sense of the absolute, as regards its own position in the world, which reigns supreme in the British and in the Gallic genius." (*Hawthorne*, Ch. VI.)

† See Van Wyck Brooks, *The Dream of Arcadia: American Writers and Artists in Italy 1760–1915*, New York, 1958.

much because of the distinction of his work as by way of recogniz-
ing the fact that the United States was now a major nation.* Thus,
to the critics of the 1920's, James's act of expatriation was one that
they could condescendingly consider that of a renegade, a deserter.
Now a curious inconsistency reveals itself again and again in
James's treatment at their hands. We have it, in the reminiscences
of one of the most influential of them. These very 1920's "were 'an
age of islands,' Van Wyck Brooks recalled, when 'almost everyone
seemed to be looking for an island,' when thousands of Americans
fled to Majorca, Capri, the West Indies and scores sailed away for
the South Seas"; and "Anywhere, anywhere out of the world, out
of the dull American world, was a general cry among those who
had returned from the war and who wished never to go back to the
Tilbury Towns of their childhood, the Winesburgs, the Spoon
Rivers or the Gopher Prairies." Precisely how general this cry was
we learn more than three decades after the author of those recollections had written *The Pilgrimage of Henry James* (1925), with
its theme of James and Deracination. Now, sparing himself least of
all, Van Wyck Brooks admitted that "I was to realize, looking
back, that I had been quarrelling with myself" in so doing: "For,
like many of my friends, I too had been enchanted with Europe,
and I had vaguely hoped to continue to live there." [81] But by 1957
time had woven a magic circle of immunity thrice around Brooks's
original charges.

Actually, Brooks had drawn his line in the dirt as far back as
1915, with his charge of artificiality in the native speech of America.
At that time he had posited that whereas in England there is only
one language (for literary is also spoken English there "and expresses the flesh and blood of an evolving race"), in this country
the literary style is still that of the eighteenth century: "But at
what cost! At the cost of expressing a popular life which bubbles
with energy. . . ." [82] A good deal of this nationalism carried over
into *The Pilgrimage of Henry James*. James, he quoted, " 'yearned

* With its own language, too, as H. L. Mencken's *The American Language*
had declared in 1919.

after the fulness of European life which he could not join again, and had to satisfy his impulse of asceticism in the impassioned formalism of an art without context.' " By divorcing himself from his homeland culture, James had performed upon himself the mutilating act of deracination. He eventually had to descend to populating his fiction with characters that his own brother had maintained were " 'wholly out of impalpable materials, air, and the prismatic interferences of light, ingeniously focussed by mirrors upon empty space.' " [83]

Although the *Pilgrimage* was a book-length, methodical exposition, its influence was probably far less than that of a fairly brief subsequent foray into detraction of James's achievement. This was the chapter "Henry James" in *New England: Indian Summer* (1940), the second volume of his Makers and Finders series. By then Brooks had become famous for his *Flowering of New England*, and now its sequel returned to the 1925 charges.* Giving them the added merit of diminution and of lessened animus, he brought them out again, nonetheless, for the inspection of a now large audience: James had an incurable and artistically fatal addiction to Europe's charm, to exalting manners above morals, and thus had invalidated his valuable American birthright.

All through the 1920's the charge would be levelled at him. In 1928, Professor Vernon L. Parrington declared Henry James's American citizenship forfeit: "The work of Henry James I choose to exclude from the classification of [realism], for despite the accident of birth James was culturally European and belongs to the history of English literature rather than to American." [84] Two years later appeared a not much longer, but much more trenchant, Parrington indictment of an apparent lack in James. As the editor of this posthumous volume pointed out, Parrington tended to equate American literature with American thought, and looked for the

---

* These volumes, written in a charming style, sold hugely. The *Flowering* was reprinted forty times in the fifteen months after its publication in 1936, and *New England: Indian Summer*, at least fourteen times in the month of its publication. (Also see Bernard De Voto, *The Literary Fallacy*, Boston, 1944, pp. 27–28, 45–46.)

imprint of economic forces not only on political, sociological, and religious institutions but on literature as well (a tendency that would grow with the incoming decade, to James's misfortune). Accordingly, this agrarian-minded scholar regretted James's cosmopolitan affinity, "for the flavor of the fruit comes from the soil and sunshine of its native fields." How like Whistler, who also "sought other lands," and "how unlike he is to Sherwood Anderson, an authentic product of the American Consciousness!" Like Brooks in 1925 and Boyd in 1927, so now Parrington too found James a "*déraciné*" in 1930.[85]

But from the beginning of the decade on, it was the fact of his residence abroad that made Henry James so favorite a Judy for the influential Punch of Baltimore, Henry L. Mencken, and his powerful dark-green literary weapon of the 1920's, the *American Mercury*. No matter that years before Mencken had introduced to America the best of the foreign writers (Shaw and Nietzsche, among others); no matter that Mencken himself found America a ludicrous assemblage of boobs and that he consented to live in it only because it provided him with all the entertainment of a zoo: still, it was along the hair-sights of Americanism that Mencken lined up the famous deserter, and his bullets went out toward the target year after year. One of the "evils of the situation" of The National Letters in 1920, he wrote, is "the tendency of the beginning literatus . . . to desert the republic forthwith, and thereafter view it from afar, and as an actual foreigner." (This is the language of the *Scribner's* reviewer of 1881, barely changed after forty years.) "More solid and various cultures lure him; he finds himself uncomfortable at home. Sometimes, as in the case of Henry James, he becomes a downright expatriate, and a more or less active agent of anti-American feeling. . . ." Later in the volume Mencken returns to the theme: among the "lesser men," he says, "we have Henry James a deserter made by despair; one so depressed by the tacky company at the American first table that he preferred to sit at the second table of the English." And in the following volume of his widely selling *Prejudices*, he repeats the charge: "Henry James,

Ezra Pound, Harold Stearns and the *émigrés* of Greenwich Village issued their successive calls to the corn-fed intelligentsia to flee the shambles, escape to fairer lands. . . ." *

Rare indeed were the opinions that dissented from this verdict, and they are amply worth the examination. It is interesting to note that one comes from the decade preceding the 1920's, and the other from that following them; so that one seems rendered before the patriotic heat engendered by the war and the other by a change of domestic circumstances in which the charge had lost its sting. Back in 1913 John Macy waved aside the charge of expatriation, saying that

The world is small nowadays, and since Mr. James does not deal with rooted people, but with persons, whatever their nationality, who . . . travel freely, he carries his country under his hat; and he can study it just as well in London as in Florence, in Rome as in Chicago. His expatriation is really less significant than Washington Irving's long sojourn abroad.[86]

And in 1934 Edmund Wilson also re-examined the charge. James did not "uproot" himself from his native land simply to live in England, he insisted: actually he had travelled so much between America and England and Europe, when not between New York and New England, and from such an early age, that "he had never any real roots anywhere." Not only this, but his essential sympathy was, notwithstanding, always with America:

James . . . is an American who . . . finally chooses to live in England; and he is imbued to a certain extent with the European point of view. The monuments of feudal and ancient Europe, the duchesses and princes and princesses who seem to carry on the feudal tradition, are still capable of making modern life look to him dull,

---

* *Prejudices: Second Series*, New York, 1920, pp. 50–51, 97; *Prejudices: Third Series*, New York, 1922, p. 12. In the *Fourth Series* (1924) he finds James "as thoroughly American as Jay Gould, P. T. Barnum, or Jim Fisk." (See "The American Novel.") For subsequent volleys at James in the series, see the indexes of the individual volumes.

*undistinguished and tame. But the American in the long run al-
ways insistently asserts himself.*

Literally, always. James could sneer at the "petty miseries" of
Flaubert's Emma Bovary, but if he doesn't sneer at those of an
equally "little bourgeoise" like his own early Daisy Miller, it is
simply because "Daisy is an American girl," Wilson points out:
and the "great popularity of her story was certainly due to her
creator's having somehow conveyed the impression that her spirit
went marching on." As for the Midmores and Ralph Pendrel of
The Sense of the Past—the last story that Henry James worked on
in this life—: "Is it the English ghosts or is it the American himself who is a dream? . . . [W]hich is real—America or Europe? It
was . . . the American who was real." Then, by way of summation, "Yes, in spite of the popular assumption founded on his expatriation, it is America which gets the better of it in Henry James.
In his shy circumlocutory way," in short, "he was genuinely democratic." [87]

Now closely related to, if not inextricable from, the factor of
expatriation in the shaping of James's reputation is the factor of
taste. And to explain taste is to explain something "so mystical and
well nigh ineffable" that one may, with Ishmael, "almost despair of
putting it in a comprehensible form." But some guidelines have
already been laid down.

A valuable one, and possibly the earliest, is Van Wyck Brooks's
of 1915. In " 'Highbrow' and 'Lowbrow' " he spoke of "two main
currents in the American mind running side by side but rarely
mingling":

on the one hand, the transcendental current, originating in the piety
of the Puritans, becoming a philosophy in Jonathan Edwards, passing through Emerson, producing the fastidious refinement and
aloofness of the chief American writers, and resulting in the final
unreality of most contemporary American culture; and on the other
hand the current of catchpenny opportunism, originating in the
practical shifts of Puritan life, becoming a philosophy in Franklin,

passing through the American humorists, and resulting in the atmosphere of our contemporary business life.[88]

Now in the 1900's and 1910's, these currents found voice in the classical-humanist critics and in the romantic-radical critics, as one of them deplored who eventually had spoken for both:

The leaders of one party sulk like Achilles, in the universities; the leaders of the other party rail, like Thersites, in the newspapers. "Academics!" cry the journalists. "Barbarians!" cry the professors. The antagonism is acute, and the consequences of this division are a tendency toward sterility in the Party of Culture, and a tendency toward ignorance and rawness in the Party of Nature.[89]

Some years later, Philip Rahv annotated this division in *Image and Idea*. First, he points out that our literature "suffers from the ills of a split personality" of "Paleface and Redskin":

At his highest level the pale-face moves in an exquisite moral atmosphere; at his lowest he is genteel, snobbish, and pedantic. In giving expression to the vitality and to the aspirations of the people, the red-skin is at his best; but at his worst he is a vulgar anti-intellectual, combining aggression with conformity and reverting to the crudest forms of frontier psychology.[90]

Now it is curious how this antipathy emerges as criticism of the Paleface when the Redskin speaks out in his own person.* Mr. Rahv's instance of the spontaneous antipathy between James (his typical Paleface) and Whitman (his typical Redskin) is familiar to all. To it one might add instructive collateral examples from well-known practitioners of the theory of human conduct as motivated by "the ineluctability of flesh and fate and instinct and environment" that Sherman speaks of. We have heard of Mencken's

---

* For a book-length exposition of the thesis that "in the American writer of genius the ability to function has been retained—with the exception of James —by depreciating the intelligence" see Wright Morris, *The Territory Ahead.*

stiletto thrust about James needing a "whiff of the Chicago stock-yards." In a well-circulated piece, his "Puritanism as a Literary Force," he identified Howells and James as having "both quickly showed that timorousness and reticence which are the distinguishing marks of the Puritan." * Then, when his *American Mercury* began, its first issue (1924)—on whose first page Carl Van Doren wrote Henry James's obituary—contained an article by a contributor named Ernest Boyd who was identified at the back of the issue as none other than "the well-known Irish critic, author of 'the Irish Literary Renaissance.' " Several years later this truculent man,† an expatriate himself ("He came to America in 1914 and is now living in New York") would have at James again and at much greater length. Now, in "Aesthete: Model 1924," he reviewed the lamentable progress of the artistic mind in America during the recent past. In the years leading up to the Great War, the budding aesthete "went to the cemetery to contemplate the graves of William and Henry James, and noted in himself the incipient thrill of Harvard pride and acquired New Englandism"; and although "these gentle pursuits did not mean so much to him at first as the more red-blooded diversions of week-ends in Boston," from the moment of his conversion to Aestheticism (a change induced in part by Harvard professors revealing "American literature to him as a pale and obedient provincial cousin"), "while the stadium shook with the hoarse shouts of the rabble at football games he might be observed going off with a companion to indulge in the subtle delights of intellectual conversation." [91] Thus does Boyd equate *aesthete* with *effete*.

But more serious, as the years passed, was the effect on James's reputation of the practicing Redskinism of important writers of

---

* A *Book of Prefaces*, New York, 1917, p. 218. Ezra Pound objected to this blanket accusation in a letter to Mencken dated November 28, 1917. "James was, I admit, touched with a sort of Puritanism but . . . he HAS written the MOST obscene book of our time, puritan or no puritan." (D. D. Paige [ed.], *The Letters of Ezra Pound*, New York, 1950, p. 125. Pound does not identify the novel.)

† Notice the titles of two of his books: *Appreciations and Depreciations* and *Literary Blasphemies*.

fiction in America. Consider Ernest Hemingway. It is true that he insists that the "good writers" are Henry James, Stephen Crane, and Mark Twain, but this is an obscure passage in *The Green Hills of Africa* (1935), itself one of Hemingway's least familiar books, and in any event, it is merely a point of departure for his extended lecture on Twain as the great source of modern American literature. In Hemingway's even more out-of-the-way, burlesque novel *The Torrents of Spring* (1926), there is a touching anecdote about Henry James receiving the Order of Merit on his deathbed; but it is told by a waitress in Brown's Beanery, Petoskey, Michigan, in a something less than respectful context, prefaced as it is by Scripps O'Neill's silly reverie:

Henry James, Henry James. That chap who had gone away from his own land to live in England among Englishmen. Why had he done it? For what had he left America? Weren't his roots here? His brother William. Boston. Pragmatism. Harvard University. Old John Harvard with silver buckles on his shoes. Charley Brickley. Eddie Mahan. Where were they now?

and followed by the surly comment of the drummer reading the *Detroit News:* " 'What was the matter with James? . . . Wasn't America good enough for him?' " *

Certainly *The Sun Also Rises,* because of its perennial popularity, continues to publish to modern readers the calumny that James's own contemporaries so freely recorded. For what could an author claiming, as we have seen James do, the justification of "operative irony" (for his stories of the literary life) expect at the hands of the garrulous Redskins Jake Barnes and Bill Gorton as they fish and drink in the mountains?

---

* Yet the *Torrents* also pokes fun at H. L. Mencken, to whom the book is dedicated (in part); and the other popular writers of the 1920's such as Fitzgerald and Dos Passos are not so much satirized as given walk-on parts in a vast comic pageant of literary America. It is quite possible, then, that Hemingway here (as in *The Sun Also Rises*) is expressing a kind of admiration for Henry James, but in a devious way.

"*Aren't you going to show a little irony and pity?*"
I thumbed my nose.
"*That's not irony.*"
As I went down-stairs I heard Bill singing, "Irony and Pity. . . .
Oh, Give them Irony and give them Pity. Oh, give them
Irony. . . .*"
"*What's all this irony and pity?*"
"*What? Don't you know about Irony and Pity? . . . They're mad
about it in New York. It's just like the Fratellinis used to be.*"

What wonder that in the next breath, the fire is directed at the
great Ironist? From mention of *impotence* and *accident*, Bill goes
on to:

"*Never mention that. . . . That's the sort of thing that can't be
spoken of. That's what you ought to work up into a mystery. Like
Henry's bicycle. . . .*"
"*It wasn't a bicycle,*" I said. "*He was riding horseback.*"
"*I heard it was a tricycle.*"

That Bill lamely concludes this serio-comic banter with his breathlessly brief (as well as unenthusiastic) tribute that "I think he's
a good writer, too," can hardly matter at this point as far as James's
reputation is concerned.*

Thus easily, incidentally, does expatriation, in James's case, fuse
with the even more damning connotations of mutilation. Glenway
Wescott gives us this quasi-free association from his youth: "Henry
James; expatriation and castration." [92] And still another novelist
(and critic) reads into the central issue of *The Ambassadors*—the
decisions that Strether must make—the voyeurism and impotence
of its own author:

---

* The derisive discussion above is about James's much commented-upon con-
cealment-revelation of a disability he incurred early in the Civil War (the
"horrid even if . . . obscure hurt" of *Notes of a Son and Brother*, Ch. IX)
that kept him from military service. By 1924 this would elicit Mencken's remark that he (along with Mark Twain, Walt Whitman, and William Dean
Howells) was a "draft dodger." (See "The American Novel" in *Prejudices:
Fourth Series*.)

. . . *Strether's choice of impotence is a willed, a moral act, and
. . . his very voyeurism is insight and "vision." . . . But Strether
is . . . his own author: the Henry James who began with "pedestrian gaping" along Broadway, and remained always the big-eyed
child, imagining "the probable taste of the bright compound wistfully watched in the confectioner's window, unattainable, impossible. . . ."* [93]

Then, there is Faulkner. Even if we permit him the obviously
flippant (and possibly not even sober) retort to a journalist's question about Henry James ("the nicest old lady I ever met")*: its
implicit rejection is of a kind with Faulkner's own impatient par-
rying of the intellectual questions asked of him about his own art
(as reported in *Faulkner in the University*), not to mention the
careless English he is known to have spoken in the company of
friends.

Is it any coincidence that by and large these men and other de-
tractors of James were men of the outdoors,† so that Rahv's facetious
distinction may be taken at a literal level? For all that—as Carvel
Collins's recent collection of early Faulkner pieces [94] reveals—the
early Faulkner imitated Verlaine and that he spoke in religious
terms at Stockholm, the writer of "Spotted Horses" and *Old Man*
had a basic affinity for fishing and hunting (and, for a while, barn-
storming in airplanes). And was there not as much truth as jest in
Mark Twain's confession in 1890 to "an Unidentified Person" that

*as the most valuable capital, or culture, or education usable in the
building of novels is personal experience I ought to be well
equipped for that trade. I surely have the equipment, a wide culture
and all of it real, none of it artificial, for I don't know anything
about books.* [95]

* Of a kind with this is Mark Twain's suggestion that Henry James be re-named
"Henrietta Maria." (Thomas Beer, *Stephen Crane*, p. 105.)
† Even as late as 1930, Ernest Hemingway could explain to Josephine Herbst
that " 'My writing is nothing. My boxing is everything.' " (Morley Callaghan,
That Summer in Paris, Ch. 28.)

And although that other celebrated Redskin, Stephen Crane, did not belittle Henry James (they respected each other greatly, as is well known), Crane too took—if he did not actually feign—this stance toward all that Henry James stood for in his reactions to inquiries about his literary origins or taste. He hadn't read "Dostoywhat'shisname" and didn't "know much about Irish authors" such as Mallarmé.[96] Notice, too, Crane's condescending reference to the Pullman passengers from the east passing through the west in the opening lines of "The Blue Hotel."

Whether vulgar or not, these are the voices of the "anti-intellectual, combining aggression with conformity and reverting to the crudest forms of frontier psychology." They are the arrows shot at the paleface "at his highest level," where he "moves in an exquisite moral atmosphere" beyond their ken or even their toleration. In an earlier day they were shot at James's own great master, Hawthorne, as he tells it in the fable about Owen Warland in "The Artist of the Beautiful" * or elsewhere.

Personality—its facts or its myth; foppishness and reputation for snobbery; purported Anglophilism and actual expatriation; the simple matter of taste. . . . Yet even these do not account for all of the extreme reactions to Henry James from the time of his death until yesterday. At least one other faction must be considered (if it can be separated from the others at all): that is the factor of politics and economics. For as the 1920's became the 1930's—that period of depression and turmoil both here and abroad—the rising tides of doctrine and action washed around James's reputation as well as around national boundaries, and made it (as well as others') the darling or the demon of feud and schism.

Edmund Wilson has provided a useful division of literary critics into two kinds. One, the non-historical, he defines as arriving at his judgments either "under the aspect of eternity" (T. S. Eliot, for

---

* Oscar Cargill, in fact, thinks that Owen's situation suggests that of James's Roderick Hudson in Northampton. (*The Novels of Henry James*, New York, 1961, p. 33.)

example) or through a kind of connoisseurship (Saintsbury). The other, the historical, group, deriving from Vico and coming up through Herder and Taine to Marx and Engels, interprets literature as a product of geography, economics, politics, and the like.[97] It was no wonder that in troubled times such as The Great War gave rise to, Henry James came under the cross fire of literary judgments stemming from these frequently irreconcilable points of view. H. G. Wells practically admitted this in that sublime inverted compliment of his letter to James, wherein he confessed that "writing that stuff [Boon] about you was the first escape I had from the obsession of this war," that "there was no other antagonist [i.e., someone believing that "literature like painting is an end" in itself] possible than yourself." [98]

Of a small number of critics who, for whatever reason, admired James's work because of its excellence (whatever its failures) in what it attempted (whatever its limitations), one of the earliest and most influential was Stuart P. Sherman, whose continued eulogy of James has been cited above. And Sherman was for long a New Humanist, a group with attitudes roughly corresponding to those of the non-historical critics. Then there was the Henry James Issue (August, 1918) of the *Little Review* with its two appreciations by T. S. Eliot; and although review and contributor were then quite limited in reputation, the growth of Eliot's importance as a poet and critic was rapid. By 1930, in fact, we find the Communist Vernon F. Calverton noticing that Irving Babbitt (another New Humanist) and Eliot (a former pupil of Babbitt's) had become "the mixed inspirations of our college-boys"; * and what emphasis Eliot gave to his own position by his proclaimed affiliation with royalty, Catholicism, and classicism gave added weight, eventually, and heightened

---

* "Humanism: Literary Fascism," *The New Masses*, V (April, 1930), 9–10. Quoted in Daniel Aaron, *Writers on the Left*, New York, 1961. Aaron also writes, "During the [early 1930's] Eliot's lofty pronouncements began to be taken seriously, as Malcolm Cowley wrote [in *Exile's Return*], by dozens of young men who followed his example 'and called themselves royalists, Catholics and classicists.' "

significance to his 1918 dictum about the fortunate imperviousness of Henry James's mind to ideas.*

For to the literary critics who sympathized with the various groups of the Left during the surge toward Russian socialism in the years of the Thirties, that very tribute of Eliot's stated exactly their quintessential objection to Henry James. To them, the writer's part in the ideal society was doctrinally utilitarian, and if to enlist his pen in the cause of class warfare—even by producing mere propaganda—was only fitting and proper, then to turn his pen to the use of mere art—even if of sheer magic—was to be frivolous and irresponsible. Was not the first such objection, H. G. Wells's in *Boon* (1915), raised by a Socialist who wrote to James that to him (Wells) literature "is a means, it has a use. . . . I had rather be called a journalist than an artist. . . ."? [99] But the party-line attacks were characteristically American. Of these possibly the earliest was by Waldo Frank. Anticipating Parrington's association by some fourteen years, Frank coupled James with Whistler. Their "ivory tower," he said, resulted from "lack of strength to venture forth and not be overwhelmed . . . ;" and their form of art was the extreme one of "those who gained an almost unbelievable purity of expression by the very violence of their self-isolation. . . ." †

Now Edmund Wilson has pointed out that the "insistence that the man of letters should play a political role, the disparagement of works of art in comparison with political action, were . . . originally no part of Marxism. They only became associated with it

---

* Pound's endorsement, in the same issue of the *Little Review*, would have been equally influential had he not gone beyond royalism to fascism, or had his reputation as a literary critic ever approached his pupil's.

† *The Seven Arts*, I (November, 1916), 73. Quoted in Aaron, *Writers on the Left.* Alfred Kazin notes that back in 1886 H. H. Boyesen in his "The American Novelist and his Public" had ridiculed the "boarding school" standard of the novel-reading public and attacked James (with Howells) for not writing about American politics. (*On Native Grounds*, New York, 1942, p. 26.)

Yet Wright Morris praises James for not succumbing to such pressures: "Caught between the past and the future, immersed to the eyes in the destructive element, he remained true to his genius—one on whom nothing, no, *nothing*, was lost." (*The Territory Ahead*, p. 112.)

later." * Still, it was just this requirement of commitment, of engagement, of affiliation with the causes of political freedom, economic reform, or whatever, as the index of a writer's worth that loomed larger and larger as the hopefully acute paralysis of the financial structure of the country began to settle down to a chronic disability. Indeed, the Thirties were a decade not very favorable to politically disengaged writers, whether quick or dead. The current writers, of course, felt the change at once. F. Scott Fitzgerald underwent an involuntary retirement (in terms of his vogue in the Twenties). Another un-idea'ed romantic of the Angry Decade of domestic depression and international political overthrow now beginning, Thomas Wolfe, felt the critical arrows that by the end of that decade (and of Wolfe) would make him a native Sebastian: for the social-consciousness "boys who write book reviews in New York," as Wolfe spoke of them, the decade was saved by Dos Passos, Farrell, and finally by Steinbeck's *Grapes of Wrath*,† which seems to have drowned the memory of Wolfe's solipsistic insolence (as for the critics of the 1920's it had been Sherwood Anderson).

The Thirties were a time for action, not for good taste, and the Far Left soon became strident in its demands on literary artists. The decade had barely opened when the Left launched a notorious attack on another romantic, Thornton Wilder. Its perpetrator was Michael Gold, the particulars of whose denunciation do not differ basically with those, whether spoken or implicit, of the attackers of Henry James. Gold, who had just demanded in *The New Masses* that the writer "must decide now between two worlds,—coopera-

---

* He dates the association from 1924 and the appearance of Trotsky's *Literature and Revolution*, "in which he explained the aims of the government, analysed the work of the Russian writers, and praised or rebuked the latter as they seemed to him in harmony or in conflict with the former." Thus, Wilson concludes, it was that this point of view, "indigenous to Russia, has been imported to other countries through the permeation of Communist influence." ("The Historical Interpretation of Literature.")

The very same appraisal of the value of the poet's work in terms of its usefulness to the state's dogmas had, of course, been made by Plato in his *Republic*.

† As in art criticism, praise of the native-theme and social-consciousness painters (Wood, Curry, Benton, *et al.*) was the order of the day.

tive or competitive, proletarian or capitalist," now accused Wilder "of peopling a devitalized museum . . . with moldy characters and of brooding over their 'little lavender tragedies' with 'tender irony.' " [100] What wonder then, if, only two years later, in a densely printed, 500-page survey entitled *The Liberation of American Literature*, the critic Vernon F. Calverton does not once mention the name of Henry James (although he does give extended treatment to so non-literary an entity as the I. W. W.)? * Or that in the following year Granville Hicks identifies the "tradition" of the title of his *The Great Tradition* as that of socialism in America, and ends that book with encouragement to writers in that tradition to "give their support to the class war that is able to overthrow capitalism"? A good deal of what he writes about James is reminiscent of Parrington, Brooks, and Frank. James appears, we note, in a section labelled "Fugitives." Although there is "a kind of James cult," Hicks declares that most readers have been "wise" in their decision to "reject" him. After all, for James, literature was not life but a game. Unhappy in his own land and unable to accept life on British terms, he had no course but to create an imaginary society that alone could be to his liking: "His refuge was not England but the realm where art was sacred—and sufficient." In these terms and practically in these words Harry Hartwick censured James the next year, for all that—as Harry Hayden Clark stated in his foreword—Hartwick spoke as a partisan of a theory of literature (naturalism). Defend James though he might against the old related charges of expatriation and snobbery of subject matter and assert (if feebly, yet assert) that *"The American, The Portrait of a Lady, The Wings of the Dove*, and *The Ambassadors*, do not merit the neglect to which they are at present being subjected," yet Hartwick complained of James's esotericism, stylistic virtuosity, obscurantism, and even of a lack of the humanism that seemed so characteristic of his art at first glance: it was merely a kind of relation-ism, to invent a term. No, alas, "like Howells, he was a man born out of his time,

* In an earlier volume he had cited James, and approvingly, as a theorist about literary criticism. (*The Newer Spirit*, New York, 1925, p. 177.)

an anachronism, a last survivor of the Hawthorne-Emerson-Lowell [that is, the genteel] tradition, whose backbone was severed by the Civil War," and that is one reason "why James's books are gathering dust on the shelves today. . . ." [101]

The voice of Ludwig Lewisohn, speaking out wistfully at this time, reminds us today of the vagaries of literary popularity. Looking upon James as, for all his faults, "probably the most eminent man of letters America has yet to know," he declared that he knew "of no more unhappy symptom of the spiritual confusion of our immediate day than the noise, as of cracked trumpets, that surrounds the name of Herman Melville, and the silence which has fallen about that of Henry James." [102] And Edmund Wilson, one of the most knowledgeable historians of that confusion, was saying that there had occurred an "eruption of the Marxist issues out of the literary circles of the radicals into the field of general criticism. It has now become plain that the economic crisis is to be accompanied by a literary one." [103]

Even disciples were falling off, disturbed by the times and responding to polemics inspired by them. Such, we are told, was the change in Dorothy Canfield Fisher. In her *Seasoned Timber*, there is evidence of the change "from instinctive allusion to Henry James, recurrent in the earlier works, to inevitable allusion to Sinclair Lewis"—in particular, to the latter's tongue-in-cheek arraignment (in *It Can't Happen Here*) of fascist tendencies in the materialism of American life. "She acknowledges that Vermont . . . is losing its basic resources. . . . Vermont has one final defense—its native backbone. Henry James cannot help her in this crisis; but she is [very] conscious of her new ally [Lewis]." [104]

Whatever their form, it should be noted, the strictures about James or other writers akin to him have thus far tended to be sober and reflective. But if Gold's were a striking exception, so too were those contained in a chapter-long attack in a book by Ernest Boyd, who, midway in the Twenties, had stooped—in language as crude as his friend Mencken's but without Mencken's essential good-naturedness—to pronouncing James "a literary gent" whose later manner "fulfilled all the requirements of an intellectual cult" [105] (as well as to such other scorn as has already been cited). Unlike Gold's, however, Boyd's attack seems based on aesthetic, not political, grounds.* The reverse, more or less, is true of Mr. Geismar, author of the most recent James polemic. He is willing to concede a certain merit (as an "entertainer") to James, but his Boyd-toned denunciation of the Jamesians is dedicated to Van Wyck Brooks and echoes the censure of James that the collectivist critics of the 1930's produced. Indeed, Mr. Geismar echoes his own pronouncements of around that time. Twenty years before his *Henry James and the Jacobites* he had written that the bias of his *Writers in Crisis* "is democratic, its belief is in the potential of democratic society, and especially American society"; yet late in this book (with its rejection of the earlier "Henry James figures . . . paralyzed by nuances in the vain effort to escape the American vulgarity, pacing up and down their foreign piazzas, trying to decide whether to offer each other a cigarette, perhaps, or refrain"), prompted doubtless by his recommendation of the leftist writers Muriel Rukeyser, Horace Gregory, Albert Halper, Robert Cantwell, Richard Wright, and Clifford Odets, he feels it necessary to insist that notwithstanding his stressing "the . . . finale of [American] artistic individualism, the merging of the 'I' and the 'we' in our literary tradition," he does "not wish to be taken as the advocate of collectivism." [106] Thus his 1963 reflections on the 1930's are noticeably nostalgic: for the Thirties were an "age of social concern and radical belief, of thwarted hopes and twisted careers, of disenchantment, yes, but of vitality and excitement too"; † and as he proceeds, he uses the very terminology of the collectivists of that age:

---

* He did write a sympathetic introduction to V. F. Calverton's *The Newer Spirit* (1925), but its remarks seem more those of a man demanding a hearing for than endorsing "A Sociological Criticism of Literature" that the book's subtitle announced as its approach to its materials. Elsewhere he writes, like Mencken, as an independent spirit, not easily labelled.

† *Henry James and the Jacobites*, p. 3. This last emphasis may incriminate Mr. Geismar far more surely of the charge of being "non-historical" than he can Henry James. Shall we admit the group of witnesses that the collectivist Van Wyck Brooks himself has assembled? "[In the 1930's] humanity seemed

*In this leisure-class literary cosmos, the idea of making a fortune
. . . was unthinkable, except for those vulgar American financiers
of James's work, or those quaint, childlike, sweet millionaires. . . .
James thought the function of the artist was to teach the rich how
to use their money better. Wasn't he in fact the perfect novelist of
our primitive finance-capitalism in its first flowering of titans and
robber barons . . . ?* [107]

As for the Jamesians, nothing less than imputation or personal
abuse will suffice: they are snobs, escapists, lazy, clever holders of
academic sinecures, cultists brain-washed into mistaking for art
mere entertainment produced by an elegant literary pretender who
had first had to brain-wash himself in order to remove an intolerable
awareness of failure.

To the fury of this resentment toward the Jamesians, no rational
refutation is in order; but to Mr. Geismar's charges about Henry

---

to pass into a dark night of the soul. Nothing could have been more marked
than the transformation of the literary world from the state of mind of a
dozen years before when, as Waldo Frank had said, at the time of *The
Seven Arts* [1916 ff.], 'There is a murmur of suppressed excitement in the air.'
It was, he added 'like that which hovers over a silent crowd before the
appearance of a great procession.' Had this procession come and gone? Certainly no one in 1930 looked for any such thing to appear in the future, for
'a dreadful apathy, unsureness and discouragement is felt to have fallen upon
us,' Edmund Wilson wrote in the following year. Gertrude Stein said, in fact,
that there was no future,—there was 'no future any more'; while Paul Rosen-
feld, editing *The American Caravan*, noted that after 1930 every contribution to this yearbook was tragic. In the great number of papers that were
submitted to it, he said, there was not one cheerful composition. Paul was
dismayed by this uniform note, so different from that of the time when he,
like all our contemporaries, had begun to write and when he had half expected to see 'ideas at every street corner and rivers of living water in the
street.' Over the gate of the thirties one seemed to see the words, 'Abandon
hope, all ye who enter here.' " (*Days of the Phoenix*, pp. 183–184. From a
chapter entitled "A Season in Hell.")

In 1952 Edmund Wilson, to be sure, also recalled the early 1930's as "not
depressing but stimulating," and himself as "exhilarated" at the collapse of
American finance capitalism ("that stupid gigantic fraud") but he precedes
this with the admission that only a few years previously he had "caught a
wave from the impulsion of the Marxist faith." (*The Shores of Light*, New
York, 1952, pp. 498–499, 496.)

James, the record of that novelist's own work is the most effective witness for the defense.

To say that James "converted every loss . . . in his own career, into an imaginary victory," [108] is to be ignorant of the fact that James disowned a good part of his literary creation in assembling the contents of his New York edition and that his prefaces to that edition abound with apologies and embarrassing admissions.

Next, to state that "[e]ven more than the late nineteenth century British nobility, James preferred the early nineteenth century English scene simply because the older nobility appeared to be more noble" [109] is either to be unaware of or to suppress two of the first principles about Henry James, statements of feeling that he entered on the record time and time again, speaking both in his own person and in that of his fictional creation. For one, the author of a long, critical appraisal of the eighteenth century beginning "No other age appeals at once so much and so little to our sympathies, or provokes such alternations of curiosity and repugnance" is Henry James himself; [110] as he is of the declaration, apropos a collection of eighteenth-century letters, that they "would do something toward blunting the edge of our admiration for the eighteenth century, of our envy of it as a kind of golden age of 'society,' in so far as these feelings are at all tinged with superstition." [111] Does this sound like a man who, Mr. Geismar implies,* worshipped a society in proportion as it receded from the present? For another important principle, in the preface James wrote to the *Aspern Papers* volume of his selected works there is a long passage stating why he preferred the Regency period of English history (as opposed to the periods *both earlier* and later) that has been as widely quoted since its appearance half a century ago as any passage of James's prose: to read it is to see at once that James's preference has nothing whatever to do with comparative degrees of nobility. †

* In its earlier appearance (in *The American Scholar*, XXXI [Summer, 1962], 373–381), Mr. Geismar's above-cited passage had actually had James preferring "the eighteenth century English scene."

† James Thurber had cited this passage back in 1930. (I take it up at length in Chapter V, B, below.)

Equally mistaken is Mr. Geismar's statement that James preferred, even to the early nineteenth-century English scene, "the great and glorious French Empire of the *ancien régime*. James was non-historical, since his notion of 'history' was that of legend, romance and the picturesque. The French Revolution of *The Ambassadors* is a matter of blood and terror; and of those delicate, cultivated, ancient French noblewomen who gallantly await their turn at the guillotine." [112] Is not Lambert Strether's eventual (and emphasized) revulsion *against* this very romantic projection of the history of Paris the underlying *theme* of *The Ambassadors*? For the Strether who has caught his glimpse of Chad and the Countess on the river is a man who finds himself stripped of every lingering trace of "legend, romance and the picturesque" in his being. With a sinking feeling, he insists to himself that he has been Time's fool to have speculated so romantically *at first* about the glory of the First Empire, to have conjured up vaguely "the world of Chateaubriand, of Madame de Staël, even of the young Lamartine." For Paris, he now sees, is no such matter, and to the waking mind that is now his, the old dream will no longer suffice:

. . . beyond the court . . . came . . . the vague voice of Paris. Strether had all along been subject to sudden gusts of fancy in connexion with such matters as these—odd starts of the historic sense, suppositions and divinations with no warrant but their intensity. Thus and so, on the eve of the great recorded dates, the days and nights of revolution, the sounds had come in, the omens, the beginnings had broken out. They were the smell of revolution, the smell of the public temper—or perhaps simply the smell of blood.

But least defensible of all is for Mr. Geismar to declare that Henry James's "view of womankind was essentially that of a child-life purity, sweetness, goodness. . . ." * for it is to ignore a lifelong

---

* *Henry James and the Jacobites*, p. 6. This is by and large a revival of Van Wyck Brooks's distortion of many years before: ". . . especially there were young girls who were variously enchanting. . . . There were prettily innocent Daisy Millers who lived in a round of dressing and dancing. . . . How

gallery of unflattering, even offensive, female portraits. Were they not indeed his very trademark? Look wherever in his career we may, they confront us. In the first chapter of Howells's *The Rise of Silas Lapham* (1884), is not Silas's wife described by a reporter as "one of those women who, in whatever walk of life, seem born to honour the name of American women, and to redeem it from the national reproach of Daisy Millerism"? "Purity"? Newton Arvin has noticed that the Baroness in *The Europeans* is not concerned about "lights and shades, but . . . hard cash," and she is a familiar type in James's repertory, as he demonstrates. Like her, James's other women—and his men—want to know about other people "not what they might learn from philosophy, but from Dun & Bradstreet's, and they go to some trouble to learn it." He instances Esther Blunt, of the early "A Landscape Painter," as "the first of a longish line which reaches to Kate Croy . . . and Charlotte Stant. . . . If these women are not good mathematicians . . . , good bookkeepers . . . they are nothing." [113] "Sweetness"? Edmund Wilson has called our attention to the various females in James's fiction who can be classified as "frustrated Anglo-Saxon spinster" and who are patently deceitful: Olive Chancellor of *The Bostonians*, Adela Chart of "The Marriages," and very possibly the governess of "The Turn of the Screw." [114]

If James's own literary criticism and his fiction reduce what Mr. Geismar calls the "cluster of limitations" in him to mere distortion

---

light their figures were . . . ! Their profiles were delicate. . . . There were Francie Dossons, Bessie Aldens, Pandora Days, and Linda Pallants, and Isabel Archers who moved in a realm of light. . . ." (*New England: Indian Summer*, pp. 290–291.)

It is also a theme that has recently received wide attention, surely, for the stress given it in Leslie Fiedler's *Love and Death in the American Novel* (1962), but here the interpretation of James's "Fair Maiden, the Good Good Girl" and "Nice American Girl" is given a depth and a comprehensiveness that deserve study. (See pp. 288–295, especially.)

Neither of these critics—both of whom are using their examples to support a thesis about James—is aware of Howells—who was writing literary history—when he singles out De Forest and James as both having "offended 'the finer female sense' " of their audience (the difference between them being that James also "lastingly piqued" that sense). ("Mr. James's Masterpiece.")

or even fabrication, what can be said about Mr. Geismar's insistence that these "limitations" are indeed James's very charm for "all those contemporary critics who had turned away from the radicalism of the thirties; or who had been against it in the first place; or who, in the next generation of the forties and fifties no longer wished to concern themselves with anything remotely bearing on the social question," [115] except that it leaves him, and *not* "this particular Emperor . . . naked"? For in his claim that in "the epoch of the cold war, of McCarthyism, . . . of governmental purges and investigations, of both a forced conformity of thought and a natural, self-induced one, Henry James was the perfect symbol of safety, propriety and gentlemanly behavior" [116]—in it, does Mr. Geismar not at last disclose the provocation for his entire attack? Does he not exemplify the uncomfortable truth that literary criticism can be as much a victim of the poisoned air we breathe as are the bones of growing children?

The record itself shows how grossly the Geismar charge misrepresents the radical critics, who, as often as not, have been capable of maintaining political conviction and esthetic values simultaneously —have been, that is, capable of a pre-Trotskyite objectivity that Mr. Geismar might well observe. Shall we begin with the example of Randolph Bourne? Here is a man who, as Daniel Aaron puts it, "had written a Whitmanesque hymn to 'Sabotage,' proclaimed the I. W. W. as the harbinger of industrial democracy, and had attended the Paterson pageant in Madison Square Garden"; yet who as early as 1914 wrote a letter in which he placed Henry James with Emerson, Thoreau, William James, Royce, and Santayana: they were all "great men" in that they "express the American genius and those ideals of adventurous democracy that we are beginning to lose, partly through having filled our heads with admiration of English rubbish and partly through having formed a stupid canon of our own with Poe and Cooper and lifeless Hawthorne and bourgeois Longfellow and silly Lowell." And of his six "the most thoroughly American" was—Henry James: because of his "wonderful sensitiveness to the spiritual differences between ourselves and the

Older World," and "the subtle misunderstandings that follow our contact with it. . . . To be sure, . . . he always makes the English-man far too charming; but then his Americans are apt to be charm-ing, too, so I suppose the proportion is kept right." [117] This inde-pendence from party-line dogma of Bourne's artistic appreciation is the more remarkable for coming from the man who with Van Wyck Brooks led the "League of Youth," a group that "wanted a socialist society . . . that would provide a literature . . . authentically American, that might inspire a 'true social revolution.' " [118]

To come up to the 1920's and 1930's is to be confronted often by the name of Edmund Wilson, whose index entry in Daniel Aaron's *Writers on the Left* is one of the longest there, sharing that distinc-tion with Michael Gold, Vernon F. Calverton, and Granville Hicks (as well as with Leon Trotsky and the Union of Soviet Socialist Republics), yet who has always had "an ethical vision that pene-trated the ideological miasmas of Right and Left and kept him intellectually unsubmissive." [119] In the very year (1934) that Wilson objected to a proposed lampoon of "my old friend Mike Gold," and joined the editorial board of Calverton's *Modern Monthly* [120] he contributed to the Henry James number of *Hound and Horn* what has since been recognized as one of the major insights into James's art. In it, after dwelling at some length on the ambiguity of "The Turn of the Screw," he directs his attention to the question of James's stature. Milly Theale, of *The Wings of the Dove*, he feels, is "the kind of personality, deeply felt, which only the creators of the first rank can give life to"; moreover, it is a greatness that so far from rooting itself in unreality and gossamer glamour has as its very roots "the industrial background" whose absence in his fiction James had always been reproached with:

The industrial background is there. . . . [W]e never get very close to it; but its effects are part of the picture. It is for those things of which that background has starved them that James's Americans come to Europe and it is their inability to find in other societies something with which their own society has never supplied them that is at the bottom of their most poignant disappointments.[121]

Perhaps it is a similar concern with and knowledgeability about economic determinism in this period that prompted Newton Arvin, defined by Daniel Aaron as one of "the fellow-traveling Left intellectuals," to analyze James's world in terms of it: just as it is his equal ability to steer a sure course between art and politics. Certainly the light he has thrown on the motivation of James's main characters has, with Wilson's, answered the frequent charge that these people live in a world all of James's own. I have already cited his enumeration of the money-minded heroines of that world; his study also includes its over-all venality, its ubiquitous greediness. Arvin concedes that there are "fine examples of the opposite" in James; but though James criticized this greed only from the "angle . . . of a refined individualism . . . he was too honest, too responsible, too scrupulous a writer to white-wash his society as he found it." [122]

Coming up to the mid-forties, to the period when, as Mr. Geismar accurately reports, "James was 'discovered,' and rediscovered, and discovered again, until he took on, with each passing year of our own period, a greater and greater importance" [123]—a rather significant fact inheres in the particular identity of the two James critics who were most responsible for this rediscovery. Looking back in 1957, one of them, Philip Rahv, has recorded that "the revival of this classic American novelist, a revival long in preparation . . . was finally brought to a head, in the fall of 1944, by the simultaneous appearance of two anthologies of his fiction." One must recall that the year he is speaking of is that of the Allied invasion of the Normandy beaches if one is to appreciate his further recollection that "As the editor of one of those anthologies I was quite as surprised as anyone else by the unexpected dimensions of the interest in him. . . ." [124] Now it happens that the man partly responsible for this James Revival and pleasantly surprised at it all was no T. S. Eliot or Stuart P. Sherman—is, in fact, a man whose own affiliations were originally Leftist: witness his essay in 1932 on Plekhanov (the chief exponent in Russia of Marxism as a philosophy, as he has been referred to); his membership in the New York City John Reed

Club; and his founding (with William Phillips) of the *Partisan Re-view* " 'to put forward the best writing then produced by the Left.' " But they quarreled with " 'Party-line notions' governing the 'literary movement,' " protesting " 'against the official idea of art as an instrument of political propaganda.' " [125] In Rahv, too, then, so far from apostasy, from the very first there was possible the separation of politics and art indispensable to respectable literary criticism.

The editor of the second of the two anthologies that Philip Rahv mentions, namely Professor F. O. Matthiessen, presents a similar moral. Speaking of his Harvard undergraduates "during the tense winters of 1942 and 1943," he writes: "When I said, half meaning it, that a book on Henry James was to be my overaged contribution to the war effort, they urged me to be serious. They believed that in a total war the preservation of art and thought should be a leading aim. They persuaded me to continue to believe it." [126] Again, what is interesting in this reminiscence is the intellectual backgrounds of the man who wrote it, is the evidence it furnishes of the complexity of feelings that Henry James has always aroused in the James critics whom we respect the most. For the Matthiessen who is referring above to the genesis of one of the most valuable of all appraisals of Henry James's art (*Henry James: The Major Phase*) and had already written an equally valuable appraisal of T. S. Eliot (who, as we have seen, had early taken up the cause of the counter-Revolution) is the same man whom the historian Daniel Aaron groups with "a number of the liberals . . . who . . . were [in 1930] already moving leftward" and of whom (with various others) he says that they "were already radicals or half radicalized" [127] and who as late as 1950 left behind at the time of his death a note identifying himself as "a Christian and a socialist." And if Howard Mumford Jones pronounced an unofficial valedictory of the 1940's when he found that "we are still arguing whether it is better to be aware of *Finnegans Wake*, W. H. Auden, and Henry James than it is to be aware of Damon Runyon, *Strange Fruit*, and the prose of Ernie Pyle," [128] he may also have been prophesying the Fifties, a period when research on and reprinting of Henry James's works at least vied with those of William Faulkner, who combines the technical virtuosity of the first of Professor Jones's groups with the topical immediacy of the second. And it is to the point to note that the year (1962) of the opening round of Mr. Geismar's attack was, as well as a trying year in the Cold War, also the year of the publication of the first four volumes of the projected complete edition of James's shorter fiction, of the republication of the first volumes of the New York Edition of his Novels and Tales, and of the appearance of the middle two volumes of a four-volume biography of Henry James—volumes which were awarded a prominent prize for non-fiction writing for that year. As to whether the man responsible for most of the above-enumerated publishing activities (Professor Leon Edel) or the man whose veritable encyclopedia of information and comment on James's novels (Professor Oscar Cargill) of the preceding year provoked Mr. Geismar's attack, so far from being complimented for their monumental contributions to this cause, should reproach themselves, I leave to their own consciences to decide: why a man or woman is attracted to a writer and when, is a problem in motivation that even psychiatrists would be most reluctant to have to rule on. For a layman, then, to impute to Jamesians the ignominious and craven motives that Mr. Geismar does, is to descend to the level of the McCarthyism that he professes to abhor.

In any event, the above evidence proves that the outcome of the battle over Henry James does not depend on the vicissitudes of history, does not become stronger or weaker with the heat of political unrest or even of world upheaval, but will, as a matter of course—as all art must—offer itself for judgment again in the 1970's. Then, as now, doubtless the man and his work will bestride the literary scene, if not like a colossus, yet as a reminder of a rare—or even a rarefied—area of the human consciousness, possibly of what Hawthorne spoke of in the preface to his last romance as "a sort of poetic or fairy precinct, where actualities would not be so terribly insisted upon as they are, and must needs be, in America."

One fall day only the other year, when nuclear attack seemed quite possible, my wife dragooned me into carrying down into our basement quantities of bags of sand, jars of water, cans of meat and fish for five humans and two cats, as well as bars of soap and rolls of toilet paper. (Could Hawthorne have imagined that "actualities" would ever be so "terribly insisted upon" in his "dear native land"? Can we not imagine him turning to his nearby slumbering veterans of the astral New Mexican mushrooms of the early 1940's with the cry, " 'Rappaccini! Rappaccini! and is *this* the upshot of your experiment!' "?) But not a single volume of Henry James. As for me, if I myself did not remedy this neglect, it was not for her reason (namely, that like most of my friends, she prefers to hold James at a greater distance than the confines of our basement afford), but because I took the situation for what it proved to be—a scare. Yet the Great Depression was no mere scare, and one of the last physical acts the hero of that haunting nocturne of its middle years, William Saroyan's "Daring Young Man on the Flying Trapeze" (1934), does on the day he dies of starvation is to perform the homage of an hour's reading, not of Henry George, but of Marcel Proust. And it could be remembered at best by only three or four of us who heard a well-known contemporary European man of letters confide it, that one of the two books he carried with him through World War II was by the very author he had minutes before been finding grievous fault with on the public platform—James Joyce's *Ulysses*, a dish equally caviare to the general. It seems predictable, then, that in times of stress to come, Henry James will prove, as well as an outlet for tension, a frequent source of comfort and even of inspiration.

PART TWO:

THE BOOKS

II. A BEGINNING: WATCH AND WARD IN TIME AND PLACE

. . . the very poorer, the poorest . . . I am . . . for this formal appearance in society, "cutting" without a scruple. These repudiated members, some of them, for that matter, well-nourished and substantial presences enough, . . . I fondly figure as standing wistful but excluded, after the fashion of the outer fringe of the connected whom there are not carriages enough to convey from the church— whether . . . to the wedding-feast or to the interment!

(*The Novels and Tales of Henry James*, XII, Preface)

Henry James's beginning seems unremarkable in the light of his ending. He ventured into print as a writer of book reviews and travel pieces interspersed with short stories and then novels. Understandably, his first imaginative attempts displayed enough marks of the apprentice to cause embarrassment to the much written about and widely imitated man of letters of the later years. The very volume of recollections, anecdotes, and intricate appraisals comprised by the prefaces that Henry James lovingly lavished on the inner fringe of the connected of his works during these years, added to the magnitude of importance that edition would acquire in the years to come, has of course had the effect of discouraging inquiry about the numerous members of the outer fringe. And only ten years later Joseph Warren Beach, by examining the "repudiated" children in his *Method of Henry James* showed good cause for their repudiation. But the great and still increasing interest in James since that time has led more than one scholar to reconsider James's discarded writings, now with the purpose of finding out what value they have or what promise of the later James they reveal.* The present inquiry will limit itself to his first novel, *Watch and Ward*, which appeared in early issues (August-December, 1871) of the *Atlantic Monthly*. James was then only twenty-eight years old. Beach suggests that James would probably have been glad to blot it out of existence. But James bestowed a great deal of care (and hope) on it, and if he eventually disowned it, this was only after he had gone to the considerable trouble of revising it "minutely" for book-form appearance in 1878, of providing "many verbal alterations," as he wrote in a Note.[1] In any event, examined in its original form —that is, seven years before its appearance as a book, by which time he had completed two more novels—*Watch and Ward* yields various interesting disclosures about James's art.

The leading character, Roger Lawrence, is a "solemn little fop." As he prepares to propose (for the third time) to Isabel Morton, he carefully draws on his lavender gloves. He is "remarkable for the spotlessness of his linen, the high polish of his boots, and the smoothness of his hat. He carried in all weathers a peculiarly neat umbrella. He never smoked; he drank in moderation. His voice . . . was a mild deferential tenor." Isabel refuses him again, but his humiliation soon shades into a different and more complex emotion. Before his interview with Isabel he had been buttonholed in the hotel by a seedy-looking stranger who desperately asked a hundred dollars of him. Roger had of course refused him. The next morning he discovers that the man has blown his brains out in the next room, orphaning his twelve-year-old daughter. To contemplate the forlorn, sweet and—even this early in James—homely girl is to bring tears to Roger's eyes. "Was it the inexpugnable instinct of paternity?" we find Roger wondering. "Was it the restless ghost of his buried hope?" Whatever it was, it serves to make Roger adopt

* Cornelia P. Kelley's *The Early Development of Henry James* (1930) is a treasure house of information about James's beginnings.

Nora. He goes zealously about his new responsibility, this labor of love. Even this early in James, too, we find the curious observer making minute notations: at first he fears that Nora may be "simply stupid"; later, however, that she may become "too clever."

As a matter of fact, as the years pass, Nora begins to meta-morphose from nondescriptness into attractive, even stately young womanhood. She likes the piano and adores Roger. While she is away at school, Roger (thinking, these days, that if she is to become his future "perfect" wife, he in turn must become a wise, educated husband) travels extensively. After he has successfully withstood the temptation of Teresita, a childlike Peruvian enchantress, he returns confident of his steadfastness. But it is at this point that his troubles truly begin. For lo, enter George Fenton. Nora is sixteen by now, and with Fenton begins the first rivalry for Nora's affec-tions. A young Missourian, Fenton has come East ostensibly to claim kinship with her (actually, the villain is after Roger's money). However, by the time Roger sends her off to Rome to spend a year with the now widowed Isabel, Nora has become infatuated with Hubert, Roger's cousin, a dilettante of a young parson who devotes the Sabbath Day to the Lord and the other six to His choicest fe-male creations.

Thus it is Hubert who receives her on her return to the United States (Roger has just caught pneumonia); and he takes advantage of his opportunities until Isabel threatens to expose his engagement to yet another girl. Nora ministers lovingly to the ailing Roger, who forthwith proposes marriage to her. After her first reaction of aston-ishment, Nora bursts into laughter; but when she learns from Isabel that during all the years of his solicitude and generosity Roger has lived on the hope that she will eventually marry him, she runs away to George in New York (begging Roger by note not to follow—and offering any future Lawrence offspring free music lessons).

But after the maturing influence of her stay in Rome, Nora finds George as vulgar as his scrap-iron yard; and, in truth, he comes within an ace of holding her for a ransom of $5,000 from Roger. This leaves as possible asylum only Hubert, who, of course, receives her with apprehension, his confusion becoming confounded by the sudden arrival of his fiancée. But by now Nora's eyes are open; and, fortunately, the pursuing Roger is already coming into view (holding his hat in one hand and wiping the perspiration from his forehead with the other). " 'My dear Nora,' " he asks, passing her hand through his arm and listening to her confession of shame, " 'what have *we* to do with Hubert's young girls?' " And so they marry. "Roger, the reader will admit," his youthful creator concludes, "was on a level with the occasion,—as with every other occasion that subsequently presented itself." *Finis.*

While it is true that in *Watch and Ward* we are at least spared the villains and "sophisticated heroines" of James's even earlier, short story efforts, the fragility of this first novel is undeniable, particularly its plot. We notice that, surely as a concession to popular taste, the story ends with a wedding; and we recall that in a similar concession he would transform Daisy Miller's tearful demise into the joyful peal of marriage bells when he rewrote the story into play form; * but later in his career so little use did he make of this predictable ending that Edmund Wilson hardly overstates in his observation that in James's fiction "the men are always deciding *not* to marry the women." [2] As for the suicide with which *Watch and Ward* opens and its near-kidnapping, episodes like these or their equal would disappear from James's novels, but only gradually. Oscar Cargill speaks of the "old fashioned French melodrama" of *Roderick Hudson* (1876), with Christina's forced marriage to the Prince, and of *The American* (1877), with its "skeleton in the closet"; [3] and if a reviewer would complain in 1878 that Daisy Miller "is sacrificed to Mr. James's incapacity to get his dramatis personae off the stage in any way except by killing them," [4] his remark would fit not only the earlier *Roderick Hudson*, which ends

---

* Similarly, in the final form of its play version, the Jack of *The American* gets his Jill and even Valentin is allowed to keep his life.

with the hero's body at the bottom of a mountain cliff, but *The Princess Casamassima* (1886), in which the hero, unable to solve the dilemma besetting him, shoots himself. If only gradually, yet so completely would James eventually forswear such familiar contrivance that in 1905 Joseph Conrad felt the need to take it upon himself to defend James against the often-voiced complaint that James's novels were disappointing because they *lacked* the clear-cut endings of conventional romantic fiction. His fiction lacked "finality," Conrad declared, only "when contrasted with the usual method of solution by rewards and punishments, by crowned love, by fortune, by a broken leg or a sudden death." [5] So surely had it grown up by then.

But while today we may say about *Watch and Ward's* plot what Dr. Johnson said about *Pamela's*, still James's first attempt at a book-length fiction already displayed certain merits not found with such frequency in the new national letters as to be disregarded by the modern student of that period. For any ambitious novel by an American author in 1871 would have had to venture forth most diffidently into the midst of several formidable literary forces and fashions.

From the one, the eastern side, for many years each ship had brought to the Atlantic ports the literary outpouring of the still-mother nation, to be circulated as far west as the Pacific. Speaking of the younger men of literary ambition in Columbus, Ohio, during the late 1850's, William Dean Howells recalled that "We looked to England and the East largely for our literary opinions; we accepted the *Saturday Review* as law if we could not quite receive it as gospel." [6] Much was in the monthly issues of the variously colored influential magazines. To the grudging tribute of Poe's "How to Write a Blackwood's Article" should be added the deposition of the historian of that magazine that "for one reader of *Blackwood's Magazine* in the old country, there cannot be less than fifty in the new." [7] Then during James's boyhood there came *Blackwood's* successors in popularity in this country. James himself recalled *Punch* fondly a half-century afterwards,* and Bret Harte recalled that "the illustrated and satirical English journals were as frequently seen in California [in the 1860's] as in Massachusetts . . . ," that he had "more difficulty in procuring a copy of 'Punch' in an English provincial town than . . . at 'Red Dog' or 'One-Horse Gulch.' " [8] And all the while, of course, there were the great English novelists: Scott, Dickens, and Thackeray, to begin with. Scott's *Ivanhoe* would be discovered to be one of the three best-sellers in America as late as 1896. Dickens, of course, was a star that shone as brightly after his death in 1870 as before.† A historian speaks of a short span of years around this time when *Harper's* ran "three novels of Dickens, four of Thackeray's, one of Bulwer's, two of George Eliot's, six of Trollope's." [9] The 1870's brought the novelists Hardy and Eliot (with whom James inevitably began to be compared, his novels appearing, for example, side by side with Hardy's in *Harper's*). And along with all this for years there had been coming the fashionable literature from France, penetrating even remote areas. "You, who live where you can see all the new books as soon as they appear," the narrator of a story in an American magazine for young readers writes to his "old friend" in the city, "can hardly imagine the eagerness with which we poor country people, far away from publishing-houses and foreign bookstores, welcome the sight of this monthly parcel. We passed over the green and yellow duodecimos, glancing at Féval, About, Berthel, Sand, and the rest,

---

* Just as he thought more (in *Notes of a Son and Brother*) of the files of the *Revue des Deux Mondes* in his Cambridge closet as an educational force than he did of Harvard University, so (in *A Small Boy and Others*) he tells us that earlier *Punch* "contributed in the highest degree to our education" about Europe. See F. W. Dupee (ed.), *Henry James: Autobiography*, p. 34.

† See Bret Harte's 1870 essay with its concluding belief that "his grave is in every heart, and his epitaph on every hearthstone"; his tearful "Dickens in Camp" of the same year, with its miners sitting by as though entranced by a firelight reading of "Little Nell"; not to speak of his imitation of "The Haunted Man" of even earlier date.

That there was no exaggeration in this account, one gathers from a contemporary editorial statement of the effect of Dickens' death on his popularity: "Innumerable lives of Dickens have been issued, and new editions of his novels in every conceivable shape, and with every sort of title. . . ." (*Scribner's Monthly*, I [November, 1870], 111.)

each looking for his particular favorite among the authors. . . ." *
(Just as lovingly, the elderly James would recall, he had fondled
the pink monthly numbers of the *Revue des Deux Mondes* long
years before; and certain yellow duodecimos were the ones that the
young Strether took home from Paris in *The Ambassadors*.) In only
a few years, such literature would get its rude jostling from the scandalous naturalistic fiction of France which, by the end of the century, would have influenced James's younger contemporaries Crane
and Norris. Its manifesto (the preface to the Goncourts' *Germinie
Lacerteux* [1864]) reads in part:

*Living in the nineteenth century, at a time of universal suffrage,
and democracy, and liberalism, we asked ourselves whether . . .
"the lower orders" had no claim upon the Novel . . . , whether in
these days of equality, there were still for writer and reader un-
worthy classes, misfortunes, that were too low, dramas too foul-
mouthed. . . .*

* *Our Young Folks*, January, 1865, 9–10. Some of "the rest" deserve individual
mention. For one, there was that veritable factory of fiction, Alexandre
Dumas. Recalling his 1864 interview with Dumas in Paris, an American journalist wrote that he had told Dumas "that he was scarcely better known in
France than in America; that he could not write a book that would not sell
[there]. . . ." (John Bigelow, "A Breakfast with Alexandre Dumas," *Scribner's Monthly*, I [April, 1871], 597.)

Equally popular imports were Eugene Sue and Victor Hugo. In one 1863
issue of his magazine, Louis Godey warned his (female) subscribers about the
"lax morality" of "the sensation school of modern French novels" with their
insidious effect of obscuring hitherto-clear boundaries between right and
wrong, and singled out Sue and Hugo for particular mention. Instead of
"wading through one of these evil works of passion, pollution, and false sen-
timent," he urged readers to "take up a healthy English or American novel."
Three issues later, in calling attention to the success of the New York publisher, Will Carleton, he cited statistics that in themselves prove how timely
his warning had been:

Among the Pines	35,000	copies sold	
Rutledge	30,000	"	"
The Sutherlands	30,000	"	"
Les Miserables	120,000	"	"

("Editors' Table," *Godey's Lady's Book and Magazine*, LXVI [March,
1863], 305; "Godey's Arm-Chair," *Ibid.*, LXVI [June, 1863], 582.)

The very next year (1865 being the publication date of Mark Twain's story about a Californian frog) there would begin to arise from America's own far west a native literature, in origin equally democratic (and occasionally as scandalous) *—a wind that would blow in upon the civilized east and even Europe with the same tonic but startling force, some years later, of Rudyard Kipling (that *enfant terrible*) on the London of the *fin de siècle* languor.† This was the work of the local-color writers of a country rapidly expanding and discovering the variety and richness of its own resources. For the year of the publication of *Watch and Ward* was also the year of Edward Eggleston's *Hoosier Schoolmaster*,‡ of John Hay's *Pike County Ballads*, of Joaquin Miller's *Songs of the Sierras*, and the year straddled by Mark Twain's *Celebrated Jumping Frog* volume and his *Roughing It*. No matter that this home-grown product aimed chiefly at the picturesque, the outlandish, the grotesque, or the comic; that its most popular practitioner—a true son of Artemus Ward—scoffingly disclaimed any pretensions to serious literary art at the conclusion of his *Roughing It* or in the prefatory "Notice" to *Huckleberry Finn*, and that he was embodying in *Innocents Abroad* at this very moment his disdain for European culture: exactly this kind of entertainment was charming eastern § and transatlantic readers as well. We are familiar with the stories of the triumphal personal entry onto the London scene of the hopefully grizzly-bearish Bret Harte and Joaquin Miller; to them we should add the evidence, twenty years later, of Henry James himself. For the cele-

---

* See Bret Harte's reminiscence about the first reaction to the prostitute in his "The Luck of Roaring Camp."

† And on the anything but languorous scene in America. Such, at any rate, despite the great success of his *Red Badge*, is Stephen Crane's sad reflection: " 'Yes. I'm just a dry twig on the edge of the bonfire.' " (Thomas Beer, *Stephen Crane*, p. 233.)

‡ For all its unique regional quality, derived as much from European art as was Hardy's or George Eliot's fiction. One could not go far enough west in this country to escape the damned shadow of Europe, apparently.

§ "Americans have as a general thing a hungry passion for the picturesque, and they are so fond of local colour that they contrive to perceive it in localities in which the amateurs of other countries would detect only the most neutral tints." (Henry James, *Hawthorne*, Ch. I.)

brated English portrait painter of "The Liar," exploring the guest room he has been given in the country house, notes that "the literature, as usual, was mainly American and humorous. . . ."

And all the while, midway between them in space as a kind of tertium quid and overwhelming them in popularity by sheer volume, there was that ceaseless torrent of Female Fiction, that ever-replenishing well of piety, passion, and pathos, whether the exquisite imports (*Wuthering Heights, Jane Eyre*) or the derivative literary hollyhocks of "the ink-comparable women of America"—as the completely American and humorous R. H. Newell phrased them in his own travesty of "harrowing Romance as inflicted by the intellectual women of America." [10] Their name was legion (Mrs. A. J. E. Wilson, Mrs. E. D. E. N. Southworth come to mind first) and they would continue to shore up the native bulwark of morality against the nasty tides of French filth when these started washing up against our coasts. As would soon happen! Only six years after Henry James's *Watch and Ward* came out, Emile Zola would write that unspeakable novel whose arrival in translation would be greeted as a plague: "We would as soon introduce the small-pox into our homes as permit this unclean volume [*L'Assommoir*] to come in contact with the pure-minded maidens and ingenuous youth who form their chiefest ornament," * the reviewer hissed; but fortunately consolation and reassurance were to hand: "In strong contrast with this sensational novel are two graceful religious tales [Rose Porter's] *In the Mist*, and [Jennie M. Drinkwater's] *Tessa Wadsworth's Discipline*, in which the fragrant lives and the virtuous loves of two pure women are depicted, in the one case with gentle pathos, and in the other with innocent and cheerful gayety." [11]

Yet for all of these formidable competitors, a serious native literary art was also coming into life in the year 1871. Two practi-

---

* Issued in book form in 1877 after a scandalous, relayed serialization, *L'Assommoir* sold 100,000 copies in a matter of months in its native land, where it was just as angrily denounced. (Matthew Josephson, *Zola and His Time*, New York, 1928, pp. 230 ff.)

tioners were in fact at work. For this was also the year of William Dean Howells' *Their Wedding Journey*. Ten years earlier, when the weary and aging Hawthorne had found it refreshing to contemplate this young man from a place (the Ohio River) "upon which the damned shadow of Europe had not fallen," he could not know that the young man in question had fed his youthful hunger on Heinrich Heine; yet for this the less wonder that Henry Adams would find in *Their Wedding Journey* a "remarkable delicacy and lightness of touch" and venture the prediction that "if it can throw over the average bridal couple some reflection of its own refinement and taste, it will prove itself a valuable assistant to American civilization." [12]

And is it not fitting, then, to wonder whether, with the exception of Howells, any other American novelist could have displayed the literary skill that *Watch and Ward* is capable of here and there? Even by 1868 a critic in the *Nation* was saying that "within the somewhat narrow limits to which he confines himself, Mr. James is the best writer of short stories in America." [13] Yet those limits, narrow or not, already included a variety of qualities in which American readers might find much promise. The pictorial realism that he admired in Balzac is already in evidence. Leon Edel has recently reminded us that "When it came to painting scenes he was unmatched in his precision and genius for essential detail: Washington Street in Boston, snow-piled and jammed with horse-cars, lives for us in his tales, as do the people within the large-windowed houses in Beacon Street. . . ." [14] Here, when the fleeing Nora steps off the train in New York in the hours of early morning, the city immediately comes into focus by virtue of just such a precision:

A Dutch grocer, behind her, was beginning to open his shop; an ash-barrel stood beside her, and while she lingered an old woman with a filthy bag on her back came and poked in it with a stick; a policeman, muffled in a comforter, came lounging squarely along the pavement and took her slender measure with his hard official eye. . . . She ventured into an establishment which had Ladies

Café *inscribed in gilt letters on a blue tablet in the window, and justified its title by an exhibition of stale pies and fly-blown festoons of tissue paper.*

This is part of what James was to recall at the end of his exiled life as "a squalor wonderfully mixed and seasoned," a "vast succulent cornucopia." And the passage displays an etching-like minuteness of description that would not only characterize the other early work (*The Bostonians, The Europeans, Washington Square*) but would linger on, even into the final, the difficult, novels. Is the street scene above merely apprenticeship work, even when placed beside a description from *The Ambassadors* (1903) of

the mere way the bright, clean, ordered water-side life came in at the open window. . . . —the mere way Mme. de Vionnet, opposite him over their intensely white table-linen, their omelette aux tomates, their bottle of straw-colored chablis, thanked him for everything almost with the smile of a child, while her gray eyes moved in and out of their talk, back to the quarter of the warm spring air. . . .

As the excerpts already cited reveal, the style is surprisingly straightforward, without the precious bane of the involutions of the later novels. Furthermore, even at the start of his career James could achieve a dramatic effect that is both restrained and eloquent. Here, for example, is Roger starting uptown in search of Nora:

The weather was perfect; one of those happy days of February which seem to snatch a mood from May,—a day when any sorrow is twice a sorrow. Winter was a-melting; you heard on all sides, in the still sunshine, the raising of windows; on the edges of opposing house-tops rested a vault of vernal blue. Where was she hidden, in the vast bright city?

Also worthy of our note is the refreshing way young James was practicing the art of satire. This emerges early, with Isabel rejecting

Roger: "She esteemed him more than any man she had known,—so she told him; but she added that the man she married must satisfy her heart. Her heart, she did not add, was bent upon a carriage and diamonds." * But the vignette of Teresita is even better. "Her charm was the charm of absolute *naïveté*, and a certain tame unseasoned sweetness,—the sweetness of an angel who is without mundane reminiscences; to say nothing of a pair of liquid hazel eyes and a coil of crinkled blue-black hair. She could barely write her name. . . ." Or consider the appraisal of the adolescent Nora: "She had . . . an elusive grace. She had reached that charming girlish moment when the crudity of childhood begins to be faintly tempered by the sense of sex." To which he adds: "She was coming fast, too, into her woman's heritage of garrulity"—an observation as early as lasting in the novelist's consciousness, and not always, as here, introduced for comic purposes. After Hyacinth Robinson, for example, in Ch. 17 of *The Princess Casamassima*, listens to the Princess tell the story of her life, he reflects, apropos this "chatter," that "a vulgarity of confidence was indeed a leading characteristic of the sex as he had hitherto learned to know it. . . ."

Finally, who among his fellow-countrymen could have produced such simple melodic effects as "he trod on tiptoe in the region of her early memories" and as "the summer twilight of her mind, which seemed to ring with amorous bird-notes"?

But what is perhaps most impressive in the novel is James's infinite care for characterization, manifested as the hero's personality unfolds. For Roger Lawrence is by no means merely a hasty sketch. His first reaction of annoyance and anger at Fenton's attentions to Nora soon merges into shrewdness: it occurs to him that Fenton's "precursory love-making" may eventually awaken the naïve girl to his own aspirations. Consequently he adopts a policy of watchfulness and courtesy toward his adversary, very much like that which

* Shades of Cervantes! " 'For that and nothing more?' said Don Quixote. 'And do they, then, send lovers to the galleys?' 'But it was not the kind of love your Grace has in mind,' the prisoner went on. 'I loved a wash basket full of white linen. . . .' "

Rowland Mallett in *Roderick Hudson* was to adopt toward Christina Light, or Maggie Verver toward Charlotte Stant in *The Golden Bowl*. All are instances of the "fine measurements," the "intimate impressions," for which, James maintained in the preface he wrote for the New York edition of *The American*, "ninety-nine readers in a hundred have no use whatever." *

There was yet another kind of "intimate impression" that in time became perhaps as characteristic of Henry James's art as any other: namely, his "historic sense," his feeling for what T. S. Eliot would call the "presentness of the past." And although Eliot himself would insist that this sense was more genuinely a part of Hawthorne than of James,[15] the point is impossible to establish. Certainly one finds it *hic et ubique* in James's art. Even in *Watch and Ward* it lurks in a nostalgic lecture which Hubert delivers to Nora as she prepares to go to Rome. This, it will be recalled, is the Rome of the period of great excavation. It is the Rome about which the narrator of another James story of this early period indulges in "super-sensitive flights" on the Campagna; he refers to "times when the air seemed so heavy with the exhalation of unburied death, so bright with sheeted ghosts, that I turned about and galloped back to the city." [16] It is of this Rome that James would tell his readers a year or two later that, as he lounged on a sunny day over the railing guarding the excavations of the Forum, he both rejoiced and winced at seeing "the past, the ancient world . . . bodily turned up with a spade. . . . The pleasure is the same—in kind—as what you get at Pompeii, and the pain the same." [17] In truth, even at the age of seventy he could quote from memory the following "faint thin shred" of an unpublished poem by a boyhood friend which this brooding aspect of Rome had contributed to his phantasy:

> Harold, rememberest thou the day,
> We rode along the Appian Way?

---

* For the theme of *Watch and Ward* in terms of literary history, see Leon Edel's introduction to the Evergreen edition of this novel.

> *Neglected tomb and altar cast*
> *Their lengthening shadow o'er the plain,*
> *And while we talked the mighty past*
> *Around us lived and breathed again!* *

Thus it is that Hubert Lawrence expands into another dimension of himself when he tells Nora of the two pasts that he has left in Rome:

"Your real lover of Rome oscillates with a kind of delicious pain between the city in itself and the city in literature. They keep for ever referring you to each other and bandying you to and fro. If we had eyes for the metaphysical things, Nora, you might see a hundred odd bits of old ambitions and day-dreams strewing that little terrace [where Hubert once stayed]. Ah, as I sat there, how the Campagna used to take up the tale and respond to the printed page! If I know anything of the lesson of history . . . I learned it in that empurpled air!"

That air of the past—of Rome or Chester or London or Paris or even of old New York—provided an enchantment to Henry James and his fiction from the very first. Whether the Clement Searle of "A Passionate Pilgrim," the Hyacinth Robinson of *The Princess Casamassima*, the Lambert Strether of *The Ambassadors*, or the innumerable, quickly forgotten heroes of the other pieces—old houses, old cities, and old civilizations make deep "metaphysical" inroads in their consciousness, until, as we shall see, in the last, post-humous novel, *The Sense of the Past*, Ralph Pendrel takes the final step and physically enters into a relationship with a group of Londoners of almost a century before. Fantastic as that step might seem, it was merely the ultimate extension of a persistent passion in Henry James that may be found budding briefly in the first novel he wrote.

* William James appears to have recited these lines, which Henry recalls, were "to stick in my remembrance for reasons independent of [their] quality." *A Small Boy and Others* (1913). (F. W. Dupee [ed.], *Henry James: Autobiography*, p. 220.)

III. THE PUPIL BORROWS

The James who wrote *Watch and Ward* was a fledgling novelist, a sensitive young man of letters and, if a good short-story writer and the son of an illustrious, energetic lecturer, yet fairly unknown. The James who had been dead almost ten years by 1925 was, however, a man whose name and literary creation were, as we have seen, on their way to becoming a national issue. If in that decade he had been awarded the tribute of association by T. S. Eliot with the revered figure of Nathaniel Hawthorne, he had not escaped the imputations of the now-famous reproach by Van Wyck Brooks:

Countesses, duchesses, great ladies, noble gentlemen were so obviously the heroes and the heroines of the wondrous European fairy-tale! That was the New York idea [of his boyhood], and all the stories he had read, all the pictures he had absorbed, had prepared him to believe it. . . . He had "read too many novels." [1]

And severe though this reproach is, it is gentle by comparison with the allegations contained in Thomas Beer's review of the Brooks volume in which this reproach had appeared:

> The princess faraway of the young man's mind had already robed herself [by 1865]. She glittered in . . . novels. . . .
> Where did this stuff come from? Let the literary Breasted dig in the remains of George Whyte-Melville [whose novels James had not read for thirty years yet the "jolly rubbish" of which he recalled vividly one day in 1913 when talking to a group about "the fashionable trash of Victorian times"]. He will come face to face with some ghosts related to the Princess, some scenes of aristocratic life as imagined by a placid hunting squire akin to peers [of limited] ideational quality. . . . This treacle had passed into him as a lad and [in later years] in moments of miserable speculation over situations utterly beyond his "sensations of society" it sweated out. . . .[2]

Now, justice requires that this journalistic literary judgment be recognized as just that. Like all sweeping indictments, it contains a tiny truth; but unless the facts about these ignoble backgrounds of James's art are examined with the care for accuracy of the Breasted that Beer proposes, his judgment is of value merely as a study in malice.*

Such an examination has in fact been underway for some time now: the literature of source studies of James's fiction has been growing with his reputation. Its extent can fairly be grasped from the text and footnotes of Oscar Cargill's *The Novels of Henry James* (an exhaustive volume that of necessity excludes investi-

---

* The next year he renewed his aspersions in a book on the American *fin de siècle*, *The Mauve Decade*. Here he scattered his shot throughout the volume. Again his favorite theme is imitation in fiction (George Moore on Howells as an imitator of James; Constance Fenimore Woolson as an imitator of James; James as—by insinuation—an imitator of Woolson); but he strays into James's obscurity (his intention at the close of "The Beast in the Jungle," his point of view with regard to "Julia Bride"), his over-fastidiousness as a person, and—surprisingly enough—his generosity in regard to charity solicitations.

Beer dedicated this volume to Ernest Boyd, whose anti-Jamesian *Literary Blasphemies* the next year would in turn be dedicated to Beer.

gation of James's many short stories and novelettes). To read that literature, in turn, is to realize that James's art, like that of all other major authors, was derivative. Not only this: much evidence is at hand of his thorough acquaintance with and uncannily accurate recollection not only of the classic works of his age but of such literary trash as Beer mentions.* To learn this, however, is to learn nothing of any importance in itself. What could be of less ultimate literary value to a writer than the lowest trash, the veriest treacle, of all—his childhood reading? James himself has recalled for us such long-vanished items as *The Wide Wide World* and *The Initials* (not to speak of the gas lights hissing in front of the dramatized *Uncle Tom's Cabin*, as its tearful religiosity swept the country in those years). And has any other writer, however important, ever sated his boyhood thirst on anything less nectar-like? What *is* of importance is the way by which a writer inevitably transforms the raw materials of his craft, whether these are noble or base; in fact, it is partly by studying this very process that we can derive our first insights into a writer's art. In James's case such a study will lead to the discovery that, whatever his borrowings, when it came to the act of writing he was always his own man.

For the present I wish to pick out three novels from the limitless range of literature that Henry James either read from preference or was obliged to read (he was for years a book reviewer for various journals, it will be remembered); and to try to view three works of Henry James the novelist in their light.

* For his own confession of indebtedness to such sub-literary French practitioners of fiction in the nineteenth century as "Gyp" and Henri Lavedan, see *The Novels and Tales of Henry James*, IX, Preface; also, Oscar Cargill, *The Novels of Henry James*, pp. 263–279.

A. HAWTHORNE AND "THE LIAR"

Readers of James's commentary on *The Scarlet Letter* in his *Hawthorne* will recall that he explains that romance's qualities, in part, by comparing it with *Adam Blair*, a J. G. Lockhart novel of half a century before, saying that Lockhart's "interesting and powerful little tale has a great deal of analogy with Hawthorne's novel—quite enough, at least, to suggest a comparison between them. . . ." And now we, a few years ago, were more or less invited by Marius Bewley's "Appearance and Reality in Henry James" to a comparison between *The Scarlet Letter* and a story that James himself wrote a few years later, "The Liar." Professor Bewley asks us to think of the central figures in that story as being "on the point of committing that crime which for both Hawthorne and James was the worst possible: of violating the integrity of another man's personality, of seeking to take possession of it through false images and conventional laws." [3] Is this man, in truth, to be thought of in terms of such a person as Chillingworth? Can any correspondence be discovered between James's other couple in that story—the lovers—and Hawthorne's? If we pursue the Bewley suggestion, we come, in James's words, to the conclusion, that "if one has read the two books at a short interval, it is impossible to avoid confronting them." And this aside from any question of indebtedness: for, as James himself pointed out, the interest in such a comparison is that it "speedily leads us to larger considerations than simple resemblances and divergences of plot."

As "The Liar" opens, a portrait painter named Oliver Lyon who had courted a young Englishwoman in Munich during his student days finds himself in her company at dinner in an English country-house. Unobserved in the midst of a group, he ferrets out about her what he can from his neighbors at the table and concentrates on her actions, particularly her solicitous, even affectionate, attitude toward her husband nearby. She is a strikingly handsome woman, and if her name, Everina Brant, sounds somewhat un-English, it matches her person, for she is dark-haired and Mediterranean-looking and gives the appearance of passion or sensuousness (enough to have inspired him in the Munich days to paint her with "vine leaves and a leopard skin—a kind of Bacchante"). Yet inasmuch as, he remembers, she was a most proud and reserved woman, he is the more impressed with her present gestures.

After dinner, he seeks her out, and they consider past and present. Twelve years before, she had rejected his marriage proposal; her reason then was apparently that although she was from a "noble" English "house," it had decayed financially and she felt obliged to it to marry as well as she could. She is now in at least comfortable circumstances: her husband, the affable Colonel Clement Capadose, if not wealthy, is well enough off, and much in demand at country-houses. Also, they have a daughter, Amy, of whom both are fond. Oliver, who has progressed from studenthood to prominence, is both jealous of Clement and most curious about Everina's devotion to this man, for Capadose has a reputation as a teller of outrageously tall tales. Oliver rebukes Everina for ignoring his presence at dinner, and expresses the hope that she doesn't mean to "repudiate" him. We learn that she had rejected him years before not because she did not think that he would become successful but possibly because she was aware that his restless, prying nature was ill suited to her own. Indeed, their incompatibility is manifest: as this warm, affectionate woman now tells him, " 'When you come to see me in London . . . I shall see you looking all around.' "

Actually, he has already begun this, so to speak. For Oliver finds himself progressively curious about her true relationship to Clement. Isn't she "consumed by a hidden shame" in having rejected him, Oliver, for a man patently so ignoble—even ridiculous? Or is it possible that by now she was "so perverse that she thought it a fine thing" for her husband to be "striking" at the expense of his "honour"? Given Oliver's personality, he cannot rest until he finds out. And for the remainder of the story, for what we must consider a rather long amount of time, he sacrifices all other concerns (including several lucrative commitments) to this investigation.

In response to her invitation, he begins visiting her and Amy in London (her popular Clement being off on visits much of the time), watching her every mood and gesture as he queries her about her husband. Curious even about her relationship to the little girl, he observes "that she had the maternal passion, in spite of the bad blood in the little girl's veins." Soon he cloaks his true objective in the guise of painting Amy. Although he can execute such a painting in a matter of days, Amy's he allows to go on week after week, thus making possible prolonged observations of and conversations with her mother, who of course accompanies her to the studio. It is Oliver's notion that this sustained propinquity will elicit some sign from Everina of her old affection for him, "some sign she was sorry" for rejecting him for this buffoon. If she does not (and she doesn't), then he has prepared another trap for her, this one, infallible. He is, in fact, already plotting Clement's exposure; has a "legitimate treachery" in mind. He will paint the Colonel as what he is in the eyes of any honest person; will "draw" Clement "out" in the sittings, so that "none but the initiated would know" that he "was vulgar, in spite of his talents, his fine person, his impunity." Then Everina, confronted with the subtly but inescapably graphic evidence of her husband's baseness, will have no choice—if she is still the honest woman Oliver once knew her to be—but to acknowledge that baseness and to writhe in embarrassment and humiliation.

In view of what she knows about his cold, prying self from of old, Everina is at once suspicious. She wants to know from him why painting Clement will do Oliver (who is already famous) "a lot of good"; and just what the painting will be "expressive" of. Although she is obviously in no position to turn Oliver's request down, she does tell him that " 'Nothing would induce me to let you pry into *me* that way!' "

Soon, as Professor Bewley has pointed out, Oliver's morbidly jealous passion causes his original plan of a highly limited revenge to degenerate: as the sittings begin, Oliver determines "that his character should be perceptible even to the meanest intelligence" at the Academy, where in fact he plans to exhibit it. And draw Clement out (the idea "which he had been nursing for so many weeks") he does, with no difficulty: "He encouraged, beguiled, excited him, manifested an unfathomable incredulity. . . . He lashed him on when he flagged; his apprehension became great at moments that the Colonel would discover his game. But he never did, apparently: he basked and expanded in the fine steady light of the painter's attention."

The result is a masterpiece, but Oliver is not destined to display it in the Academy and thereby advertise Clement's contemptibility to the world. Everina, catching sight of the almost finished portrait, discovers the revenge that Oliver has been preparing and betrays her distress to the unwitting Clement, who slashes the portrait to ribbons while Oliver is secretly watching it all from the balcony of his studio. Later, when questioned about this vandalism, Clement disavows any part of it (a disavowal, because of the exact circumstances of the portrait's destruction, difficult to disprove), and Everina—to Oliver's chagrin—supports Clement's lie. This leaves Oliver merely the satisfaction of believing that her love for her husband and her loyalty to him have exacted from this "honest and straightforward" woman the heavy price of her integrity.

In looking back, we may wonder that there can be so many correspondences in situation with such widely diverging final effects. It is as though James had vaguely or subliminally set himself the task of transposing Hawthorne's historical romance into a contemporary novel, so to speak, without in any significant way taking liberties with its basic concerns or structure. There lay the trap for James, and it would seem that he fell into it.

If we merely compare their surface features, we see in both the progressive degeneration and self-corruption of a rejected and malicious leech as he goes about perpetrating his revenge on a victim whose own wrongdoing seems more and more condonable by contrast. Accordingly, we have the eventual defeat of hatred by its very triumph. Just as Arthur had been an adulterer without in any way lessening his value as spiritual leader of the community (in fact, his preaching increases in effectiveness as a *result* of his sin), so Clement's captivating person endears him to all despite the harmless failing of his of telling outlandish lies that harm no one and that even give him the added charm of the story-teller. In his act of slashing the portrait of himself to ribbons after learning from Everina of his close companion's true purpose, does Clement not effectually echo Arthur's judgment on Roger? " 'We are not, Hester, the worst sinners in the world. There is one worse than even the polluted priest! That old Man's revenge has been blacker than my sin. He has violated, in cold blood, the sanctity of a human heart. Thou and I, Hester, never did so!' "

Of course, to equate the situation of the two men in this quantitative way alone is silly; but this is by no means true if we direct our scrutiny to the correspondences between the painter and the woman. For the James triangle only apparently lacks the element of drama that Hawthorne's managed by having the predator fasten himself on one of the most revered and ethereal yet intelligent of victims (whereas James's victim Clement is merely amusing, kind —as his name suggests—and endowed with a childlike simplicity of mind): in its duel between Oliver and Everina "The Liar" presents a situation exactly the counterpart of this of Hawthorne's. If for Arthur we substitute Everina, what we have is no less than a retelling of Hawthorne's story. For again we find the author's focus on the man plotting revenge, the suspense (will he or she betray his guilt?), and the effect on the secret sinner of the act of concealment. If the price of Arthur's immunity is concealment, so is Everina's. Just as his fall from spirituality should be a sin in Arthur's eyes, so (notwithstanding her charm and the viciousness of her adversary) should Everina's bearing false witness.

But if she is properly analogous, in terms of function, to Arthur Dimmesdale, Oliver Lyon is even more closely analagous to Hawthorne's Chillingworth. Hawthorne introduced an outlandish monster; James's is a monster in modern dress. Hester examining Roger's incredible sinisterness is reproduced in Oliver speculating about his own deviltry and even in James's added editorial reminder of his morbid state of mind. Moreover, in each case the villain is the only one who knows the guilt of his victim.

And yet, from this point on the stories diverge, pursuing opposite courses and producing opposite effects. Arthur eventually has his own conscience to confront and does, so that Roger is reduced to a mere catalyst, rather than an agent. (Remember that he confesses his guilt not because Roger has thwarted his escape by ship —of which Hester has not had the opportunity to apprise him—but because, in the most carefully managed bit of suspense in the story, in the act of re-writing his Election Day sermon late the night before he had completely changed his mind about escaping.) In telling the truth, Arthur literally shames the devil and thus destroys him. Everina, to be sure, is until Oliver springs his trap on her, guilty of nothing:

1) She commits no sin by hearing her husband tell his lies, since everyone knows that they are lies and since being merely outlandish, they are more properly entertainment than deception;

2) She is guilty in the leech's eyes only, rather than in her own, so that she can be excused for her lie, for countering treachery with loyalty;

3) Consistently with his character and reputation, Clement's lie about the destruction of the portrait has harmed no one: he attributes the act to a drunken street-walker who had actually trespassed in Oliver's studio once before and whom he is not likely to see again.

Yet unlike Roger, Oliver at least gets the satisfaction of knowing that she has lied and that she knows that he knows that she has lied.

It is in this divergence that we begin to understand what was wrong with James's idea. To the extent that Everina steadfastly refused to reveal her "secret" to Oliver, she is a fit counterpart to Arthur Dimmesdale; but in resorting to a lie at the last instead of confronting her pursuer, she is in no way to be thought of in terms of the sublime Arthur. Her lie is a most believable one, yet it demonstrates how the very success of James's story from one point of view turns out to be its failure from another. For in replacing with a novelistic plausibility the melodramatic apotheosis of Hawthorne's romance, James forfeited this last effect without a compensatory gain. If the charm of *The Scarlet Letter* is a very fragile one, an essence most volatile if enchanting, still Hawthorne's triangle of tormented love and hate here seems to have been summoned up, like Glendower's devils, from vasty deeps, from Dante's haunting and picturesque circles of hot carnality and icy-cold malice, as unforgettable as they are phantasmal, and pursuing as relentless and inevitable a course as fate in their "dismal," their "gloomy maze." Roger is paradoxically both a phantasmal nemesis and a disturbingly real presence, a distinguished scholar and outraged husband and vampire who knows that although he is the one sinned against, his was the earlier sin and that what he is now engaged in is a terrible sin; that he, the hunter, and his quarry alike are victims of a "dark necessity," a cruel fortune against whose slings and arrows he, Arthur, and Hester are utterly helpless. He is Revenge incarnate. No matter that *The Scarlet Letter*, as James wrote, has "a want of reality and an abuse of the fanciful element," —still, we cannot at any time believe that Roger's sense of grief and of the violation of his honor are not real. *His* is the "legitimate treachery."

Oliver's, however, is thoroughly implausible and contrived. We cannot imagine him capable of the grief of a rejected suitor—for it is a palpably factitious grief—far less of nourishing his sense of loss for a dozen years. It is impossible to believe that one of the distinguished artists of England would abandon himself utterly to such an obsession. In truth, there is so little correlation between offense and revenge that character and author alike feel the need for accounting to the reader for the oddity of his behavior, thereby forcing us the more to think of him as a bloodless animation of mere Curiosity, and as incapable of true passion as Hawthorne's own prying Miles Coverdale. Even though Oliver justifies his behavior toward Clement on the grounds that he had been in love with Everina, so that Clement's "delinquencies . . . turned to the tragical in his mind," still "he had a sense that his solicitude might also have been laughed at"; but in the most unforgivable artistic blemish of James's story we find him almost remonstrating against our disbelief in advance by pleading with us to accept this manifest obsession as justifiable behavior: "Lyon's curiosity on this point may strike the reader as fatuous, but something must be allowed to a disappointed man"!

Hawthorne's nemesis is a figure as proud and awe-inspiring as he is, in James's words, "livid and sinister,"—a Puritan Agamemnon who, betrayed, wounded and harassed, mournfully asks his repentant victim to believe that the Delusion that prompted his indignity to him was Zeus's own daughter:

> . . . . *I am not responsible*
> *but Zeus is, and Destiny, and Erinys the mist-walking*
> *. . . . It is the god who accomplishes all things.*

James's, however, is merely vile, a fanatical insect wildly whirring and secretly hoarding its venom for one intense sting that will hurt exactly no one. Of *The Scarlet Letter* James had written that "it belonged to the soil, to the air; it came out of the very heart of New England." Of his own analogue of it we in turn may say that it smells of the lamp, it came off a chessboard.*

---

* Actually, Oliver Lyon dimly suggests a picture at a Dostoyevsky Exhibition of the Sick Mind. With Oliver's outrageous sense of affront and planned revenge, compare the Underground Man's plot to humiliate a certain officer who is not even aware of his existence: he will write a satire in which (at first) the innocent victim will easily be recognized by the reading public.

B. VICTOR CHERBULIEZ AND
DAISY MILLER

As early as 1865, when James was first beginning to appear in print, he reviewed for the *Nation* a novel entitled *Paule Méré*, translated into English from the French of a prolific writer whom we may fairly term one of the Whyte-Melvilles of the Continent: a man who wrote novels of the "popular" kind, relying heavily on action, suspense, and romance, who enjoyed a great vogue, and yet who has become as completely forgotten as though he had never existed. It is true that in a moment of pique James could refer to Cherbuliez as "that pitiful prostitute" (in private),[4] and an American reviewer could charge Cherbuliez with devoting "all his energy to the flimsiest entertainment of an idle generation of novel-readers"[5] (as though he were an earlier Edna Ferber or Daphne Du Maurier); but to accredit James's own printed judgments at the time that Cherbuliez was "the novelist of literary people" and a "novelist of incomparable talent"[6] and to read that James was surprised and hurt that the literary *cénacle* of Paris (Turgenev, Daudet, Maupassant, and others) contemned such *Revue des deux Mondes* novelists, including Cherbuliez, as James admired,[7] is to recognize that we are considering a man who loomed large on that bygone horizon.* For the discovery that James was familiar with this particular Cherbuliez novel, we have Viola Dunbar to thank.[8] But for the purpose of discovering what *Paule Méré* may have contributed to the development of James's art, we must place it side by side with *Daisy Miller* (1878).

To do so is at once to be surrounded with similarities—of characterization, of plot, of theme. Although the heroine Paule is artistic,

---

* For other data about Cherbuliez's reputation, see Ch. IV ("Dotting the I's"), below.

she is essentially as headstrong and independent as Daisy. Like Daisy, she has been slandered: various of her innocent but unchaperoned outings in the vicinity of Geneva have been falsely interpreted, and scandal has even had her accompanied on one of these occasions by a "lover." Marcel Roger, Cherbuliez' hero, also bears an interesting resemblance to James's. Like Winterbourne, he is about thirty, wealthy, a self-styled *"spectateur desoeuvré,"* and cosmopolitan in upbringing and point of view. The ambivalence of his attitude toward the maligned heroine corresponds to Winterbourne's: one is a Swiss who has lived abroad long enough to be able to discredit local gossip but not long enough to outlive his provincial morality; the other, an American who has lived abroad long enough to relish American freshness but not long enough to recognize innocent flirtation. Like Winterbourne's, Marcel's love withstands scandalous insinuations (of his mother and others) and supports his faith, albeit waveringly, until he observes the heroine late one night in an apparently compromising rendezvous. At this he rejects her with finality.

In their larger outlines, then, James's and Cherbuliez' tales are so remarkably similar that it is most difficult to believe that one was not based on the other: both relate, with varying sympathy, the sad fate of an admirable girl whose actions run afoul of rigid Genevan standards of deportment. In both, the action opens in a provincial Swiss *pension* and closes in Italy; in both, a young, leisured idler half representing, half resenting, Genevan propriety irresolutely opposes a close female relative in his affection for a young woman who does not "belong" there; in both, this young woman is ostensibly immodest, yet actually quite chaste. Finally, in both an apparently compromising situation destroys the hero's faith; and both heroes learn of their mistake too late. It is also true that—as we have seen a reviewer of *Daisy Miller* complaining—James, like Cherbuliez, relies on melodramatic contrivance to bring his story to its unhappy conclusion.

Yet so far from being a plagiarism, or even an imitation, *Daisy Miller* both in fine and in large is like no other novel of the nineteenth century. One would have to search prodigiously in *Paule Méré*, for example (or even in the later James, for that matter), for the likes of one Randolph C. Miller. Or, more important, for the tempestuous Marcel Roger in James's *Winterbourne*, whose name is a revealing index to his personality. He seems a most satisfactory combination of various contradictory elements: of candor and reticence, of courtesy and aloofness; of impressionability and haughtiness. And if, as with the male protagonists of the later James, the reader wishes that a warmer blood directed his movements, he is entirely credible as a person. Cherbuliez' hero, Marcel Roger, is more of a melodramatic stereotype begging for alteration into individuality. Cherbuliez, indeed, invests him with a huge capacity for romantic passion which not only eventually threatens his sanity but continually tries the modern reader's patience. When belatedly he discovers Paule's innocence, he penitently pursues her to Venice, but the story ends as emotionally as it has proceeded, with Paule at the point of death from heart-break. It all fairly exudes Byronism.

The novel as a whole is also permeated with a tearful sentimentality, a proclivity toward heroics, posturing, and rhetorical bombast as unpalatable to modern taste as the cumbersome ornateness of the Victorian and Ulysses S. Grantian interiors in which Cherbuliez' art was so popular. Indeed, James's own contemporary remark that the book is "rather youthful in its unsparing ardor" [9] merely euphemizes *Paule Méré's* limitations without denying them. By comparison James's yet fresh laconic artistry, his ironic understatement are a sophisticated modern stage play using the same materials yet reducing the original thereby to the level of a silent movie dependent for its effects on the familiar exaggerated facial gestures and body attitudes.

But after all we must reckon with the fact that the title of both *Paule Méré* and *Daisy Miller* is the name of a young woman; and the most telling difference between them is in the characterization of their heroines. When we look back at Paule, we can see why she could serve James as a model only initially; for although she seems to resemble Daisy, she actually resembles only a situation. She is simply Innocence Wronged. "In 'Swiss Notes,' contributed to the *Nation* for September 19, 1872," Miss Dunbar has noted, James

speaks of the moral individuality of Switzerland and of its want of a sense of humor. To support his own observation of the highly artificial character of life in Geneva, he refers to a novel [that] Cherbuliez has . . . written . . . expressly to prove that frank nature is woefully out of favor there, and his heroine dies of a broken heart because her spontaneity passes for impropriety. . . . The book is Paule Méré, which he described the next year [in the North American Review, CXVII (October, 1873), 462] as "an attempted exposure . . . of the narrowness and intolerance of Genevese society." [10]

James had quite another purpose in mind with Miss Annie Miller, of Schenectady, New York, it is clear: just as in the Miller family he enables all America (and possibly some of Europe) to see its innocents abroad—wide-eyed but boorish, culturally underprivileged but vital and venturesome—so in Daisy he creates at last an unmistakably *American* young lady. No one had really "done" her as yet, even though she fairly begged to be done, swarming as Europe was beginning to be with the likes of her and of her family, the New Americans freed from the restrictions of a long war and flourishing from native commerce (and thriving on it, as "An International Episode" would soon show them). There was a second Cherbuliez heroine—the "English" Miss Rovel—who, James had insisted, was no such thing, but a Parisian in disguise; and he had reproached Cherbuliez: "Why cannot a French novelist draw, with any approach to verisimilitude, a young girl brought up in the Anglo-Saxon fashion?" [11] Two years later James himself achieved a very masterpiece of verisimilitude. Paule, James had found "not absolutely natural"; Daisy's utter naturalness became and remained both the target and the toast of a vast female American audience. As Howells was to recall a quarter of a century afterwards, "Mr. James . . . lastingly piqued ["the finer female sense"], and to read him if for nothing but to condemn him, is the high intellectual experience of the daughters of mothers whose indignant girlhood resented while it adored his portraits of American women." [12] James's novel, then, prompted no less reaction than this mixture of extremes. For Daisy was, after all, an original. Transcending the limitations of her continental genealogy, she was the universal that Aristotle spoke of, as well. Let the continent revel in amusement and self-satisfaction from contemplation of her gaucherie and that of her family:

No American who has not been abroad can really appreciate this story. One must have shuddered at the approach of Randolph C. Miller's type to understand the full horror of that child seen in a land of well-trained children. One must have listened in a railway-carriage to the confidences of a young lady (seen for the first time at the station), poured out for the benefit of all chance fellow-travelers; one must have painfully struggled between a sense of snobbishness in not acknowledging one's country-people and a conviction of untold miseries consequent on the other line of action; in short, one must have suffered in order fully to understand the fine quality of this story. We hope . . . [that] the American people . . . , being quick-witted, may see themselves here truthfully portrayed, and may say, "Not so, but otherwise will we be." [13]

For all that, her fellow-Americans would look upon her as inescapable, as something even to be proud of—the New American Woman, an early instance of American literary concern for what Howells recalled as "the rising tide of national life." And an unforgettable instance, too. For like Roger Lawrence in Watch and Ward, Henry James took someone else's creation only as his materials, not as his finished product.* These he could shape, with a lov-

---

* As even Thomas Beer was capable of discerning: "The memory is strange: in 'The Bostonians' a dozen sentences from cheap, forgotten authors whose stuff Henry James read on the beach of Newport, and an epigram of Thomas Wentworth Higginson, appear transmuted in the slow, inimitable medium projected by that scrupulous mind." (The Mauve Decade, New York, 1926, pp. 243–244.)

ing discipline, into someone of his own making. And the dew still glistens on the petals of her name.

C. WILLIAM BLACK AND
THE TRAGIC MUSE

From that dross, this gold; from that muck, this pearl. Of the many enthusiastic testimonials to *Daisy Miller's* excellence, one might single out—as I have just done—the review in the left-hand column of page 387 of the *Nation* for December 19, 1878, upon the publication of the story in book form. It is anonymous, of course; but so is a long review (in the *right*-hand column of that very page) of a novel by one William Black entitled *Macleod of Dare*. William Black, like Victor Cherbuliez, was highly regarded by his nineteenth-century English audience and like him is completely unknown today—another Whyte-Melville. He was, we learn from an entry of some length in the Eleventh Edition of the *Encyclopedia Britannica*, "for nearly thirty years . . . successful in retaining the popular favour. . . . He died [in 1898] without having experienced any of that reaction of the public taste which so often follows upon conspicuous successes in fiction"; yet the current edition has no entry on him at all.

Now one or two interesting observations may be made about the review I have mentioned above of this forgotten novel by its forgotten author. First, Henry James himself wrote it. Next, a close comparison of *Macleod of Dare* with a novel that James himself published twelve years later,* *The Tragic Muse*, cannot help lead-

---

* Almost exactly the time span between *Paule Méré* and *Daisy Miller*, it happens.

ing one to believe that for many of its qualities *The Tragic Muse* made considerable use of the Black novel (as well as such others as Professor Cargill has called our attention to); [14] but that at the same time, appraised in terms of its own real accomplishments, *The Tragic Muse* remains as underivative a novel as James ever wrote.

Here is the plot of *Macleod of Dare* as Henry James gave it in his review:

The story relates the fortunes of a gallant and simple-minded young Scotch laird, the last of an ancient fighting line who dwell in their legendary castle in one of the islands of the west coast of Scotland. The action takes place at the present day, and the author brings his hero up to London and introduces him to the complexities of contemporary manners. . . . Macleod falls in love with a London actress, a young woman of irreproachable life and with the prospect of a brilliant career, and induces her without difficulty to listen to his suit—which is purely honorable—and to promise to become his wife. She comes to pay a visit to his mother on the island of Mull, and otherwise induces him to believe that she intends to keep faith with him. But she breaks faith, throws him over, becomes engaged to a member of the theatrical world. The young man, who has loved her devotedly, takes her infidelity so terribly to heart that it finally affects his reason. He sails down from Scotland to London in his yacht, induces the young lady, by false representations, to come on board; then, closing the hatches, puts to sea with her and hurries away northward. The most violent recriminations naturally ensue between the love-crazed Caledonian and the bewildered and outraged actress, which are finally eclipsed by the fury of the elements themselves. A terrible storm overtakes the yacht, which goes down in darkness and thunder.[15]

To this should be added the supporting details of a not particularly memorable story. The English actress, Gertrude White, and her father, Septimus White, live in modest respectability on "Gerty's" earnings from light stage parts. A collector of objects of art, Mr. White has given his money and time to preparing Gerty for a stage career. Sir Keith (Macleod of Dare) meets her through Norman Ogilvie, an old school-mate, who is acquainted with sophisticated London society. Sir Keith has left two women behind at Castle Dare. One is stately old Lady Macleod, who sorrowfully contemplates this unfortunate involvement of her last son; who has only memories of the past valor of the family to console her and worsening financial circumstances to face. She looks upon Sir Keith's intended marriage as a veritable fall from honor and wonders whether death would be better for him. The other woman is Janet Macleod, a half-cousin, who has urged (unsuccessfully) that Sir Keith use a letter of credit for a large sum of money as he departs for his first trip to the metropolis, and whom Lady Macleod is hoping Sir Keith will marry. Gerty promises to marry Sir Keith. When she is invited to Dare much against Lady Macleod's wishes, she is bored by the dreariness of the Highlands and the seriousness of talk at the castle; she rejects the thought of a life-time of dullness there, even as a Scotch nobleman's wife. She meets L. Lemuel, the man she eventually becomes engaged to, during the absence in Scotland of the enamoured Sir Keith. He is a painter and devotee of art who has her sit for a portrait of Juliet that, she hopes, will further her stage career, a career in which he has great faith.

The Tragic Muse, of course, developed into two interlocking stories: one about art, with Nick Dormer and Julia Dallow, the other about the theatre, with Peter Sherringham and Miriam Rooth; and both a centripetality and a gratuitous complication are added by Miriam Rooth's becoming a magnet for Nick as well as for Peter (and accordingly a cross-purpose for Julia and Biddy). Nevertheless, parallels both vague and close with *Macleod of Dare* can be seen in James's story. The English Miriam Rooth and her mother live a meagre bohemian existence on money left by the late Mr. Rooth [Roth], a dealer in art objects. Mrs. Rooth is devoting her life to making an actress of Miriam. Both Nick and Peter are introduced to the demimondaine Miriam by Gabriel Nash, an old college classmate of Nick's. Nick forsakes two women for an art career in a London studio. The first, his mother Lady Agnes

Dormer, has only Nick to look to for financial support, which can result only if Nick takes up the political heritage of his late father. After Nick's final refusal, "She draped herself in [her wrongs] as a kind of Roman mantle, and she never looked so proud and wasted and handsome as now that her eyes rested only upon ruins." The other is Julia Sherringham Dallow, Nick's second cousin, who insists on giving him money (which he refuses) for his campaign for the Harsh seat in Parliament; Lady Agnes wants Nick to marry her. Miriam actually appears to promise to marry Peter late in the story. Lady Agnes recoils from familiarity with the unfashionable Rooths when Peter arranges for Miriam to display her talent before them. Miriam, in turn, cannot stomach the dullness of the socially enviable life she would lead as a diplomat's wife. She meets Basil Dashwood, her eventual husband, during Peter's prolonged absence from her at the time of his first courting. He recognizes and appreciates her talent, whose greatest test, in the story's closing pages, is her performance of Juliet. Meanwhile, Nick is struggling along with portraits of Miriam which will, she hopes, help accelerate her rise to prominence.

In addition, there are correspondences in themselves minute enough to seem trifling, but, as collateral, impressive in their aggregate:

(1) Norman Ogilvie is identified as Sir Keith's "mentor" in London, and the second chapter of Black's novel bears that title; Gabriel Nash is identified to Julia by Peter as "Nick's new Mentor or oracle."

(2) Madame Carré, the drama teacher who develops Miriam as an actress, lives in quarters that strike Peter as a "theatrical museum" and Nick Dormer as a "little temple of art." L. Lemuel, Gerty's painter-sponsor, lives in what Gerty calls a "palace of art," "a temple dedicated to high art."

(3) Gerty aspires beyond modern comedy parts to the greatness of Rachel, of Mrs. Siddons. She is even written of by one admiring critic (of the provinces) as having "the beauty of Mrs. Siddons and

the genius of Rachel." In James's novel, Mrs. Siddons has become the title, of course; Peter suggests to Nick that he paint Miriam as such; and associations of Miriam with Rachel, whether by herself, Peter, or Dashwood, are numerous.

(4) Gerty writes to Sir Keith her disgust with her tour: the rigors of travel, the poor accommodations, the vulgarity of the provincial audiences—the noise, the drunken antics of sailors, etc. Gabriel Nash, as we notice, lectures Peter on the crassness of the theatre audience: their "essentially brutal nature . . . flocking out of hideous hotels and restaurants gorged with food, stultified with . . . sordid preoccupations of the day, squeezed together in a sweltering mass. . . ."

(5) Apropos her debut in London as Juliet, Gerty writes to Sir Keith:

"I hear there is to be a grand supper afterward somewhere, and I have no doubt I shall be presented to a number of ladies who will speak for the first time to an actress and be possessed with a wild fear; only, if they have daughters, I suppose they will keep the flut-tering-hearted young things out of the way, lest I should suddenly break out into a blue flame, and then disappear through the floor." (257–258)

With this compare Miriam's remarks to Nick apropos Mrs. Rooth's apologetic confession that she has had Biddy Dormer in to meet her and Miriam: " 'Your sister *is* charming—awfully pretty and modest. If you were to press me I should tell you frankly that it seems to me rather a social muddle, this rubbing shoulders of 'nice girls' and *filles de theatre*; I shouldn't think it would do your young ladies much good." (Ch. 44) (It is true that she goes on to add scoffingly—as the hypocritical Gerty did not—that " 'However, it's their own affair, and no doubt there's no more need of their think-ing we're worse than we are than of their thinking we're better. The people they live with don't seem to know the difference . . . ,' " thereby evincing a blunt candor that, as we shall see, is one of her distinguishing traits.)

(6) In the closing action of *Macleod of Dare*, Sir Keith makes anchorage in some remote island and issues an ultimatum to Gerty to marry him; when she tells him that she hates him, he drowns her and himself. In the middle of *The Tragic Muse* there is a faint, joking, yet curious variation of this situation: Nick, openly annoyed at Julia Dallow's attempts to take him away from art, remarks as they set out for the island in the lake, " 'I could kill you for that' "; Julia asks, " 'Shall you drown me?' "; and Nick retorts, " 'Oh, let me perish with you!' " And toward the end of the novel: "Nick had an unexpressed conviction that if . . . he had embarked with Mrs. Dallow in this particular quest of a great prize, disaster would have overtaken them on the deep waters."

Moving from plot and situation to characterization, we come upon correspondences between Black's title hero and the dual male protagonists of James's novel. Sir Keith is a handsome, virile young laird who worships his venerable home and is suspicious of the new. His satisfaction at the "pretty little old-fashioned courtesy" that young ladies in London render their elders is offset by his discovery that their gowns are open in back to the waist. His consciousness is filled with the storied history of the Macleod and other Scotch clans, particularly of their part in the last events of the Stuart rebellion of the preceding century. Imparting this affords him one of his few pleasures during his uneasy stay in the capital. Another is his acquaintance there with a couple—Admiral Maitland and Miss Rawlinson—who are in their nineties. One can note in all this faint hints for the "muscular and musing" Nick Dormer of James's novel who has to steel himself to rub elbows with the man in the street, whose vote he doesn't really want; and although to look for precedents for characters in a James novel who are enchanted by the living past of people and places is in itself the ultimate in redundance, still it should be submitted that Nick is attracted to the wily, ancient Mr. Carteret, whose present is in his remote youth, and to the ancient abbey at Beauclere, with the message of time that it whispers in his ear.

Sir Keith is, however, somewhat more suggestive of James's other leading male character, Peter Sherringham. Sir Keith comes from the aristocracy and betrays its characteristic aloofness from, even reprobation of, the stage in a way that dooms his romantic intentions. When Black imagines Gerty's future interpretation of Sir Keith's attitude toward her as " *'This man hates the stage because he is jealous of its hold on my life,'* " he is stating but half the case: Sir Keith also hates the stage *because it is the stage.* He reveals what James called his "literal mind and purely moral development"—the fact that he is "a Puritan and a precisian"—in his literal recoil from the disreputability of every aspect of stage life. He goes most unwillingly to see Gerty act, only once or twice at that, and tells her that " *'I desire that all the theatres in the kingdom of Great Britain and Ireland—with all their musical instruments, lime-light, and painted scenes—may be taken and dropped into the ocean.'* " Although this is a sort of jesting, and knowingly cruel, he finds it necessary to an honest statement of his feelings. His marrying her, accordingly, rests on the understanding that she will forsake her present way of life. When her news that she is going to take another part in a London play first suggests the possibility of rejection of his affection, he tells her: " 'You are going forward to a new triumph, Gerty; and the first step you will take will be on my heart.' " And when he discovers the identity of his successful rival, Lemuel, he assails him silently as " 'the woman-man, the dabbler in paint-boxes, the critic of carpets and wall-papers!' "

Similarly, Peter Sherringham is a genteel diplomat who is uncomfortable at thoughts of the hand-to-mouth existence of Miriam and her mother; is shocked that she has accepted money from Gabriel Nash and insists that she return it; feels ill at ease in bohemian quarters; conceals his closeness with stage people from his friends ("he carried the apprehension of ridicule too far"); and while "neither a pedant nor a prig," considers the possibility of giving up his career for love unthinkable: his proposal is in effect to take Miriam away from the stage in marrying her. He cries out, when she first rejects his attention: " '. . . you must destroy and torment and consume. . . . You must forage and ravage. . . . You use us, you push us about, you break us up. We are your tables and chairs, the simple furniture of your life.' " And to his calling his rival, Basil Dashwood, " 'a young mountebank,' " she retorts, " 'How you hate us! Yes, at bottom, below your little taste, you *hate* us!' "

On the other hand, there is equally impressive evidence that if James did in truth use the materials of the novel he had read over ten years before in shaping *The Tragic Muse*, this in turn became manifestly his own superior creation. Nor may this be concluded only from the obvious differences in the two stories: the multiplication of personal relationships in James, as compared with Black's sparse tale; and the happy curtain scene in James, with its two marriages and its suggestion of a Nick-Julia reconciliation, as compared with Black's "dusky pall of fatality [of the] 'Bride of Lammermoor,' " as James had defined it—the melodramatic murder of Gerty and the suicide of Sir Keith. These are mere differences in plot and structure; they are no measure of the superiority of James's book as a work of fiction. His alterations in the major characterizations, however, are.

Let us consider the men first. Here we see at once that if it was the simple hero of Castle Dare that went into James's crucible, he has emerged two men; and this in turn is not so worthy of consideration as that these two men are themselves divided into two men. Sir Keith Macleod is, in James's own reliable analysis,

the portrait of a deep and simple nature, with an hereditary disposition to brutality and violence, wrought upon by a grievous disappointment and converted into the likeness of one of his highhanded ancestors. Macleod is meant for a man of strong and simple passions, a hero . . . who loves . . . with consuming intensity, and for whom a sentimental disappointment is of necessity a heartbreak. [Sir Keith has a] formidable sincerity and dangerous temper.[16]

The old Britannica article would note that in general, "subtlety of intuition plays no part in [Black's] characterization." Surely Macleod of Dare bears this out. Once he has seen Gertrude, his passion is aroused; once she has promised to marry him, he will allow nothing to change her mind. With a melancholy that seems in keeping with the savage scenery and weather of his home, he broods about his future grave and has a morbid preoccupation with the image of a sinister, fatal serpent. His are outdoor pastimes; one learns with surprise that he has been reading *Pendennis*, his only concession to the world Gerty is a member of.

James's men, on the other hand, are engrossing personalities such as James had admired in Turgenev's fiction; and if viewed together (for they are one, in terms of temperament, of sensitivity), they represent their creator's attitudes toward art, whether pictorial or histrionic. It is true that Nick's representation in a political context is "factitious," [17] but this need not distract us from his actual complexity. For he is both aware of his mere facileness as an artist and of his fate to try to rise above that limitation. He finds Miriam's essence "irresistible" yet not her self; conversely, although the femaleness of Julia's presence causes in him an "agitating blur of vision," still once she is out of sight, her influence vanishes. For there are, as James puts it, "reciprocities and special sympathies, in such relations; mysterious affinities . . . , divinations of private congruity."

Peter Sherringham too may be said to begin where Sir Keith leaves off. The secretary of the British Embassy in Paris is a much more interesting character because of his contradictory impulses. Side by side with his distaste for actors and stage effects, and doing battle with it in a way whose inconsistency he is embarrassedly aware of, is a genuine and consuming interest in the theatre as an esthetic force. He carries this conflict of impulses, this "mixture of impulse and reflection," into his dealings with Miriam: he too is capable of an irresistible romantic attachment, but with him passion is merely one facet of that attachment. Roughly combining the aggressive persistence of Caspar Goodward toward Isabel Archer and Ralph Touchett's disinterested affection, he seems at first to have "taken" Miriam "up," to be "struck with her rich type," yet shortly has to confess to himself that "he had been in love with her

from the first hour." He shrinks from deciding "whether Miriam
would be an interest or only a bore," and confesses to his sister that
" 'I do care for [Miriam] in a way. . . . She's interesting. . . . And
she's awful!' " His discovery that he is in love with Miriam wars
with his suspicion that he may make a fool of himself about her;
and if he foresees that she is vulgar, the prescience is distasteful
since he knows that he is in love with her. He is capable of assuming minor melodramatic stances, such as precipitately requesting
and sailing for an unenviable post in some little Central American
country to hide his romantic hurt, and of marrying little Biddy
Dormer almost out of hand when it is established that Miriam is at
long last married; but characteristically he divides his time between
the proper pursuit of his official responsibilities at his office in Paris
and of furthering Miriam's career (improperly), whether by paying
for her lessons, for her admission to plays, recommending books to
read, and even by buying a play for her at great expense to himself.

But his most important claim to our interest today is his ability
to transcend his self-conscious distaste for the physical aspect of the
play-house, for rehearsed lines and properties and stage business: he
can view a fine dramatic performance of human action as a deeply
satisfying coalescence of spirit and artifice, its capacity to satisfy
him due as much to his awareness of the artifice as in spite of it. In
keeping with the puritanism that Henry James noted in him, Sir
Keith Macleod is so shocked by his discovery at a Caledonian fancy-
dress ball in London that the dark-eyed, mischievous-looking Lady
Devonshire is really the light-eyed, demure Gertrude White of his
affection in disguise that "the cold austerity of his look" frightens
her. He does not seriously believe that such "social misdemeanours"
as flirtation, adultery, heavy drinking by women, or marriage for
money exist outside the depraved minds of the authors of the paper-
backed French novels that he flings contemptuously aside, unfinished, at Castle Dare. Thus, seeing Gerty he is ashamed and wonders: "What was she doing . . . amidst all this glaring sham—
before all these people?" When the impending immoral outcome
of the piece on the stage turns into virtue triumphant, he leaves the

theatre relieved, breathing "more freely when he knew that Gertrude White was now about to go away to the shelter of her own home." Compare this severely limited consciousness with the welter of sensations, as exciting and mysterious as they are pell-mell, that Miriam's stage performance calls forth in Peter:

Miriam had never been more present to him than at this hour; but she was inextricably transmuted—present essentially as the romantic heroine she represented. His state of mind was of the strangest, and he was conscious of its strangeness; just as he was conscious, in his person, of a cessation of resistance which identified itself absurdly with liberation. He felt weak at the same time that he felt excited, and he felt excited at the same time that he knew, or believed he knew, that his face was a blank. He saw things as a shining confusion, and yet somehow something monstrously definite kept surging out of them. Miriam was a beautiful, actual, fictive, implausible young woman, of a past age and undiscoverable country, who spoke in blank verse and overflowed with metaphor, who was exalted and heroic beyond all human convenience, and who yet was irresistibly real and related to one's own affairs. But that reality was a part of her spectator's joy, and she was not changed back to the common by his perception of the magnificent trick of art with which it was connected.

To make the comparison is to watch entertainment become art, is to observe the novelist merging with the psychologist as he presents the human personality in all the dimensions with which modern knowledge credits it.

As regards the supporting male characters, it would be hard to believe that James's enigmatic Gabriel Nash could have been cut from any pattern as ordinary as Black's Norman Ogilvie. Not that resemblances even between these two intermediaries are not discernible. Although Ogilvie is in the military, there is a definite suggestion of delicacy, even of effeminacy, about him. Sir Keith tells Janet, " 'I said to him, "Do you wear gloves at Aldershot?" His hands were as white as the hands of a woman.' " And at one time

Sir Keith thinks of him as "lily-fingered and gentle-natured." Ogilvie is correctly, even foppishly, dressed, and Black's description of him as a "facetious boy" is apt. It is no great distance from this description to the "fair," "fat," "young," and "mellifluous" person who is Gabriel Nash. Moreover, the knowledgeability of both is an operational one. It will be recalled that it is Gabriel Nash whose unerring sense about the Rooths makes it possible for him to predict to the infatuated Peter the future course that Miriam will follow with regard to marriage. Norman performs a parallel function. He is the one who early tries to correct Sir Keith's sudden passionate idealization of Gerty:

> "Well, I should say [that giving a charity performance] was exactly the thing that Miss White would like to do—get mixed up with a whole string of duchesses and marchionesses—a capital advertisement—and it would be all the more distinguished if it was an amateur performance, and Miss Gertrude White the only professional admitted into the charmed circle."

And it is Ogilvie who finally divulges to the distressed Sir Keith the perfidious Gerty's plan to marry the man Lemuel. But even if Sir Keith in moments of irritation at Norman's levity thinks of him as a "lily-fingered jackanapes" and both Peter and Nick at such moments wonder whether the mentally dextrous Nash isn't an "ass," still Norman is by and large a rather proper, tactful young man, and no important part of this simple young Scotsman from Aldershot seems to have carried over into James's will-o'-the-wisp philosopher from Samarkand—if not James's most gratifying character, possibly his most original.

This originality is even more prominently in evidence in a comparison of the two authors' characterizations of women. Black's are typical of their time, either passive and loyal or coquettish and fickle, but consistently the weaker, submissive sex. James's are strong, overshadowing the men, who yield the supremacy to them or devote their energies to combatting it. Black's Janet Macleod, for example, is a fairly nondescript young female of the Highlands aristocracy. Sweet, quiet, gentle, and plain-featured, she seems a Celtic "Madonna"; generously offers all the money she has saved to Sir Keith with no conditions; is compassionate to the sick in the vicinity; and while quietly trying to be a companion and confidante to Sir Keith, always remains in the background and makes no attempt, however timid, to attract him romantically.

The Julia Dallow who is her counterpart in *The Tragic Muse* is a veritable antithesis of this. A handsome and high-handed young woman, she is a passionate practitioner of the *vita activa* and seems the English opposite number of the New American Woman of James's novels. She is familiar with current periodical literature on politics (*e.g.*, the Hoppus article on "The Revision of the British Constitution" that evoked Nick's exasperation in the previously cited lake episode) and works at making Nick a politician, to the extent of campaigning with him. Utterly lacking in feminine softness, this "imperious and generous" widow cannot accept Nick on any terms but her own; and although it is old-fashioned jealousy of another woman (Miriam) that causes her break with Nick, the end of the novel finds them still apart notwithstanding Miriam's marriage. In view of her deep-seated incompatibility with Nick, James can say no more finally than that she has not married anyone else, however enthusiastic a Liberal: it would have been faulty workmanship to reconcile her "personal passion" for an artist with her admitted hatred of art.

Striking though this re-shaping of Black's simple, stage-property Janet Macleod into the bustling Julia Dallow may be, it seems almost inconsiderable by contrast with the great achievement of James's novel, namely Miriam Rooth, who as The Tragic Muse replaces Black's laird as hero. This might have been expected of a writer who cared so little for political life and so much for all arts, particularly the theatre. Not only this: it might have been predicted from James's own dissatisfaction with Black's Gertrude White. In fact, we can place the strictures of his apparently casual review side by side with the studied remarks of his that are already associated with the origin of *The Tragic Muse* and even see the seed of his own actress in the process of germinating.

Having pointed out that the merit of *Macleod of Dare* was "in its grace and picturesqueness, and in the romantic portrait of the hero," he goes on to maintain that

the weak point of the tale is the figure of the heroine. . . . Gertrude White is not in the least the study of an actress, nor indeed . . . the study of anything at all. The author had an admirable chance; nothing could have been more dramatic than to bring out the contrast between the artistic temperament, the histrionic genius and Bohemian stamp of the femme de théâtre, and . . . her stalwart Highland lover. But . . . Gertrude White . . . is nothing of a Bohemian, and we doubt very much whether she was anything of an actress. It was a very gratuitous stroke on Mr. Black's part to represent her as one. Her profession plays no part in the story, and the hero greatly dislikes the theatre and goes to see his mistress but two or three times on the stage.

Just as, a dozen years earlier when he conceived Daisy Miller, James was impatient with the European Cherbuliez for his inability to portray an Anglo-Saxon girl, so now, he insists, it would have been possible to manage the whole matter of the characterization of the actress much more credibly: "The reader involuntarily thinks of the very different manner in which two or three French novelists he could name would have attempted the portrait of Gertrude White—of how minutely they would have studied it, how different a type they would have suggested, and how many details and small realities they would have given us."

Thirty years later, when James wrote the Preface to his *Tragic Muse*, while he confessed to a "certain vagueness of remembrance in respect to the origin and growth" of his novel, we still find him returning to the question of the handling of the characterization of the actress by the French novelists. Now he even identifies one of them as Anatole France, even if only as the creator of "vivid monsters" on a lower level than his own Miriam Rooth. For us, who have access to his review of Black's novel, watching this buried seed unwittingly come to life in the Preface is like watching Lambert Strether's "lemon-colored volumes" of thirty years ago come to life the moment he returns to Paris in *The Ambassadors*; it also is in effect to measure the intensity of James's otherwise unrecorded desire to "do something about the stage," as he would have put it. Small wonder, then, if for James this turned out to be a more engrossing intention than the original one—his Preface has it—"To 'do something about art.'"

But in order to do something about the stage, it was necessary to present a theory of the dramatic medium of which the actress herself would be an inevitable outcome. To explain Miriam Rooth, he must explain the requirements to which she is subject. Such an explanation can be found in several places in *The Tragic Muse*. In essence, it is: to be a good actress, a woman must either have no personality of her own or must learn to efface it completely. This theory is like the one of the artist's model in "The Real Thing," and like it rests on a paradox—here, that to the degree that a woman creates a striking impression of her own, she has limited her range as a stage performer. Conversely, the best—that is, the most varied—actress is the one with least personality of her own. As Peter realizes, Miriam's whole existence is a "series of parts assumed for the moment, each changed for the next"; as he tells her, " 'You are always playing something. . . . You're an embroidery without a canvas.' " And to her " '. . . do you think I've got no character?' " he retorts, charmed by her "plastic" quality, " 'Delightful being, you've got a hundred!' " (Or, as the equally charmed Howells put it in his review of James's book, Miriam is "most herself when her whole nature is straining toward the realization of some one else. . . .") [18]

Now, so far from this theory being original with James, it can be found even in *Macleod of Dare* itself, where it has more than one articulator, chiefly the pontifical Mr. White. He lectures his inconstant daughter:

"The artist loses himself. He transfers his soul to his creation. His heart beats in another breast; he sees with other eyes. . . . [Gerty] ought to be ready at any moment to project herself . . . into any character. She ought to practice so as to make of her own emotions an instrument that she can use at will. It is a great demand that art makes on the life of an artist. In fact, he ceases to live for himself. He becomes merely a medium. His most secret experiences are the property of the world at large, once they have been transfused and moulded by his personal skill."

Sir Keith echoes this in his remonstrance with Gerty: " 'Do you have a chance of believing in anything . . . on the stage? . . . What must the end of it be?—that you play with emotions and beliefs until you have no faith in any one—none left for yourself; it is the only material of your art. Would you not rather like to live your own life?' "

Gerty is both inspired and troubled by the rigorousness of this esthetic:

"It isn't the life of a human being at all . . . ; it is the cutting one's self off from everything that makes life worth having. It is a continual degradation—the exhibition of feelings that ought to be a woman's most sacred and secret possession.
And what will the end of it be? Already I begin to think I don't know what I am. I have to sympathize with so many characters—I have to be so many different people—that I don't quite know what my own character is, or if I have any at all."

This, to her father. And to Sir Keith she confides that she doubts " 'whether I have got any opinions—whether, having to be so many different people in the course of a week, I have any clear notion as to what I myself am.' " It is this inability to comply with the requirements of her art because of qualms about their morality that justifies James's charge that she "is almost as much a Puritan and a precisian as her lover." It is the essentially moral young Englishwoman who confides to her father her feelings of guilt that the hypocrisy of her dealings with Sir Keith inspires: " '. . . I feel now as if I was called on to act a part from morning till night, whereas I was always assured that if I left the stage and married him it was to be my natural self, and I should have no more need to pose and sham.' " And it is the Puritan in her again who pleads with her father, citing a street accident that she has recently witnessed: " 'When I walked away . . . I caught myself trying to recall the way in which the woman threw her arms up when she saw the dead body of her child, and I was wondering whether I could repeat it. And then I began to wonder *whether I was a devil*—or a woman.' " (Italics mine.)

Now these are precisely the qualms that Peter has about the young actress to whom he feels himself attracted:

It struck him . . . that a woman whose only being was to "make believe," to make believe that she had any and every being that you liked, that would . . . produce a certain effect, and whose identity resided in the continuity of her personations, so that she had no moral privacy . . . but lived in a high wind of exhibition, of figuration—such a woman was a kind of monster, in whom of necessity there would be nothing to like, because there would be nothing to take hold of. [Italics mine.]

But the difference is that only in the latter instance are the fears justified. For as James quickly saw, Gerty was not an actress, except by author proclamation. To the extent that she is anything, she is an average middle-class young woman whose ability to act is never made credible. She is naturally domestic. She insists on mixing the salad dressing for Sir Keith herself; her younger sister Carry reports that Gerty has been " 'far more anxious about these cutlets than about her new part' "; * and the author reminds us that "Gertrude White was at all times and in all seasons a precise and accurate

---

* Is it possible that in this "spiteful" and "cruel" younger sister who is capable of heckling Gerty with provincial reviews of her acting there is another source for James's Rosie Muniment of *The Princess Casamassima?* (See Cargill, *The Novels of Henry James*, p. 184.)

house-mistress [who] allowed nothing to interfere with her domestic duties." In fact, our *soi-disant* actress is basically a "shifty, practical, industrious person" who is the mainstay of the little old-fashioned house in South Bank, Regent's Park: "Her father had to confess that there was no one but herself whom he could trust to arrange his china and dust his curiosities. And how could he resent her giving instructions to the cook, when it was his own dinner that profited thereby?" It is this middle-class quality that is partly accountable for her responding originally to Sir Keith's proposal, for she is impressed with the gentility she will acquire by marrying him: as Lady Macleod she will be able to play Lady Bountiful to the Scotch poor and to share ownership of the sumptuous Macleod yacht Umpire.

Partly, of course, it is mere changeableness. In fact, it is as though by this one, arbitrary label Black thought to establish her identity in the story; as though, for Victorian readers' acceptance of her as an actress, it was merely necessary for her to be presented as asking, " 'Would it surprise you if the new day brought [to me] a complete new set of feelings?' " This trait accounts for the coolness of the letters ("She might have written thus to one of her school-companions") she writes to the love-sick Sir Keith. With as unconvincing a change of heart as prompted her to adopt a stage career, she promises to give it up for marriage, then decides to give up marriage for her stage career (her marriage to Lemuel in no way detracting from this new decision but being responsible for and even reinforcing it). Fickleness and conceit, desire for self-advancement, jealousy of other actresses, and sensitiveness to criticism—these are Gerty White, even if they are qualities that are merely announced, and not so much manifested as reiterated.

Now Miriam Rooth is at least all of these. Peter knows that she is "noisy and pert," "grossly vain," and conceited; by her own admission she is "capricious"; and the prestige of Nick's initials on his portrait of her is a most gratifying prospect to this little "Philistine." But with these touches James's characterization of her merely begins. These are her secondary traits, for in essence her character is exactly opposed to Gerty's.

In fact, if there is any real parallel with Gerty, it is James's Nick Dormer. To match the Gerty of bohemian yearnings and domestic affinity who goes from career to thoughts of marriage back to career, is James's divided painter-politician-painter. There are "two men in him, quite separate." Although "he longed for [Julia], . . . yet without her the place was more filled with what he wanted to find in it." His situation even parallels Gerty's: does not Julia besiege him with a Macleod-like persistence? Is not the chief attraction for him (rather, for his mother and sisters through him), the country estate of the "mistress of Harsh"? Yet basically he is more faint and pliable than he is fickle.

Miriam Rooth, on the other hand, has a character that is inflexible, unyielding in its devotion to and enslavement by the need to be an actress, to the exclusion of all else. She is the woman of the One Idea, the "magnificently stupid," vacant-looking splendid girl with the cold, largely-gazing eyes, the strange tragic beauty, the "natural felicity," even "sort of grandeur" of movement. Refusing to acknowledge discouragement, she memorizes quantities of lines, practices gestures by the dozen, consistently and innocently exploits all men who offer their help yet belongs to none of them. (Even her husband is merely a convenience to her career, as Peter and Nick have been before; she will discard him when the need arises.) The middle-class Gerty was a snob who had rationalized her change of mind about Sir Keith as a protest against the unbearably dull life in the Highlands; the classless Miriam openly admits to Nick the value to her portrait of his initials on it and admits to Peter that life as the wife of a rising diplomat is not to be traded for a stage career. To be sure, like Sir Keith, Peter Sherringham is astonished to discover that after several months' separation the woman he wants to marry "had no personal emotion in seeing him again," and after several months' absence from Nick, to whom she has been visibly attracted romantically, she breezes unexpectedly into his studio with Dashwood, "giving her left [hand] to Nick (as she might have given it to her own brother) . . ."; this, however, is not because she is a chameleon like Gerty but because "the cold passion of art had perched on her banner."

Finally, whereas Black's statements about the stage sounded memorized, we never do not think of Miriam Rooth as The Actress. All of James's many details lead us persuasively to that realization. Rachel Félix is merely a rote phrase in Gerty White's day-dreaming; to the assiduously toiling Miriam Rooth it is a shrine worthy of a life-long pilgrimage.* No one, herself included, believes her statement that " 'I'd give it all up in a moment, my odious trade—for an inducement.' " That odious trade, in fact, becomes the supreme achievement of James's story, if not of all his stories. Her late, shadowy father, Rudolf Roth, "with his love of old pots and Christian altar-cloths"; her self-effacing, novel-reading mother with her pathetic claims to being "a Neville-Nugent of Castle Nugent" (her naivete and abjectness so different from Septimus White's self-conscious urbanity and sententiousness); the sojourns in Italy and other dimly perceived yet vividly sensed precincts of Bohemia; the tawdry yet evocative salon of Madame Carré (she of the atrocious wig); the dressing rooms of the theatre; the smells, the flaming of the gas lights—it is all there in *The Tragic Muse*. There, captured for modern pleasure is the eternal Mrs. Siddons: the cold yet appealing, ruthless yet innocent, latter-day Melpomene. While only by digging deeply in the bottomless accumulation of Victorian light reading can one find the faceless flibbertigibbet who was probably responsible for bringing The Tragic Muse to life.

---

* Some indication of the awe with which the Paris of the 1850's held this actress emerges from James's own autobiographical *Notes of a Son and Brother* (1914). There he recalls sitting "in a dusky upper chamber" and reading " 'French literature' " with a M. Toeppfer: "He had haunted the parterre of the Théatre Français, and when we read Racine his vision of Rachel, whom he had seen there as often as possible, revived; he was able to say at moments how she had spoken and moved, and I recall in particular his telling me that on her entrance as Phèdre, borne down, in her languorous passion, by the weight of her royal robes—'Que ces vains ornemens, que ces voiles me pèsent!'—the long lapse of time before she spoke and while she sank upon a seat filled itself extraordinarily with her visible woe." (F. W. Dupee, [ed.], *Henry James: Autobiography*, pp. 242, 243.)

IV. FIGURES IN THE CARPET

A. DOTTING THE I'S

It is an unfortunate fact of Henry James's reputation that, if any one impression persists, it is that his fiction raises barriers to comprehension forbiddingly high except for a handful, a devout "few." Even so early a member of this group as Stuart P. Sherman, while referring to "the thirty or forty volumes which any one can read with ease" adds "the fifteen or twenty richer volumes which demand closer application." [1] And there is ample evidence that James himself sensed this distance between his art and his audience. Numerous are the passages, throughout his long career, in which he speaks, whether peevishly or regretfully or both, of the demands which that art makes on that audience. In his *Hawthorne* (1879) there is an edge to his reference to "an American reader with any turn for analysis," [2] and the much later Prefaces are literally sprinkled with more direct opprobrious reflections on the audience's native equipment for its task. He notes a "certain extraordinary benightedness on the part of the Anglo-Saxon reader"; protests against the general "numbness" of Anglo-Saxon sensibility, against "our so marked mistrust of anything like close or analytic appreciation"; and complains that "It is dreadful to have too much, for any artistic demonstration, to dot one's i's and insist on one's intentions. . . ." [3]

Yet he never chose merely to retreat into an arrogant obscurity, to write his poem and pare his nails. Obscurity might result, to be sure, but it was not a deliberate one. If communication between writer and reader was not always immediate, this may have been owing to James's relaxation of his usual care for the reader's grasp of his pages, to his allowing the relationship to become like that of the cousins Percy Beaumont and Lord Lambeth in "An International Episode." Their conversation, we read, with its "many odd silences, lapses of logic and incongruities of transition," is like that of "a pair who have grown old together and learned to guess each other's sense; or, more especially, like persons so conscious of a common point of view that missing links and broken lights and loose ends, the unexpressed and the understood, could do the office of talk." Moreover, frequently we find him inviting the more "sensitive" among his readers to join him in what he considered a joyous intellectual game in every sense except the literal, and at times even in that. Leon Edel has called our attention to James's "love of patterns and figures, secrecy and 'mystification,' " to the fact that in planning the "architecture" of the collected edition of his works, he "created an unlabelled but artfully arranged edition leaving it to the reader to ferret out his figures in the carpet." [4] In fact, just as in so many of his tales he creates a tri-partite relationship of Obtuse and Hostile Public, Abused Representative Artist, and between them, Understanding and Sympathetic Initiate, so for the benefit of these last—his fit audience though few—in the real-life reading public, he wove into his stories threads by which to bring the overall design of his tapestry into greater prominence. Of these, there was a variety.

1. NAMES

Poetry . . . is a more philosophical and higher thing than history; poetry tends to express the universal, history the particular. The universal tells us how a person of given character will on occasion speak or act, according to the law of probability or necessity; and it is this universality at which Poetry aims in giving expressive names to the character. (Aristotle, the Poetics, Sec. 9)

First of all, like all story-tellers of his and all other times, Henry James made use of devices of rhetoric to catch, not only the minds of the superior, but the eye and ear of the average. Chief among these devices is that of names, whose importance has been demonstrated by James's fellow craftsmen from John Bunyan to James Jones. Consider a story from James's middle period, that too-angry fable of the man in an unfeeling world, "The Death of the Lion." A mere inventory of its names is enough to designate the reaction that James wishes the reader to share with him. On the one hand, the victimized man of letters, Neil Paraday: one *kneels* to the current literary favorite only *for a day*. On the other, the varying degrees of vulgarity, insensitivity, or even animosity. The editor is named Pinhorn, with all the images and sensations of angularity and pain associated with *pin* and *horn*. How Hawthorne would have approved! * The predatory autograph hunter is a *Hurter*; the importunate publisher wants his results on the *Morrow*; the shallow, fickle hostess is a veritable *bush* of mere *whims* (Wimbush); and her estate, named Prestidge, is—minus only one letter—just what the status-seekers who flock to it want and need.

In general, however, it was to such sensitive observers as the unnamed narrator of this story that James dedicated his art; and, like

---

* Shortly after the publication of *The House of the Seven Gables*, Nathaniel Hawthorne wrote to a man actually named Pyncheon that he had used this name for his grasping, malicious villain because "its unhackneyed singularity, and a certain indescribable fitness to the tone of my work, gave it a value which no other of the many surnames which suggested themselves to me seemed to possess."

Hawthorne, he enriched their reading fare with somewhat more select garnish, for he provided their journey with touchstones that would open to them the further and more elaborate dimensions of his art. In fact, it may even be observed that in proportion as he aimed higher than the average reader,* the less his employment of this patent literary device became. In *The American*, an early work for which, with his youthful ambition, James must have had hopes of wide acceptance, all the associations that *Christopher Newman* calls forth (for which, see its first chapter) are fairly elementary ones. *Christopher* was the explorer who discovered the *New* World, and the *New* Man is the figure by which foreigners had been asked to identify The American since the days of St. Jean de Crevècoeur ("The American is a new man, who acts upon new principles; he must therefore entertain new ideas, and form new opinions"); and the associations are immediate in their effect. Similarly, in *The Portrait of a Lady* the sounds and associations of all the characters, both major and minor, are contributory to this novel's aims. Most of the time they register immediately and simply on the reader's comprehension, for they are clues to no greatly complicated mysteries of characterization. Consider the sportive naming of the supporting cast: of Mr. Bantling, who, we are told, *is* a child; of Lady Pensil, who writes (poetry!); and of the Misses Climber, who are just that, socially speaking. And there is Sir Matthew Hope, both of whose names seem appropriate to a man (like Sir *Luke* Strett, of *The Wings of the Dove*) who is a great doctor.

Even for the major characters James need provide no more complex key for our understanding: Isabel *is* an archer, aiming with great deliberateness at her destiny. The indefatigable Caspar is practically a *good* piece of *wood*: his basic integrity is beyond question and we read that he is *hard*. If Henrietta is somewhat subtler as a characterization—being not only pushy and coarsely grained enough for her profession as journalist but an honest and generous young woman as well—still James's touch with her is a faintly derisive one,

---

* Two collections of his later tales, we note, are entitled *The Better Sort* and *The Finer Grain*.

containing some amusement; and conducive to both is the association with them that the name Stackpole seems ineffably to convey. In fact the only two characters in this novel given names that suggest a depth of characterization impossible to identify unmistakably by graphic means are two of the managers, as it were, of Isabel's destiny; one a male and the other a female. About the latter, if *Serena* suggests simply the confident, poised * woman that Mme. Merle is, still *Merle* itself is asked to bear the weight of all the association with European legend and wizardry: thus delicately does James join the antipodal Brooklyn Navy Yard and Arthurian Legend themes.† Equally imponderably successful is *Touchett*: what reactions does it call forth in us if not at least of fineness (which Ralph has copiously) and at the same time of magic (which, in effect, he helps work for Isabel)?

From this it is a natural step to the names of the work of James's "major phase," in particular to *The Ambassadors*, which he himself placed second only to *The Golden Bowl* as to the degree of reading difficulty. Here the central figure is only apparently a simple re-creation of the Newman of the early novel. And the first clue to the difference of depth of conception is his name, the curious one of Louis Lambert Strether. Now the varying associational possibilities of this name defy definitive explication; but two reasonable possibilities emerge. One is what Geoffrey Tillotson (following Lionel Trilling) speaks of as "the frustrated middle-aged personage" of nineteenth- and twentieth-century literature—the sensitive, self-appraising un-actors of Dickens' novels, or possibly Thackeray's: ‡ this type, at any rate, he feels, "exists with an Athene-like completeness in the Mr. Batchelor of *Lovel the Widower* (1860). That personage is the Captain Touchit (Jamesian name!) of *The Wolves*

---

* ". . . Madame Merle in possession of the place, Madame Merle seated, all absorbed but all *serene*, at the piano. . . ." (*The Novels and Tales of Henry James*, III, Preface. Italics mine.)

† "Mme. Merle is the old-world magician, as her name indicates. . . ." (Maxwell Geismar, *Henry James and the Jacobites*, p. 42.)

‡ "Strether is stretching for new horizons, or a new breath of life; perhaps he is also at the end of his tether." (*Ibid.*, p. 272.)

and the Lamb (1854). . . ." Whereupon Professor Tillotson establishes a correspondence between Mr. Batchelor ("ruminating his inaction at a crisis in the story") and T. S. Eliot's J. Alfred Prufrock, concluding with the reflection that "the middle-aged and frustrated and much-thinking are recurrent figures" in James's fiction, including *The Ambassadors*.[5] This very quality was, I feel, one of at least two that James was trying to achieve in the surname of his hero. As for the other quality, it took professional scholars to establish the link of Strether's given names with all the associations, in the cultured reader's mind, of the time-enchanted aura of by-gone Paris contained in a novel of Balzac's that has those very names as its title; [6] yet it will be understood that at the time of *The Ambassadors'* appearance sixty years ago, these given names would have chimed with Balzac's in far more ears—and nonprofessional ones —than they do today, when educated readers consider an acquaintance with *Père Goriot* or *Eugenie Grandet* sufficient acquaintance with this acknowledged master of James's. All in all, the impression is inescapable that the composite name of possibly the most subtly drawn of James's male characters is deliberately selected for the purpose of conveying a clue to the personality of an important character for whom the *Newman* or the *Archer* of the simpler novels would not have sufficed.*

I am simplifying, of course. The name *Pocock*, for example, of a supporting character in *The Ambassadors*, has the same cacophonous and therefore satiric ring as does the name *Stackpole* of the character in the much earlier novel, and serves as no less of a program note to this family.† Study James's explanation, in his

* The same can be said for the name Merton Densher, of *The Wings of the Dove*. If I seem to be mountaining mole-hills or even creating velleities, I invite the reader to study Quentin Anderson's interpretation (in his *The American Henry James*) of the intended associational quality of Fanny Assingham of the equally late *Golden Bowl*. But it does seem beyond dispute that James's fictional names—no less than those of the great eighteenth-century or nineteenth-century novelists—simply invite interpretation.

† But James could also keep his sense of humor about names: Edith Wharton recalled that "the magic of ancient names, quaint or impressive, crabbed or melodious [pleased him]. These he would murmur over and over to himself in a low chant, finally creating characters to fit them, and sometimes whole

Scenario for *The Ambassadors*, of *Pocock* (noting that James never even uses Jim's given name) as associated with *Newsome* and therefore as the symbol for coarseness, vulgarity, and the disgusting: "Pocock, the contact of Pocock, the mind, the manners, the conversation, allusions, ideals, general atmosphere of Pocock, rub into Strether afresh the discomfortable truth that it is in the name of the paternal heritage that he has been launched upon his own errand." [7] Had there been so incisive a commentary on the name-as-person since Micawber's denunciation of Uriah Heep? Then, too, if James ever gave his readers a more useful insight into character than he did to Kate Croy's aunt, Maud Lowder, in one of the other two novels (*The Golden Bowl*) of his final trilogy, I do not know what it would be. But in no way does this simplification seriously misrepresent James's practice with names.

If, as Oscar Cargill has suggested, the link between the *Little Bilham* of James's *The Ambassadors* and the *Little Billee* of *Trilby*, —a fabulously successful sentimental (and naughty) novel about artist life in Paris' Latin Quarter that James's friend George Du Maurier had written only a few years before—speaks for itself, what it says—and what James meant for it to say—is that he is counting on his readers to recognize the parallel with a well-known recent original and then to draw from the parallel whatever associations it is capable of yielding. This may be simply that James's Bilham is meant to stand, to a certain degree, in the relationship to the major figure Strether that Du Maurier's Billee stood toward his major figures Taffy and the Laird. Surely this would have been a most likely suggestion for James's original audience, all of whom knew

families, with their domestic complications and matrimonial alliances, such as the Dymmes of Dymchurch, one of whom married a Sparkle, and was the mother of little Scintilla Dymme-Sparkle. . . ." (A *Backward Glance*, pp. 248–249.) Miss Tita of "The Aspern Papers" tells the narrator of the "very nice" people she has known in Venice: ". . . the Cavaliere Bombicci and the Contessa Altemura. . . . Also English people—the Churtons and the Goldies and Mrs. Stock-Stock . . . ; she was dead and gone, poor dear." Also, the crabbed and comic names of "The Birthplace," discussed in "The Tug of the Fairy-Tale," below.

their *Trilby*.* And what gain accrued from this recognition? For James, this: the charm of the original would be transmitted to his own characterization; for the reader, the comfortable feeling that he has been here before, that his orientation into James's less palpable Paris life is the less difficult for the reference—actually, the clue. This, James could do fairly overtly; and, in view of the modifications he would make in his own characterization, without even the slightest imputation of plagiarism.

But he was also capable on occasion of providing the initiated reader of a fiction with a more strategic clue—in one instance, with the name of a fiction that would turn out to be nothing less than a key to the understanding of an entire fiction of his own. I have in mind *Daisy Miller*, discussed earlier. Here the subtlety with which he endowed the characterization of his heroine (in contrast, perhaps, to the leading simplicity of her name) was apparent from the first, and we have seen the controversy she aroused. Had James been too subtle? one imagines him as wondering. Even after he had gone to the trouble of inserting in the very middle of his story a dead giveaway to his meaning?

For he had done just that. The original readers, as they came to the exact center (the opening page of the second of the two parts)

---

* ". . . *Harper's Magazine* was publishing 'Trilby.' . . . This . . . novel began with the January number of 1893 and instantly came storm, cancellations of subscriptions, and an increase of circulation. In June a jeweller produced a scarfpin, Trilby's foot in gold or silver, and women wore the badge. . . . [A] craze had begun among women and now comedians in light opera asked each other: 'Where's Mamie? . . . Upstairs reading "Trilby"?' and feet and shoes were suddenly 'Trilbies' while ladies in the beginning literary clubs debated Trilby's ethics and clergymen regretted to point out to fashionable parishes that Mr. Du Maurier was no Christian. Harper's Brothers paid royalties on edition after edition. Virgins posed as Trilby in her Greek gown in the tableaux of two winters. A bathsuit, a cigarette, a cigar and a restaurant were named for Du Maurier's marshmallow goddess. Suffrage got tangled with the question of nude art. Trilby had something to do with woman's independence. Saint Gaudens said airily at a male dinner party: 'Every other woman you meet thinks she could be an artist's model,' and the hunchbacked Paul Leicester Ford wanted to know of the same group: 'What would happen to an American if he'd written "Trilby"?' " (Thomas Beer, *The Mauve Decade*, pp. 48–49.)

of this story, would be asked to read this passage from a letter to Winterbourne that his aunt had written:

"*Those people you were so devoted to last summer at Vevay have turned up here, courier and all... . . They seem to have made several acquaintances, but the courier continues to be the most intime. The young lady, however, is also very intimate with some third-rate Italians, with whom she rackets about in a way that makes much talk. Bring me that pretty novel of Cherbuliez's—Paule Méré—and don't come later than the 23rd.*"

In the first three sentences of this passage is represented the central question of James's story—Daisy's innocence; and in the fourth, the key to its answer. For the fact that *Lippincott's* editorial reader himself did not recognize the irony—did not, that is, perceive that Daisy was anything but "an outrage on American girlhood" [8]—is no sign that his subscribers would not. It happens that the works of the Swiss novelist were very much in fashion in America at this time. Henry James himself, as we have seen, had called Cherbuliez "the novelist of literary people"; T. S. Perry, in the pages of the influential *Atlantic Monthly*, had called him "as prominent a writer of French novels now living" and still another reviewer had considered him almost "the greatest writer in prose fiction." [9] At least seven of his novels had appeared in English translation by 1878, and *Paule Méré* itself, originally published in the influential *Revue des Deux Mondes* in 1864, had been separately printed as early as 1865 both in Paris and New York.* In answer to the question, then,

---

* By 1896, twenty-three English translations of Cherbuliez's works had been printed, including thirteen novels and one volume of criticism. (Professor Malcolm B. Jones of Connecticut College furnished these statistics.)

In the *Journal Intime* (1882 ff.) of Henri-Frédéric Amiel, Cherbuliez figures prominently. And in his *Notes of a Son and Brother* (1914), in attempting to measure the degree of his embarrassment in remembering "with how base a blankness I must have several times listened to H. F. Amiel" in Geneva in the autumn of 1859, James writes: "I was fit to be coupled with my cousin Anne King, . . . who, on the same Genevese scene, had had early lessons from the young Victor Cherbuliez, then with all his music in him, and was to live to mention to me that he had been for her 'like any one else.' " (F. W. Dupee [ed.], *Henry James: Autobiography*, p. 245.)

of James's motive for inserting into his own story Mrs. Costello's seeming non sequitur about *Paule Méré*, we can say: to imply disapproval of her snobbery by furnishing the initiated among his readers a parallel situation. And we can add that so far from concealing his source, James counted on having his readers recognize it—literally led them to it, no doubt hopefully as well as playfully. And if, as it turned out, this clue was not sufficient for understanding of his story—if, as we have seen, James had not sufficiently dotted his *i*'s and insisted on his intentions—he had at least tried.

Daisy Miller was an early work, its popularity in later years even an actual source of grievance, Theodora Bosanquet has written, in whose presence "he felt himself rather in the position of some *grande dame* who, with a jewel-case of sparkling diamonds, is constrained by her admirers always to appear in the simple string of moonstones worn at her first dance." [10] What sparkling diamonds James's prose in time acquired, in truth became evident in his later work. Of this, "The Beast in the Jungle" furnishes an enlightening example. About this story estimates vary sharply, it being thought of by one critic as esthetically a victim of its own plot; by another, as nothing less than a parable of modern man. But as for the basic situation it presents—namely, of the developing relationship between a man and woman—a valuable aid to its comprehension had been elaborately provided by its author in its text.

Here I am not referring simply to the obvious key to the hero's monotonously methodical progress toward his unwitting doom as it immediately appears to us in his name, *Marcher*. That much is there, to be sure; but ever so much more as well. For imbedded in the names of James's tale is a more complex imagery device: it is the imagery of the months and seasons. That the hero is, in addition to being a marcher, also a *March-er* becomes more than a fanciful possibility when we notice next that the heroine is named *May*. Next, that the month which finally and irrevocably comes between them is both as a matter of record and of repetition the month of *April*. And finally, that both the story and the year begin in autumn, rise steadily to a zenith in spring, then slope sharply to a conclusion in autumn.)

With this position of months looking out at him from the story, the reader may understandably attribute it less to coincidence than to a deliberate attempt on the part of the author to provide an underscoring to the already fairly legible lettering of his little parable. In short, it is quite possible that the calendar in James's tale was designed as a backdrop to his play. ⫮

If it was, it had the fairly familiar precedent of Hawthorne's *Blithedale Romance,* which James had liked so much that superlatives about it tumbled from his pen in his *Hawthorne* ("the lightest, the brightest, the liveliest," and "delightful and beautiful"). In *Blithedale* Hawthorne had superimposed a symmetry of the seasons —if he had not performed a fusion—on the symmetry of his plot, so that we can see the reformers proceeding from spring (growth and hope) to summer (fruition and growing disenchantment) to fall (decay and disaster). And not the least fascinating of James's comments on *Blithedale* is that it "leaves in the memory an impression analogous to that of an April day—an alternation of brightness and shadow, of broken sun-patches and sprinkling clouds." [11] For in James's own story, is not most important of all the month of April—it being required to serve as two medians, one exact and the other approximate? Can it not be seen to bear this weight in the story? Consider first its function. When, in Part IV, Marcher is finally at the point of thwarting his doom, when the reader is finally led to expect a declaration,—to expect the chill of *March*(er) to be counteracted by the warmth of *May* (Bartram),—the coldness both of his nature and of *April* fatally intervenes. For their long interview takes place "in that long fresh light of waning April days. . . ." Spring was to have come early that year (March was to have yielded to May). Nevertheless, it had not, and the treachery of Eliot's "cruelest month" emphasizes the egotism or treachery or cruelty of Marcher, whose heart fails to act at the promptings of his intelligence.

He perceives the "cold meaningless cheer" of May's room for this, "the first time of the year," of all times, "without a fire"; senses that "it will never see a fire again," * that whereas her eyes are still as beautiful as they were many years ago, they are beautiful "with a strange cold light—a light that somehow was a part of the effect if it wasn't rather a part of the cause, of the pale hard sweetness of the season and the hour." Her "cold sweet eyes" are on Marcher as she comes up to him standing by the now fireless chimney-piece, and he knows that "her light might at any instant go out; wherefore he must make the most of it." But he actually does nothing, and so she dies. That is, the chill of his loveless relationship to her kills her, for spring can come early as well as late (April can be an early May or a late March) † and in James's parable for once ("that year") spring was to have come early, but May judged wrong in dispensing with her artificial warmth, for spring came late—too late, we realize, and eventually Marcher does too. May could not bridge the gap by herself, and we are told that to the very end of his life he recalls the twilight of "the cold April when, pale, ill, wasted, but all beautiful," she had been "perhaps even then recoverable."

The other season correspondence in the story, while not as neat, may also yield an effect without wrenching. If we temporarily discount the first meeting of the man and woman ten years before the story opens, then they meet first at Weatherend, in the autumn. It is an October day that charms him, both because of itself and because of her, and for the same reason in both cases: their *light*, their power of illuminating things for him. The charm of Weatherend is "in the way the autumn days looked into the high windows as it waned; the way the red light, breaking at the close from under a low sombre sky, reached out in a long shaft and played over old wainscots, old tapestry, old gold, old colour." And May herself

---

* In William Faulkner's "That Evening Sun," Quentin senses in Nancy's cold stove an omen equally sinister.
† Robert Frost tells us "how it is with an April day" in these terms in "Two Tramps in Mud Time."

brings back all the details of their first meeting "like the torch of
a lamplighter who touches into flame, one by one, a long row of
gas jets . . . [her] illumination was brilliant. . . ." They are truly
at the *end* of the *weather* during this first autumnal encounter at
Weatherend.

But because of Marcher, May moves out of weather's end *into*
the weather; specifically she sets up house in London in order to
accompany him on his fantastic wait. Some years later (in Part II)
when he brings her the customary birthday present, it is "at a season of thick fog and general outward gloom"—the very date, note,
when she foresees her doom and his, but he doesn't. This is, by in-
ference, winter, for it is as a result of her realization (in Part III)
that she can no longer meet him anywhere except in front of her
fire, to which she now resigns herself more and more. Now it is
because of his failure to understand that, when April comes, the fire
goes out, in both senses, as interpreted above. Thus there is nothing
in life left for him but to continue to exist, now apparently to no
purpose. This he does until the final day, which, like the first, is
in autumn.

But this one is a "grey afternoon when the leaves were thick in
the alleys." Once, a year before, he had stood before her grave,
"fixing with his eyes her inscribed name and date," but "her two
names became a pair of eyes that didn't know him"—from whom
"no palest light broke." Now on this gray afternoon he is resting
with an unprecedented heaviness on "the low stone that bore May
Bartram's name." It is at this point that he looks squarely into the
face of a fellow-sufferer, and the look he sees there smites him. Now
the light breaks. The "illumination" now begun "blazed to the
zenith," and now "the name on the table smote him as the passage
of his neighbor had done, and what it said to him . . . was that
she was what he had missed." Now her two names finally illuminate
his life as she herself did that first day back at Weatherend, and he
sees that May was what he had missed. But this time there is no
longer a May Bartram to illuminate this much later autumn, and
nothing remains for him but this last, appropriate gesture: to seek

in the embrace of that name the light and warmth that she, who had once brought them to him, had taken from him forever.

2. SUBTLER CLUES

Thus far we have given our attention only to the names that James used—the functional names of people, of places, of books, and of seasons as they throw light on his shorter work. But it will be readily appreciated that whatever the usefulness to the reader of this device in works of this length, it could be—might have to be—considerably greater in the long novels, particularly those of his last creative period. These, like the novels of Joyce and Proust, which cover so short a period of time for their length and are therefore so densely packed with the minutiae of the inner lives of their major characters—with what C. Hartley Grattan calls "his pursuit of the ultimate implications and overtones of each and every situation," his "idea of infinitely expanding the moment" [12]—require of their readers an unusual degree of alertness and even of initiation.* But lest even these not suffice, James saw fit to lead his readers along the "crooked corridor" of his art by means of rays of light strategically thrown and artistically integrated.

In "The Beast" itself, for example, we are at a loss to account for the significance, in Part I, of the annoyingly vague and inexact recollection Marcher has of his earlier encounter with May Bartram ten years before; but in Part VI, the last part, we begin to see its relevance and a symmetry that encompasses the story itself. We see that just as the original flashback had revealed Marcher's absorption in self to the extent of distortion of, or at least refusal to concern himself with, the immediate and important facts of a young

---

* If not of actual dedication. There is the baffling and demanding Vereker of "The Figure in the Carpet," of course. Dr. Hugh of "The Middle Years" gives up nothing less than profession and fortune to side with the dying novelist Dencombe.

woman's self in Italy before our story proper (the May-Marcher
story) begins and thus had looked ahead for us readers to the confirmation of his original premonition; so the final scene, which is
also outside the story proper (May is dead) looks back to the original meeting and complements it: what very early he had missed
now at the last he sees.)(Just as, on a more elementary level,
Christopher Newman's renunciation of revenge in Boston before
the action proper of *The American* begins looks ahead to his final
renunciation as the story ends.)

But for the greater part of the evidence I wish to submit of
James's integration into his later fiction of clues for the discriminating reader, I rely on *The Ambassadors*, a full-length novel, treated
above in passing, which James himself thought of as his finest
achievement, and which proves a treasure trove of reader aids. Here
we see these transcending the level of what we may call meaning-
by-association links and becoming metaphors that function integ-
rally in the story. I have already indicated that the first of these is
the very surname of the hero. In the main, however, the metaphors
are objects introduced early and used sustainedly through the work
as reflectors of the inner reaches of the author's or the hero's
thought. In fact, as William M. Gibson's valuable study, "Metaphor in the Plot of *The Ambassadors*," points out:

> James's metaphors . . . are pervasive and various . . . and . . .
> contribute strongly to . . . structure and effect. They may relate
> setting and character. They may define the character to which they
> are applied, and the consciousness which formulates them, and the
> relation of one character to another. They may give body to states
> of mind. They may dramatize discoveries, psychological tensions
> and conflicts. And in . . . complex and efficient fashion . . . they
> may aid in developing plot (both action and thought) within a sin-
> gle novel, particularly if it has been revised or is of the last period.[13]

I wish to extend Mr. Gibson's list * to include another important
metaphor, The Lemon Colored Volumes, and to point out how

---

* Boat, historical figure, train, silver nail, and others.

inextricably it is woven into both character and plot, how valuable it is to the characterization of the chief ambassador and to the emphasis James evidently wished his readers to see him placing on an aspect of the plot that might otherwise not linger in the reader's mind—namely, on what James referred to (in a letter) as Strether's "discipline, development, adventure and general history."

This history began, we discover, thirty years before the disembarking at Liverpool with which the story opens. It was at the end of the Civil War, and Strether and his young bride were abroad. They had "done" Paris wide-eyed and hurriedly, had brought home to America a few souvenirs, and then given themselves over to the obligations of life in a manufacturing city. In time Strether's wife, and later his son, had died, leaving him the remaining, seldom-glanced-at token of one of those souvenirs: a dozen-odd paper-bound lemon-colored volumes bought at a Paris book-stall. Yet it is these dusty volumes which soon emerge memorably in *The Ambassadors* and take on a significance paralleling that of the *petites madeleines* in Proust's novel. For in *The Ambassadors* the past— the antiquity, as it were—that comes to life is that of Lambert Strether himself.

It is for this reason that although he has landed at Liverpool he insists on Chester for his meeting with Waymarsh—Chester, dear to him from previous, too-brief experience of many years back. Similarly, although, as Strether continues to Paris, there is the burning reminder in his pocket of a bundle of letters from Woollett, to postpone the issue he passes across the Tuileries and indulges "more than once—as if on finding himself determined—in a sudden pause before the book-stalls of the opposite quay." England, Maria—they had been the prelude: the theme of Strether's *temps perdu* is now emergent. Maria, that valuable reader escort *—that "enrolled, . . . direct aid to lucidity," James called her—has discovered for

---

* As Wayne Booth reminds us, "when Henry James says [in his Preface] that he has invented a ficelle because the reader, not the hero, needs a friend, the ostensibly dramatic move . . . is dictated by the effort to help the reader grasp the work." See *The Rhetoric of Fiction*, Chicago, 1961, *passim*.

us his relationship with the present (the Newsomes), but the book-stalls themselves will now evoke the chain of recollection that throws light on Strether's past. Leave the stalls though he may, to wander about and steel himself to read the Woollett letters, what his thoughts have reverted to is his early, brief stay in Paris so long ago. Thirty years ago. . . . *Et in Arcadia ego.* As though to com-memorate those days, he had taken a pledge "to treat the occasion as a relation formed with the higher culture and see that it . . . should bear a good harvest." But a generation's time had almost obliterated the memory of that pledge. "A good harvest"? ". . . it was doubtless little enough of a marvel that he should have lost account of that handful of seed." And now

Buried for long years in dark corners . . . these few germs had sprouted again under forty-eight hours of Paris. The process of yes-terday had really been the process of feeling the general stirred life of connexions long since individually dropped. Strether had become acquainted even on this ground with short gusts of speculation— sudden flights of fancy in Louvre galleries, hungry gazes through clear plates behind which lemon-coloured volumes were as fresh as fruit on the tree.*

He has noticed them almost from the moment of his re-entry into Paris, it seems; this nostalgic metaphor of Strether's own time there will be with him during all the months he remains in Paris. Just as, in *Ulysses*, a steamer seen entering the Liffey in the morning is kept sight of, in one way or another, throughout the course of the day and the novel, so we shall not lose sight of those volumes, for in one way or another they will guide the reader to the steps Strether's imagination is pleased to take just as effectively as the other Woollett letters and the other ambassadors dictate the steps his conscience is forced to take. The lemon-colored volumes had emerged into symbolic portentousness (all unconsciously as yet) from the moment he arrived in Europe; eventually they will merge

---

* Italics in this section of the chapter are mine.

with another symbol (Mme. de Vionnet) which looks toward the future, just as they look backward to the past; indeed they are an important clue to our understanding both of Strether and of his decision as ambassador; for it is in this symbol that both courses—of reflection and action—fuse.

He remembered . . . how he had gone back . . . with lemon-coloured volumes . . . on the brain as well as with a dozen . . . in his trunk. . . . They were still somewhere at home, the dozen—stale and soiled and never sent to the binder; but what had become of the sharp initiation they represented. They represented now the mere shallow paint on the door of the temple of taste that he had dreamed of raising up. . . .* That the memory of the vow of his youth should, in order to throb again, have had to wait for this last . . . of all his accidents—that was surely enough proof of how his conscience had been encumbered. . . . His conscience had been amusing itself for forty-eight hours by forbidding him the purchase of a book. . . . On this evidence, however, of the way they actually affected him he glared at the lemon-coloured covers in confession of the subconsciousness that, all the same, in the great desert of the years, he must have had of them.

The volumes, then, have emerged from Strether's subconsciousness and are now clearly in view, no longer a symbol of psychic submersion, but a plant springing into bloom as at the coming of a long-delayed spring. They are now part of his conscious thinking, of his intelligence.

Thus it is that consciously he realizes that he is beginning to identify himself with Chad—so inextricably, we perceive, that the image of Chad's present in Paris continually shades into Strether's past there.

---

* Writing in *Notes of a Son and Brother* about the family's return to this country in 1860, James recalled: "[I was] to fall as soon as we were at home again to reading the Revue des Deux Mondes . . . ; my chin, in Europe, had scarcely risen to the level of that publication; but at Newport . . . I speedily shot up so as quite to bend down to it: it took its place therewith as the very headspring of culture, a mainstay in exile. . . ." (F. W. Dupee [ed.], *Henry James: Autobiography*, p. 271.)

It upset him a little . . . after a while to find himself at last remembering on what current of association he had been floated so far. Old imaginations of the Latin Quarter had played their part for him, and he duly recalled its having been with this scene of rather ominous legend that, like so many young men in fiction as well as fact, Chad had begun.

So, too, he himself had, almost. Strether recalls to himself an "almost envious vision" of Chad's romantic privilege of five years before, when Chad had written that he was going to remain in the Paris of "the real thing." Even then "Strether's fancy had quite fondly accompanied him in this migration" and, significantly, Strether had searched back in his own past and had briefly rediscovered the symbol of his own time there by the Seine: "Melancholy Mürger, with Francine and Musette and Rodolphe, at home, *in the company of the tattered, one*—if he not in his single self two or three—*of the unbound, the paper-covered dozen on the shelf. . . .*"

It is at this point that Strether reminds himself of his mission. He is there to rescue Chad. And yet, does not the success of that mission depend on his ability to project himself into Chad's situation, his environment, his youth? In other words, Strether's power of re-creation is perhaps serving the purpose of his errand at the same time as it is stirring into life again those long-buried seeds of his own youth.

He wasn't there for his own profit. . . . [H]e was there on some chance of feeling the brush of the wing of the stray spirit of youth. He felt it in fact, he had it beside him; the old arcade indeed, as his inner self listened, gave out the faint sound, as from far off, of the wild waving of wings. They were folded now over the breasts of buried generations; but a flutter or two lived again in the turned page of shock-headed slouch-hatted loiterers whose young intensity of type . . . deepened his vision . . . and whose manipulation of the uncut volumes was too often, however, but a listening at closed doors. He reconstructed a possible groping Chad of three or four years before, a Chad who had . . . been too vulgar for his privilege. Surely it was a privilege to have been young and happy just there. Well, the best thing Strether knew of him was that he had had such a dream.

It is in the above passage that symbol merges with characterization and, as seen in retrospect, with plot itself. For by now the reader sees the Volumes as acquiring the magnitude of a touchstone for Strether: and a most valuable one, too, being, as it is, a touchstone to taste, which Strether has begun to identify with integrity. Accordingly, the youths above betray themselves as mere loiterers, as mere listeners at closed doors. So too, probably, Chad had been during his first days in Paris. Conversely, when James wants us to perceive the extent to which Chad has matured esthetically meanwhile—has de-Puritanized himself, as it were—he does so by having Strether make the discovery for himself during an hour that he spends in Chad's apartment toward the end of his mission in Paris when he is most in need of this assurance.

. . . an hour full of strange suggestions, persuasions, recognitions; one of these that he was to recall, at the end of his adventure, as the particular handful that most counted. The mellowest lamplight and the easiest chair. . . . [T]he novel half-cut, the novel lemon-coloured and tender . . . had been pushed within the soft circle. . . . Strether found himself in possession as he never yet had been; he had been there alone, had turned over books and prints, had invoked, in Chad's absence, the spirit of the place, but never at the witching hour and never with a relish quite so like a pang.

Chad has "arrived," Chad is in possession, Chad belongs, in short: if there is doubt lingering in Strether's mind, Chad's quarters in general and the Volumes in especial have banished it.

Now it is interesting to note in this connection that the symbol which helps in performing the vital function of attuning Chad and Strether in spirit performs quite an opposite function in Strether's relationship with the Countess and for quite an opposite reason.

That is, it serves to set Strether apart from her by placing her in another period of time, as it were: this happens in the course of his first interview with her. Even so, we note that while he is in the process of surveying her quarters with an increasing admiration and awe, a faint misgiving or questioning dawns:

> *He would have answered for it . . . that some of the glass cases contained swords and epaulettes of ancient colonels and generals . . . ; copies of works presented, with inscriptions, by authors now classic. . . . There were books, two or three, on a small table near his chair, but they hadn't the lemon-coloured covers with which his eye had begun to dally from the hour of his arrival and to the opportunity for a further acquaintance with which he had for a fortnight now altogether succumbed.*

In having Strether notice this tiny deviation from the décor of the past, James is providing us with another of the various subtle hints (whose significance Oscar Cargill has so well explained) of the faintly meretricious quality of the Countess—of the mingling of the genuinely fine (here, the ancient) and the questionable (the modern). That is, although the Countess is not the unadulterated essence of the past as it still lives for him at this moment—the past of history, of romance, of innocence—still she is a superb, a fine woman. Here James has given us, via Strether, an anticipation of the discovery that Strether will finally make about Mme. de Vionnet. That is, James's casual stroke of having Strether miss his touchstone is an early hint to the intuitive ambassador that the classic perfection of the Countess's quarters is perhaps a studied one, that art has been added to ingenuousness. Of which, more later.*

It is interesting to read in the next chapter that Strether "was

---

* In *The Europeans*, when Robert Acton's unexpected late call reveals her in an apparently compromising situation, James tells us that Eugenia spoke to him "with a certain exaggerated volubility which was in contrast with the languid grace that had characterized her manner before Clifford [the other, much younger man] made his appearance." (Ch. IX)

trying with head thrown back and eyes aloft, to reconstitute a past, to reduce it in fact to the convenient terms of Victor Hugo, whom, a few days before, giving the rein for once in a way to the joy of life, he had purchased in seventy bound volumes." This act, although apparently a mere repetition of the one which preceded his departure from Paris thirty years before, is by no means meant to serve the same purpose here: although he may not know it at this point, he will have a different, less vicarious "handful of seed" to take back with him this last time.

By now the battle of the ambassadors is being waged, but in the evening Strether can wait an hour in Chad's apartment. There are the objects so dear to him—the lamplight, the chair, and the Volumes. What these objects tell us as subtly as Chad's act of opening an opera-booth door has told Strether is that Chad's taste has been moulded along the same lines as his middle-aged advisor's, for the same touchstone to that taste is both Chad's and Strether's.

Only, in fact, if we place side by side Strether's loving admiration of Chad and the Countess as living embodiments of that brief but magical past of his in Paris and their actions and dwellings as fit backgrounds for that magic, can we appreciate the violence of the shock he experiences at the discovery of the sexual relationship—the modernity and vulgarity—of the two. For they have betrayed the giddy, romantic boyishness of the charm with which he has let his mind envelop Paris all these years. His "sudden gusts of fancy," his "odd starts of the historic sense, suppositions and divinations with no warrant but their intensity," were, it turns out, just that.

Nevertheless, as he sits with the Countess in their final interview, the thought of the "great desert" of those thirty years in Woollett consciously oppresses him, and he knows that, whatever else, he must not become lost there another time. Against his hunger before, there had been only the token, the sop to the spirit, the lemon-colored volumes. This time to sustain the disillusioned man of middle age there must be more than the works of Victor Hugo. And of course he realizes now that he has it, that it is in fact sitting before him:

He should soon be going back to where such things were not, and it would be a small mercy for memory, for fancy, to have, in that stress, a loaf on the shelf.* He knew in advance he should look back on the perception actually sharpest with him as on the view of something old, old, old, the oldest thing he had ever personally touched; and he also knew, even while he took his companion in as the feature among features, that memory and fancy couldn't help being enlisted for her.

Victor Hugo will gather dust. Strether has already relegated him, along with the earlier lemon-colored volumes, to the dusty bin of youthful playthings. They have both become flesh, which is no mere touchstone to Life but Life itself. And this is as accurate a measure of the maturing of Lambert Strether as anything in the book.

That is, through her and Paris he has, the reader sees, at last "lived." There *had* been "time for reparation," as James had called it. For him this means simply that his eyes are completely open to the fullness of the life that he has *not*, after all, missed. As James comments, "he now at all events *sees*; so that the business of my tale . . . is just my demonstration of this process of vision." [14]

To Proust was granted the almost ecstatic experience of being able to apotheosize men "as occupying in Time a place far more considerable than the so restricted one allotted them in space, a place, on the contrary, extending boundlessly since, giant-like, reaching far back into the years, they touch simultaneously, epochs of their lives—with countless intervening days between—so widely separated from one another in Time." [15] The sum total of Strether's gain is far less, to be sure, but as vital to his happiness. It is his

---

* This seems, even to the metaphor used, a fictional re-creation of James's own situation. Speaking in *Notes of a Son and Brother* of easing the hurt of having to leave Europe in 1860 by voraciously reading his beloved *Revue des Deux Mondes* (cited above), he returns to the theme of this attachment, recalling the awe with which he would "open the door of the big square . . . American closet . . . on the shelves and round the walls of which the pink Revues sat with the air, row upon row, of a choir of breathing angels. . . ." (F. W. Dupee [ed.], *Henry James: Autobiography*, p. 413.)

faith that his memory of the Countess and of Paris will succor him in the hours of need which he is certain lie ahead. Just as the gleams of half-extinguished thought, the lemon-colored volumes, had lighted up the darkness of the past, so during these last months in Paris, Strether's essential "historic sense" has provided life and food for future years. For the revelation of the dusty books has in effect added James's voice to that of Proust,* whose *petites madeleines* had assured him that

when from a long-distant past nothing subsists, after the people are dead, after the things are broken and scattered, still alone, more fragile, but with more vitality, more unsubstantial, more persistent, more faithful, the smell and taste of things remain poised a long time, like souls, ready to remind us, waiting and hoping for their moment, amid the ruins of all the rest; and bear unfaltering, in the tiny and almost impalpable drop of their essence, the vast structure of recollection.[16]

Just so, perhaps, Paris, the Countess, and her salon with its enchanting echoes of the past will fuse the long-severed halves of Strether's being into an armor against Time which, however less magical than Proust's, will be as durable.

* Edith Wharton tells us of sending *Du Côté de chez Swann* to James: "He seized upon [it] and devoured it in a passion of curiosity and admiration . . . [T]he encounter gave him his last and one of his strongest, artistic emotions." (*A Backward Glance*, pp. 323–324.)

B. THE TUG OF THE FAIRY-TALE

*I had positively encountered nothing to compare with
[the grounds at Newmarch] since the days of fairy-tales and
of the childish imagination of the impossible. Then I used
to circle round enchanted castles, for then I moved in a
world in which the strange "came true." It was the coming
true that was the proof of the enchantment, which,
moreover, was naturally never so great as when such coming
was, to such a degree and by the most romantic stroke of all,
the fruit of one's own wizardry.*
(The Sacred Fount)

In Henry James's first signed story, we come to the comment that
"Lizzie's heart sank with a sudden disappointment. Imagine the
feelings of the damsel in the fairy-tale, whom the disguised enchantress had just empowered to utter diamonds and pearls, should
the old beldame have straightway added that for the present
mademoiselle had better hold her tongue." * Almost half a century
later, toward the close of a vastly productive career, we find him
discoursing on the fairy-tale as a literary form of great value:
"[T]he whole fairy-tale side of life has used, for its tug at my sensibility, a cord all its own. When we want to wonder there's no such
good ground for it as the wonderful. . . . [T]he . . . strength [of
fiction] . . . is the charming. . . . The ideal . . . is the straight
fairy-tale. . . . [A]nd the 'ghost-story' . . . has ever been for me

---

* "The Story of a Year," *The Atlantic Monthly*, XV (March, 1865), 260. Ten
years later, this reference reappears in a piece of literary criticism: "M. Hugo's
manner is as diffuse as that of the young woman in the fairy tale who talked
diamonds and pearls would alone have a right to be. . . ." (*Nation*, XVIII
[April, 9, 1874], 238.)

the most possible form of the fairy-tale." [1] In between, the numerous appearances of the fairy-tale, in one form or another, in the literary creation of Henry James comprise a facet of that creation of real fascination, and—it is being acknowledged—possibly of great importance. It happens that just this aspect of his work has been drawing the attention of scholars in recent years as they continue to return to the question of the indefinability of the charm and strength of that work. As long ago as 1924 it had been related about James that even "as a small boy he [showed] no great aptitude for anything but a felicitous rendering of La Fontaine's fables into English"; [2] the possible effects of this early affinity have been explored by a number of later readers. Elizabeth Stevenson, for example, verges on it when she notes that "It is . . . perfectly characteristic of James to have found his inspiration in a museum, a man-made place, out of the way of man's ordinary, sweated existence. It is just as characteristic that the inspiration he found there should be genuine." [3] As does Maxwell Geismar when he writes that James is "a major *entertainer* . . . of a rare and exotic sort," that he is *"all* vision—or illusion, or enchantment, or magic . . ." [4] And Lionel Trilling, passing on from his discourse on the genre that he identifies as The Young Man's Story (in which the young man of provincial birth but great hopes, poor, of good family at times, sets out to seek his fortune), makes the point that in his own attempt at this genre, *The Princess Casamassima,* Henry James "took special delight in its ineluctable legendary element":

James was certainly the least primitive of artists, yet he was always aware of his connection with the primitive. He . . . knew that he dealt always with illusion; he was proud of the devices of his magic . . . , he wished to hold the reader against his will, to enchant. . . . He . . . delighted to work, by means of the unusual, the extravagant, the melodramatic and the supernatural, upon what he called "the blessed faculty of wonder". . . . [5]

Perhaps the greatest impetus, however, to a consideration of James's work from this important point of view comes from the scrutiny that the late Professor Matthiessen gave to *The Ambassadors, The Wings of the Dove,* and *The Golden Bowl*—the novels of James's "major phase." Since then, other studies have examined James's fiction in this light. R. W. B. Lewis believes that

the form which life assumed in James's fiction reflected the peculiar American rhythm of the Adamic experience: the birth of the inno-cent, the foray into the unknown world, the collision with that world, "the fortunate fall," the wisdom and maturity which suffer-ing produced. . . . [James's] initial treatment was realistic . . . but his last novels shared the . . . mythic orientations of Cooper and Hawthorne and Melville.[6]

Still more recently has appeared Professor W. R. Martin's ex-haustive explication, "The Use of the Fairy-Tale: A Note on the Structure of *The Bostonians.*" [7] My own purpose is to add to and document these interpretations, to furnish an embroidery for them by citing the evidence of Henry James's predilection for magic as an ingredient of realism as it reveals itself in utterances in his own person and in various fictions not as yet examined for this particular quality. To these, perhaps future investigators will in turn add their evidence from the doubtless great store that lies awaiting comment.

Whether we go back into the early, the apprentice, years—into fiction that James quickly forgot—or into the important work of his mature years, we find evidence of this affinity. Several examples have been given above. "Benvolio," James himself speaks of both early and late in that story as a fairy-tale. In "Guest's Confession" (1872), as the narrator views, self-consciously, his chances of success with the young lady, he reflects that "I was neither so young nor so idle as to fancy, and I could at any rate prove I was constant. Like a legendary suitor of old, I might even slay my dragon." In an early review of an Alcott book, he mourns the passing of traditional chil-dren's books: things in them "seemed to have the glow of fairy-land upon them. But in 'Eight Cousins' there is no glow and no fairies; it is all prose." [8] In an early travel book he records: "I obeyed [the portress in Chambord] to the letter, and my turn brought me into sight of a house as charming as an old manor in a fairy tale"; that "In the warm southern dusk [Carcassonne] looked more than ever like a city in a fairy tale." [9] The apparition James speaks of as coming upon Spencer Brydon in "The Jolly Corner" (1908) is "quite as one of those expanding fantastic images projected by the magic lantern of childhood." * And, he tells us in his preface to "The Turn of the Screw," it is "a fairy-tale pure and simple." Not only these casual references to this ageless form of literary entertainment, but references to certain favorite fairy-tale characters and situations recur as well. In "Adina" (1874) the narrator remarks that "I had vaguely taken for granted that my friend was foredoomed to dispense with [a wife], very much as Peter Schlemihl, in the tale, was condemned to have no shadow." In "The Jolly Corner," again, as Spencer Brydon, hunting for his alter ego, begins to feel hunted by it in turn and finds himself engaging in countermaneuvers, "his fully dislocalised thought of these manoeuvres recalled to him Pantaloon, at the Christmas farce, buffeted and tricked from behind by ubiquitous Harlequin. . . ." One may not wish to go as far as Professor Trilling in asserting that "so sophisticated a work as *The Ambassadors* can be read as one of those [fairy] tales in which the hero finds that nothing is what it seems and that the only guide through the world must be the goodness of his heart"; [10] but there is still the fact that for the greater part of that novel Lambert Strether is living on two time planes self-consciously, that at one point he even confides to Maria Gostrey that they are Babes in the Wood (of Parisian bohemianism and intrigue).

One can even discern the fairy-tales dearest to James, for they keep making fleeting appearances. Sinbad the Sailor is one of them. He emerges even in so obscure a place as an early bit of bookreviewing: speaking of the French literary scene before 1830, James remarks that "art and letters . . . had [long] groaned under the weight of inanimate tradition. Literature was like Sinbad the Sailor

* See the account of the narrator's boyhood magic lantern in Marcel Proust, *Swann's Way* ("Overture")—still another instance of the affinities between James and Proust.

with the Old Man of the Sea on his back." [11] When James re-
fashioned the sad story of Daisy Miller into "A Comedy in Three
Acts" in 1883, he had Act I, Scene VIII, open with Charles Reverdy
coming on stage from behind with Randolph Miller on his back
snapping a little whip to Reverdy's wearied " 'The horrid little
wretch! I'm like Sinbad the Sailor with the Old Man of the Sea!
Don't you think you've had enough?' " (Randolph Miller does not.)
In *The Tragic Muse*, Gabriel Nash complains that " 'I don't go
anywhere, but [the mountebanks, much in favor at the time] mount
on my back, at home, like the Old Man of the Sea.' " And in "The
Coxon Fund," the narrator writes, apropos the time following his
first rapture to George Gravener about meeting the brilliant Frank
Saltram, that "for long afterwards he never encountered me without asking for news of The Old Man of the Sea."

Another favorite was the Sleeping Beauty in the Wood. In "The
Passionate Pilgrim" she is Miss Searle; in "Flickerbridge," Miss
Wendam. In *Roderick Hudson* the Prince Casamassima, to
Christina Light's expression of regret at not being able to lie down
to sleep on the grass because " 'it would have been unheard of,' "
replies, " 'Oh, not quite. . . . There was already a Sleeping Beauty
in the Wood.' " Is this a double-edged remark? If so, it refers to
the just-awakened sleeper in the pines of the Villa, Roderick Hudson, whose bust of his mother, Gloriani later tells Rowland, has
been described to him " 'as a charming piece of quaintness; a little
demure, thin-lipped old lady with her head on one side and the
prettiest wrinkles in the world—a sort of fairy godmother.' "

Numerous as these instances are, they are merely a random collection. Yet a complete list would weary the reader without adding
substantially to the significance of the mention and employment
of fairy-tale motifs in James's work. Suffice it to say that this employment must be considerable.* To what end?

I have already cited Professor Trilling's interpretation. Professor

---

* Professor Robert L. Gale finds that "James refers in more than sixty figures
of speech to numerous fairy tales and children's stories." ("Henry James's
Dream Children," *Arizona Quarterly*, XV [Spring, 1959], 61–63, *e.g.*)

Austin Warren's analysis of James's later novels provides still another insight. He modestly predicates "two modes of knowing: . . . dialectic and myth," and believes that with James's last novels, in particular, the "equivalent of myth lies . . . in the metaphors" in proportion as their richness increases; and that James thinks of all his characters as having an Unconscious, ". . . a world of instinctive feelings, reactions which in art must express themselves . . . in metaphoric terms." [12] Now James himself, in his article on Zola, had made the observation about Gervaise of L'Assommoir that "the intensity of her creator's vision" of her career and of the life around her was "one of the great things the modern novel has been able to do." [13] This was just what James himself was doing in a novel running that year in the North American Review: as Professor Warren points out, the intensity of Lambert Strether's vision of the Countess transforms the heroine of The Ambassadors into a legendary and historic figure, much as in The Scarlet Letter the "A" that Hester wears on her breast is transformed in meaning into everything but its original one.* And to this example we should add that of The Princess Casamassima. For at the end of the seventeenth chapter of that not particularly rewarding novel, a remarkable thing is reported as happening. Carried away with excitement at the promise of closer acquaintance with the Princess, the diminutive and humble bookbinder spends an entire week on a labor of love: he binds a book of Tennyson's poems as a present for her. But she is disappointingly out of town when he goes to present it; unwilling to leave it with the footman, he takes it back home with him. Three months pass, and so powerful is the spell that Christina has cast over him that he thinks of the book not as merely an intended gift from a man to a woman but as a thing already *given to him*—to his own humble self—*by* "the most remarkable woman in Europe"! (Had not James himself seen her as marrying into liter-

---

* And not only in the eyes of the townspeople. As Hester tells Roger late in the story, " 'Were I worthy to be quit of it, it would fall away of its own nature, or be transformed into something that should speak a different purport.' " (Ch. XIV)

ally the *greatest house* of his title?) Here is how James accounts for this reversal of facts: "Rare sensations and impressions, moments of acute happiness, almost always, with our young man, in retrospect, became rather mythic and legendary. . . ." * Christina's presence has been powerful enough to be transformed from the day of their talk by the very "intensity of her creator's vision" of her. For Hyacinth has veritably *created* her anew in his vision of her. In *The Europeans* (1878) the reverse transformation occurs: the "mythic and legendary" turns into the real. In the second chapter of that novel Gertrude Wentworth looks up from the Arabian Nights story of Prince Camaralzaman and Princess Badoura to discover that a "beautiful young man was making her . . . a magnificent bow, such as she had never seen before. He appeared to have dropped from the clouds; he was wonderfully handsome. . . ." Thus does Felix Young, her "Bohemian" cousin from Europe, break in upon her drab New England days and nights—he, the "wondrous, delightful answer . . . to her vague wish that something would befall her," a being "engendered by the Sabbath stillness for her private use. . . ."

Just so James, by this intensity of vision, has transformed so many other characters of his fiction, who cannot be conceived as merely flesh-and-blood people but must, if we are to follow James's vision of them, be conceived as possessing qualities of the fabulous. Madame de Vionnet coming to an interview with Strether that he knows she fears may mean her doom is both a sophisticated woman of 1903 and Madame Roland approaching the scaffold a century before. That is, James is trying to endow a pen-and-ink creation with a living, even towering, existence by asking us to draw from the vast store of familiar fairy-tale and legend if we would conceive that creation in all its aspects.†

---

* " 'Orpheus and the Maenads!' had been . . . my foreseen judgement when first I turned over his correspondence," exclaims the devotee of the famous and unjustly maligned late poet Jeffrey Aspern in "The Aspern Papers."

† Like Professor Warren, Professor Leslie Fiedler comments on James's investing of Mme. de Vionnet with the dimensions of fable, but attributes it to unconscious psychosexual motivation (in part): ". . . she is an Aphrodite

Particularly, of course in its magical aspect. For of all attributes of fairy-tale and fable, the distinguishing one is magic. And magic was actually the quality whose absence from the American scene James had deplored so severely in his book on Hawthorne in 1879. Ah, Goethe's blessing on the new land

> . . . use your present happily!
> And when your child thirsts for poetic glories,
> May some good genius keep him free
> From knights, from robbers, and from ghost stories! [14]

—how misguided, if well intended, had it always been.[15] Matthiessen cites a passage from Sylvester Judd's *Margaret* (1845) "at the furthest extreme from" James's indictment in *Hawthorne*—a passage of rapturous defense of unmagical America:

"There are no fairies in our meadows, and no elves to spirit away our children. Our wells are drugged by no saint, and of St. Winifred we have never heard. . . . The Valley of the Housatonic is beautiful as the Vale of Tempe. . . .* We have no . . . shrines for the

---

figure discreetly draped to avoid shocking James's genteel readers. 'A goddess still partly engaged in a morning cloud,' James himself calls his Madame de Vionnet and lest it not be clear just what part of her anatomy the poetic cloud conventionally veils, he tells us more specifically in a second metaphor, that she is 'a sea-nymph waist-high in a summer surge.' " (*Love and Death in the American Novel*, pp. 293–294.)

* About this time, too, James Russell Lowell was writing to the sculptor Story: "One needs not to go as far as Rome to find an attic, nor would I prefer an Italian clime to an American one. As for ruins, you have there, to be sure, plenty of them, the work of . . . people with whom you have nothing whatever to do. But here we have an excellent ruin on Mount Benedict which we made ourselves. . . . [Among other things] Deacon Brown has retired from business. Will not all these things be as important to the interests of mankind a hundred years hence as that Noodle VI. sits on the throne of the two Sicilies or Loafer XXI. in the grandducal chair of Florence? If you have your Pio Nonos, we can also boast our Tommy No-nose, whom I meet every time I go to the Athenaeum." (Henry James, *William Wetmore Story and His Friends*, Boston, 1903, I, pp. 103–104.)

Half a century later, O. Henry would revive Lowell's serio-comic nativism. To the Frank-Norris-like reflection that Nashville is a place " 'where few things out of the ordinary ever happen,' " the Azalea Adair of "A Municipal

devout, . . . no traditions, legends, fables, . . . chapels or abbeys, [yet] NEW ENGLAND! my birthplace, my chosen pilgrimage, I love it." [16]

Yet, so far from loving their native land for the lack of these poetic fabulous resources, American writers from Washington Irving on have labored mightily to create an art by *overcoming* them. In fact, only a few years after *Margaret's* nationalistic rapture, we find America's first important novelists engaged in the act of supplying the need for the very magic that that rapture had disdained. We find Herman Melville weaving on his loom a variety of magical threads: a tattooed prince from an island not on the map, a wanderer out of the Old Testament onto the ship of one of its kings and then into a voyage doomed by the necromantic prophecies of the Weird Sisters in search of a whale that is ubiquitous, omnipotent, and immortal. (And in his last years, working on the story of a murder in the British navy of a sailor of unknown origins and magnificent—if sinister—bearing who is repeatedly likened to the greatest of the fallen angels; his murderer, an equally unknown man of magnificent—if angelic—bearing who unquestionably partakes of the qualities of both the first man on earth and his redeemer; the judge, equally unquestionably, less man than God himself.) We also find Hawthorne literally cursing one of *Margaret's* pristine native wells in order to sate his own hunger for the familiar magic. But, for that matter, just the year before he had created a bona-fide wizard, a misshapen demon-succubus-vampire who makes Hester wonder "whether the tender grass of early spring would not be blighted beneath him" (a fairy-tale motif that James would also use, as we shall see); and who, while he does not actually "spread bat's wings and fly away," yet, when his prey finally eludes him,

---

Report" replies that only " 'on the surface' " is it " 'a humdrum town' ": " 'I have traveled many times around the world in . . . print and dreams. I have seen . . . the Sultan of Turkey bowstring with his own hands one of his wives who had uncovered her face in public. I have seen a man in Nashville tear up his theater tickets because his wife was going out with her face covered—with rice powder. . . .' "

"positively withered up, shrivelled away, and almost vanished from mortal sight, like an uprooted weed that lies wilting in the sun." For had not Hawthorne, speaking in his own person, insisted in the preface to his second, well-drugging romance on the legitimacy of that genre as an area where the writer could "manage his atmospherical medium," where he might moderately "mingle the Marvellous . . . as a slight, delicate, and evanescent flavor"? [17] Already, in "The Custom House," he had described the effect of moonlight on a parlor: "Thus . . . the floor of our familiar room has become a neutral territory, somewhere between the real world and fairy-land, where the Actual and the Imaginary may meet, and each imbue itself with the nature of the other." And half a century later would not Joseph Conrad define the charm of fiction in those terms? "All creative art is magic, is evocation of the unseen . . . for the edification of mankind pinned down to . . . reality. . . . [T]he creative art of a writer . . . is [thus] rescue work . . . since the demand of the individual to the artist is . . . 'Take me out of myself!' . . . out of my perishable activity into the light of imperishable consciousness." [18] If, then, a recent contribution to the interpretation of American literature devotes itself to the study of the image in the nineteenth century "of the authentic American as a figure of heroic innocence and vast potentialities," [19] is this not proof—albeit not at all in the way he had in mind—of the remark of one of the most memorable writers of that century, Henry Thoreau, that "Shams and delusions are esteemed for soundest truths, while reality is fabulous"?

What greater storehouse of the fabulous, of the magic, of the imperishable than fairy-tale and myth? As the Civil War was ending, in an anecdote prefacing the telling of the fairy-tale "Thumbling" in a magazine for children, this passage appears:

"O, papa! this must be a real old-fashioned fairy-book, for it is full of pictures of fairies, and knights, and giants, and dwarfs, and dragons! Do read it to us, please!"

Now, my dear friend, you know that my youngsters have a most insatiate appetite for, and a most thorough appreciation of, real fairy stories, as they call them. . . .

And all boys and girls are alike in this, and will be so, let us hope, to the end of time. Even we old fellows recall those old-time stories with something of the same awe-struck admiration, and something of the same unquestioning belief, with which we listened to them, I don't know how many years ago. We sneer at the improbabilities and inconsistencies of modern fiction; but who thinks of being startled at the charming incongruities, the bold but fascinating impossibilities, of Cinderella, and Aladdin, and Puss in Boots? Don't we in our . . . hearts still believe that, a long time ago, before men grew too wicked for them, the gentle fairies really lived in their jewelled palaces under ground, and came out, now and then, to protect the youth and beauty they loved from giants, and dragons, and malicious genii, and all manner of evil things? I declare I should be ashamed of myself if I did not; and I am sure that none of us, who are good for anything, have altogether lost that old belief; and when we look back at those days of young romance, and remember the thrill with which we read of Bluebeard's punishment, and Beauty's reward, we feel that it would be better for us if they had more of that old childlike faith. And so I encourage my youngsters to read and listen to, over and over again, the same old stories that, when I was a boy, warmed my young imagination, and to eschew the dismal allegories with which well-meaning but short-sighted writers try to supply the places of Jack the Giant-killer and all his marvellous family. And so I was almost as pleased as the children, when I saw, from its quaint and grotesque pictures, that their treasure-trove was really a book of real old-fashioned fairy stories.[20]

As though to confirm this theory, only a few years later, in one of the earliest and most warmly embraced offerings from the "realistic" writers of the west who appeared at the close of the Civil War, Bret Harte admitted that he saw his dirty diggers in the California gold fields as nothing of the sort: he was trying, he pointed out in his first collection of tales, "to illustrate an era . . . replete with a certain heroic Greek poetry," and he would "be quite content to have collected here merely the materials for the Iliad that is

yet to be sung." [21] Not only he but his characters think Homer-
ically! When the snowed-in "Outcasts of Poker Flat" sit around
the fire and music yields to story-telling among gambler, whore, and
innocent alike, Tom Simson tells from memory the "principal incidents" from "Mr. Pope's ingenious translation of the Iliad":

And so for the rest of that night the Homeric demigods again
walked the earth. Trojan bully and wily Greek wrestled in the
winds, and the great pines in the canyon seemed to bow to the
wrath of the son of Peleus. Mr. Oakhurst listened with great satisfaction. Most especially was he interested in the fate of "Ash-heels,"
as the Innocent persisted in denominating the "swift-footed
Achilles."

Indeed, the fabulous themes of Harte's stories announce themselves
in their titles: *Tales of the Argonauts,* "The Iliad of Sandy Bar,"
"A Blue Grass Penelope,"—a California that never was on land or
sea, but in magic. (And was it not in just such terms that Harte's
student, Rudyard Kipling, envisioned his private soldiers in India,
—finishing one of his stories with Mulvaney standing silhouetted
against the landscape "I know not what vultures tearing at his
liver,"—a veritable Prometheus?)

Coming up to our own day, we find the same intensity of vision
raising the people of what Thomas Wolfe thought of as "the million streets of America" to the level of the fabulous. He himself
sounds the note of magic like a bell through *Look Homeward,
Angel:* its hero, Eugene Gant, implores his "ghost" to "return not
into life, but into magic, where we have never died, into the enchanted wood, where we still lie. . . ." Eugene transforms himself
in boyhood reverie into the many contemporary heroes of the cheap
fiction on which he so hugely feeds; and in the sequel, *Of Time and
the River,* Wolfe's vision of Eugene grows into the far outlines of
mythical might, as witness that novel's eight section sub-titles:
"Orestes," "Young Faustus," "Telemachus," "Proteus," "Jason's
Voyage," "Antaeus," "Kronos and Rhea," and "Faust and Helen."

And do we not find the most recent winner of the Nobel prize, that most "realistic" of American novelists, insisting on his preference, not for the ordinary, but for the fabulous, the heroic? I have in mind one or two disclosures from the taciturn John Steinbeck. Writing to his agents apropos his early novel *To a God Unknown,* he predicted:

> *It will probably be a hard book to sell. Its characters are not "home folks." They make no more attempt at being human than the people in the Iliad. Boileau insisted that only gods, kings, and heroes are worth writing about. I firmly believe that. The detailed accounts of the lives of clerks don't interest me much unless, of course, the clerk breaks into heroism.*

And a year later, after the book had come out and reader and critic alike had failed to distinguish its theme, Steinbeck lamented that he "had expected that the plan of the Arthurian cycle would be recognized"; that although even putting "the incident of the Sangreal in the search of the forest" had not been clear enough, perhaps, still "The form is that of the Malory version—the coming of Arthur, the mystic quality of owning a house, the forming of the Round Table, the adventures of the knights and finally, the mystic translation of Danny. . . ." * And I have in mind William Faulkner's conception of the Sartorises as he explains it on the last page of *Sartoris:* "[T]here is death in the sound of it, and a glamorous fatality, like silver pennons downrushing at sunset, or a dying fall of horns along the road to Roncevaux." Is it any surprise, then, that these are the very writers whose books have been increasingly in-

---

* *The Portable Steinbeck*, New York, 1946, xi-xii, xiii. His disappointment brings to mind Norman Mailer's after the publication (and huge success) of *The Naked and the Dead.* No one, he told an interviewer, had thought beyond the obvious Farrell and Dos Passos influences: ". . . I really was off on a mystic kick. Actually—a funny thing—the biggest influence on *Naked* was *Moby Dick.* . . . I was sure everyone would know. I had Ahab [Sergeant Sam Croft] in it, and I suppose the mountain was Moby Dick." (He concludes with the apparently no-mystical-nonsense premise that after all "the book will stand or fall as a realistic novel.") (Harvey Breit, *The Writer Observed*, New York, 1961, p. 130.)

terpreted as being suffused not only with myth, but religious myth? That in *The Grapes of Wrath* the apparently obscure Jim Casy along Route 66 has been construed as Jesus Christ along the road to Jerusalem? Or that Joe Christmas of *Light in August* offers so many parallels with the story of Christ? * And that many years later Faulkner should have written *A Fable?*

Henry James too was writing in the tradition of "our one fine romancer," and for him to recall at the age of seventy that "The Wonder-Book and Twice-Told Tales had helped to enchant our childhood" † is to project for us over the long road winding back over his "dark backward and abysm" the images of Perseus and the Gorgon, of Midas (who will reappear in a phrase in *The American*), of the Golden Apples of the Hesperides, the Miraculous Pitcher, and The Chimaera, side by side with those of Howe's Masquerade, Edward Randolph's Portrait, Lady Eleanore's Mantle, and Old Esther Dudley. Like Hawthorne's, James's imagery tends to follow more secular lines than those of the moderns; like his, it never strays far from the vast and imperishable province of the fable; yet it also heeds his caution to "mingle the Marvellous rather as a slight, delicate, and evanescent flavor, than as any portion of the actual sub-

---

* There is yet a third characterization in American fiction of a man with the initials of J and C who has been associated by literary criticism with Jesus Christ—namely the Jim Conklin of Stephen Crane's *Red Badge of Courage*. (And we are all familiar with Professor Stallman's interpretation of the "fierce wafer" of the sun in that novel as the eucharistic wafer.) But I agree with H. G. Wells's judgment that one of the "certain enormous repudiations" in Crane's art is this very eschewing of images of the fabulous: "Any richness of allusion, . . . the half quotation that refracts and softens and enriches the statement, the momentary digression that opens like a window upon beautiful or distant things, are not merely absent, but obviously avoided." (This essay of 1900 has been reprinted in Edmund Wilson [ed.], *The Shock of Recognition.*)

† F. W. Dupee (ed.), *Henry James: Autobiography*, p. 478. Around this time, too, he actually wrote a little treatise on this favorite literary genre of his childhood: ". . . the fairy-tale belongs mainly to either of two classes, the short and sharp and single, charged more or less with the compactness of anecdote (as to which let the familiars of our childhood, Cinderella and Blue-Beard and Hop o'my Thumb and Little Red Riding Hood and many of the gems of the Brothers Grimm directly testify), or else the long and loose, the copious, the various, the endless . . . : witness . . . almost any one of the Arabian Nights." (*The Novels and Tales of Henry James*, XII, Preface.)

stance of the dish offered to the public." Consider, as Professor W. R. Martin has recently done, the way James merges the two elements of *The Bostonians*—namely, the novel and the "submerged archetypal 'tale' "—in an attempt to provide lights and tones for what is apparently as far away from a "tale" as James ever gets. His "tale" is about Good and Evil and by basing his "novel" on it, "James makes us aware of the enormity of the evil and the size of the issues at stake in his novel" (which the novel's ironies and modernity might conceal). Also, it is possible for James thus to use the "tale" to highlight differences for the purpose of humor, "e.g. between the lounging Mississippian and Sir Galahad; between the earnest Olive Chancellor and a wicked witch. . . ."

He has, of course, to keep the "tale" at arm's length so that our belief that he is writing about the world we know will not be disturbed, but the distance between the novel and the "tale" is turned to positive advantage. James's gentle but penetrating irony can play freely in the wide space that separates Boston from Camelot and fairyland.[22]

What we can see in so many others of James's tales is his tendency to "mingle the Marvellous" with the matter-of-fact to their mutual advantage, as Professor Martin his suggested. That is why in these apparently "realistic" stories people act in ways that, in terms of ordinary patterns of human behavior, appear exceedingly curious but that seem to surmount our disbelief—that is, keep us reading, even if alternatively between puzzlement and unquestioning acceptance—if thought of simultaneously in terms of the fairy-tale. The fusion or intermingling of the two worlds before our very eyes then defines the strange appeal of these stories. The effect is something like that produced by the stereoscope.

In " 'Europe' " we have in one of the pictures a tableau of an extremely old woman with a delusion about the presentness of the dim past and a tyrannical hold over her daughters that keeps them from ever leaving her side; in the other, we have a fairy-tale about a fierce "vulture" ancient beyond measurement, herself enchanted

by a notion around which delusion has woven its triple circle of pro-
tection against time and enslaving her "girls" yet at the same time
transmitting to them, as long as they are subject to her enchantment, an immunity from age. That is why when Jane escapes and
the spell is broken, reality takes over and for the first time things
are seen as they actually are: Jane becomes a silly old maid acting
eccentrically on the continent and Becky and Maria metamorphose
into the old women that their years now betray them to be. Becky
Rimmle suddenly looks as old as her mother, and dies; then Maria,
the youngest, appears even older than Mrs. Rimmle—that "subtle
old witch," that "wonderful witch." It is all slightly reminiscent of
Oscar Wilde's *Picture of Dorian Gray,* that fairy-tale of the man
whose face remains that of a young man through a life-time of de-
bauchery that has its secret register on the portrait of him in the
attic until the moment of his death: then the spell is broken, and
servants forcing their way into the attic find "a splendid portrait of
their master as they had last seen him, in all the wonder of his exquisite youth and beauty," while on the floor they find "a dead man,
in evening dress, . . . withered, wrinkled, and loathsome of visage."
To see " 'Europe' " in both pictures simultaneously—or, better, to
read it on one level realistically and on the other subliminally—is
the only way in which it will yield the three-dimensional quality
that went into its making.

Without this double awareness such a story as the engrossing
"The Pupil" will continue to vex us; with it, we can account in part
for the strange power the story has of making us accept it. It is true
that "The Pupil," seen as a true-to-life story, "begs . . . for
Freud" [23] and that if, as Matthiessen believes, "there is no basis in
homosexual attraction," then there is "a consequent vagueness . . .
in accounting for why the tutor's attachment to his charge is so
strong as to make him destroy his prospects on the boy's account." [24] But the story is only alternately true to life: alternately
it is also a fairy-tale that renders a most plausible accounting for
the tutor's actions. Morgan is the Stricken Boy who revives, even
thrives, under the spell of the friendship of Pemberton, the One

Teacher in a Thousand. He, in turn, finds the Boy's person irresistible and feels himself suddenly casting off his moorings from the familiar, proper world of his past and being swept along in the fast current of the strange international adventurers who are the other Moreens (while on the realistic level his Puritan self is fascinated as much as it is shocked by the implicitly wicked demimondaine goings-on of the family). So man and boy cling together for comfort and even safety against the outside world of vulgarity and change. In a situation ever so faintly suggestive of that of the Babes in the Wood who comfort each other (and present to us the picture of victims of the furtive and self-seeking machinations of parents who are exploiting them both—Pemberton being defrauded of his wages and Morgan being used as a lure), they cling together in a bond that appears to become unbreakable. If one looks for the predictable fairy-tale clues of Sinister Scheming and the Beautiful Innocent, he finds them here at once in the vulgar, shrewd, sensual Mrs. Moreen and the delicate, honest, precociously spiritual Morgan. Eventually the spell is broken when the tutor, beginning to feel stifled by this ineffably dear boy, goes off; then reality rushes in. Although later on Pemberton does return to the pupil's side in response to his urgent summons, the old magic has lost its power and the tutor betrays his need to retrieve his own desperately needed individuality. The moment the pupil perceives this perfidiousness, he dies.

If, it is demurred, the tenaciousness of the Pemberton-Morgan tie cannot help prompting a question concerning sexuality that threatens, if it does not even defeat, James's attempt to mingle the marvellous and the mundane, certainly "The Birthplace" is free from this danger. Here the bond is between a man and the *genius loci*, a situation much more felicitous for James ("The Last of the Valerii" is successful on the same account). Inasmuch as this story in particular is saturated with the atmosphere of the fairy-tale, it would do more justice to tell it in terms of the themes of this genre than in those of the real-life level (on which, of course, it operates simultaneously).

Once upon a time there was a middle-aged couple named Morris and Isabel Gedge. They lived in obscurity and semi-poverty in a dull little provincial town in England. Although they were poor and he was very homely, they had hearts of gold. Once many years ago, their zealous ministrations brought back to health a pupil in their school that anyone else would have given up for dead. As our story opens, a position has fallen vacant far away that many people of their situation would consider the nation's greatest cynosure: the custodianship of The Birthplace, "the most sacred [shrine] known to the steps of men." Now it happens that this shrine is administered by Them, a group of undisclosed identity whose chairman is a physically large man named Grant-Jackson. He also happens to be the father of the boy we have just spoken of. Mindful of their good work in the dim past, Grant-Jackson now writes to the Gedges asking them if they want to be considered for this position. When this first letter reaches Morris at his post in the little town library, he recognizes it as an acknowledgement of the "happy spell" he and Isabel had wrought on Grant-Jackson long years before; even so, it comes as "a bolt quite out of the blue," and, in view of their present circumstances, seems "too good to be true." When the appointment is confirmed, the prospect of "the romance" it offers practically transforms Morris: noticing the look on his face, Isabel's own "lighted as if he had suddenly grown handsome," and paraphrasing his expression of ecstasy, she says, " 'Certainly—we shall live as in a fairy-tale.' " (For all her practicality, Isabel "felt also, in her degree, the spell. . . ."). Thus has "the silver shaft reached and pierced" this unknown but deserving little man at his post in the gray library of a little town; thus has the Stranger from afar rewarded Baucis and Philemon's honesty and charity by sparing their lives and transforming their cottage into a tall edifice of white marble.

From the day of their arrival at The Birthplace, they feel the "spell," the "mystic presence." But as time goes on, Morris undergoes a disenchantment that threatens his own peace of mind and —to Isabel's great concern—possibly, again, their livelihood: The Place is not at all what he had reverently taken for granted that it would be, but merely a money-making semi-imposture. So little was known of "His" life anyway; thus His birthplace has been tricked out with unauthentic stage properties and a deceptive tour legend in order to satisfy Them. There are, it happens, two of Them: one is that insatiable monster, the fee-paying tourist hordes (mostly American) with their "gluttony . . . for false facts," and the other is Mr. Grant-Jackson and his Board, with their gluttony for admission receipts. What should the little man do? Truckle to Them (and to poor, dear, but fearful Isabel) in the name of food and gratitude, or disillusion and affront Them in the name of the "morality" of the situation? When he makes his first decision, not to follow in the footsteps of Miss Putchin, his predecessor lackey and panderer, but to "give the story away" to the public, and Isabel warns him, he asks her: " 'They'd turn and rend me? They'd tear me to pieces?' " (making us understand that possibly he thinks of himself as another embittered Orpheus of old falling into the hands of his ever-to-be-delighted public). Yet he persists in his decision, for without sensing it, They have released a genie from his bottle: by exalting his humble self to his present position, They have kindled his "critical sense," have "waked it up" in him. The crisis he thus provokes now works itself out in a series of four confrontations, each of them just at dusk when The Place is sinking into the darkness. First a couple of Good Fairies arrive, Mr. and Mrs. Hayes of New York. Sensing Morris's disenchantment, they warn him of trouble and leave. Then the giant Grant-Jackson arrives, to serve his twilight warning that unless the little man lives up to the part They expect him to play, he will be dismissed. Again he must make a decision, but this time out of the desperation of his plight (by now Isabel thinks he is mad and he himself is aware of his intensity) he hits upon a stratagem that will please both Them and His ghost: he will "lay it on" so heavily that They can fill Their insensitive and romance-hungry maw to satiety with his cathedral-toned reverence and pulpit-rhetoric and yet so ironically that even He will applaud from beyond the grave! But success hangs by the slender thread of skill; will he succeed? A year or more after developing his "act," he gets

his answer, and a breathlessly awaited one it is. As before, it is preceded at dusk by the returning Good Fairies, the Hayeses. Word of
his new performance has reached them across the Atlantic and now
they are here again, alone with him as before, to see. He goes
through his act for them without introduction or explanation.
Being fine people (as no other visitors have been), they sense his
ironic approach and again express fears that he will suffer reprisal.
But if it comes, they assure him, they will themselves rescue him
from his fate—will "set" him "up" themselves. And, lo! At this
moment the giant arrives again, demanding to see Morris at once.
Morris goes off to his "execution" but returns in a few minutes to
announce that his success is to be recognized by a large raise in his
salary: They are now hugely appeased.

Never, to be sure, does James's story vanish, like Jack, up a bean-
stalk to Never-Never-Land in the sky (for all that Mr. Grant-Jackson at the final crisis takes on the formidable proportions of the
flesh-hungry giant up there). For one thing, an intermittent
drollery keeps the fable from the terrible seriousness of true fairy-
tales. Morris's appearance is funny, "with his sloping shoulders, his
long lean neck and his nose so prominent [that] he resembled more
a giraffe"; his librarianship is in "Blackport-on-Dwindle, all granite,
fog, and female fiction"; and his self-conscious mockery of a shrine
custodian's contrivedly dramatic monologue furnishes its own hilari-
ousness. For another, as usual James has provided a character to
keep his central figure's feet, if not always on the ground, yet out of
danger of soaring into the dangerous empyrean: Isabel Gedge, that
fretful and lovable little baggage caught between Them and
him and sharing the qualities of both—being like Them without
their crudity and like him without his sensitivity. All in all, even
with its pronounced flaw of prolixity, "The Birthplace" emerges as
one of the warmest and most satisfying of Henry James's later
stories, largely because James has given to its little hero a sublime
achievement: at least "the strange 'came true' . . . by the most romantic stroke of all, the fruit of one's own wizardry."

Of course, in the book-length fiction, there was so much more time in which to perform the act of transmutation of the ordinary facts of existence by the magical. The magic of the fairy-tale, its "charm . . . for the distracted modern mind," he theorized, "is in the clear field of experience . . . over which we are thus led to roam; a . . . world in which nothing is right save as we rightly imagine it. We have to do *that*. . . ." [25] And frequently he asked for this imaginative re-creation of reality, knowing that he could count on his readers to perform this willing act. In the unfinished *The Ivory Tower* Graham Fielder inherits a fortune to which he has no real claim and for which he has no real use; and even James is aware of possible objection to this arbitrary turn of events, as witness his notes for that novel, wherein he refers to "the fairy tale of his sudden fact of possession." Yet no less a transformation is wrought on Milly Theale in *The Wings of the Dove*, whom Susan Stringham regards as a princess, even "the potential heiress of all the ages," * as opposed to her own self, "a mere subscriber . . . to the *Transcript*" [26]—a juxtaposition that reminds us of Professor Martin's explanation of *The Bostonians*. And such a transformation is made possible for Ralph Pendrel in *The Sense of the Past*, as well as to Isabel Archer in *The Portrait of a Lady*. Of the latter novel, Professor Edel comments that at times it "verges on melodrama when it isn't pure fairy-tale"; "a rich uncle, a poor niece, an ugly sick cousin who worships her from a distance, three suitors, a fairy-godfather who converts the niece into an heiress, and finally her betrayal by a couple of her cosmopolite compatriots into a marriage as sinister as the backdrop of a Brontë novel. . . ." [27] And there are yet other touches. Isabel has not only been betrayed by a wizard-named woman: at long last she realizes that she is in the hands of a Chillingworthian monster with a "faculty for making everything wither that he touched. . . . It was as if he had had the evil eye."

But I wish to make my final observations about the use of the fairy-tale motif in one of James's earliest, and most widely read

---

* In the tradition of Hawthorne, who leaves Pearl "the richest heiress of her day, in the New World."

novels, *The American*. For in it he had created a hero who not only has "sat with Western humorists in knots . . . and seen 'tall' stories grow taller without toppling over," but is himself such a story, so to speak. To appreciate James's conception of him we must see him in the fabulous proportions with which James endowed him. His is the charm, the warm haze of the world of the fairy-tale, and he moves everywhere as a larger-than-life visitor on the effete European scene from the fabulously vast west of a country thought to be fabulous in itself. And not only his, but the charm of much of the rest of the story itself: for at every turn the story of an American businessman's negotiations with a mercenary French family alternates with characters and themes from the world of make-believe.*

When the anti-Jacobite Fred L. Pattee wrote about Christopher Newman, "Thrust this man suddenly into the circles of French nobility . . . and ask yourself if he will talk like this," [28] he posed an interesting and vital question, but one not nearly so rhetorical as he supposed. For to the critic who observes the magic dimensions of the hero, his social adaptability seems plausible enough. Is not Newman truly an object of wonder, through whoever's vision we see him? Since James himself sees him at the Bellegardes' "circulating freely, overtopping most people by his great height," what proportions he takes on in the eyes of the French may be imagined. Even his expatriate fellow-Americans add a stroke or two to this impression of his fabulousness, whether it is Tom Tristram's telling him " 'You talk like Sardanapalus!' " or Mrs. Tristram's facetious, " 'You are the great Western Barbarian, stepping forth in innocence and might, gazing a while at this poor effete Old World, and then swooping down on it.' " Indeed, to the French characters he seems as much an object of curiosity and even awe as though he were capable of doing just that. As Valentin tells him, " '[Y]ou strike me, somehow, as a man who stands at his ease, who looks at

---

* My interpretation will impinge, but only slightly, on Constance Rourke's: she is concerned, as I am, with the "fable" of the American character; but I am concerned as well with all the other fabulous aspects of James's novel. (See *American Humor*, New York, 1931, pp. 235–255.)

things from a height' "; and later, " 'You . . . have revolved to and
fro over a whole continent as I walk up and down the Boulevard' ";
and much later, simply, " 'You walk in seven-league boots.' " If
then, to the obese duchess * he is a Frenchman's version of Mike
Fink or John Henry (if not of Brigham Young), the exaggeration is
of a piece with the rest of the novel:

"*Oh, you have your légende.* . . . What is that about your having
founded a city some ten years ago in the great West, a city which
contains to-day half a million of inhabitants? . . . You are exclusive proprietor of this flourishing settlement, and you are consequently fabulously rich, and you would be richer still if you didn't
grant lands and houses free of rent to all new-comers who will
pledge themselves never to smoke cigars. At this game, in three
years, we are told, you are going to be made president of America."

This is the man whom M. Nioche early thinks of as "the goose with
the golden eggs"; and who later, realizing "the folly of his errand"
of disclosing the secret of the Bellegardes' crime to the duchess,
thinks of himself as Midas: "his ears tingled—he had come very
near being an ass"; and the story of whose life fascinates Valentin
as a "plain prose version of El Dorado."

Newman being the fabulous American, should his intended be
less than the fabulous European? "Her family, on each side, is of
fabulous antiquity," † Mrs. Tristram tells us, and her description of
it is as extravagantly conceived as the duchess's description (above)
of Newman:

"I was not of her *monde*; I am not now, either, but we sometimes
meet. They are terrible people—her *monde*; all mounted upon stilts
a mile high, and with pedigrees long in proportion. It is the skim
of the milk of the old noblesse. Do you know what a *Legitimist* is,
or an *Ultramontane*? Go into Madame de Cintré's drawing-

---

* She herself, for that matter, is seen through Newman's eyes as fabulous—as
a "reverend effigy in some idolatrous shrine," yet also as "the Fat Lady at a
fair."

† Italics here and above are mine.

room some afternoon, at five o'clock, and you will see the best-preserved specimens. I say go, but no one is admitted who can't show his fifty quarterings."

In the same vein, the duchess, congratulating Newman on winning Claire's consent, assures him that " 'she is as difficult as a princess in a fairy tale.' "

But no fairy-tale fate is in store for her. This we learn early from, appropriately enough, a scene about fairy tales that James presents when Newman comes to dinner at the Bellegardes'. He finds Claire telling Blanche a story about a beautiful Florabella and a young prince who

"carried her off to live with him in the Land of the Pink Sky. There she was so happy that she forgot all her troubles, and went out to drive every day of her life in an ivory coach drawn by five hundred white mice. Poor Florabella," she explained to Newman, "had suffered terribly. . . . but when the six months [of starvation] were over, she had a plum-cake as big as that ottoman. . . . That quite set her up again."

Is this sad little whimsicality, we wonder, introduced as a magic converse of a drab fact-to-be? Confirmation of such a suspicion comes on the next page: in response to Newman's uneasy questioning, she admits her own shortcomings and anticipates the final outcome: " 'I have very little courage; I am not a heroine,' " she tells him; " 'I could never have gone through the sufferings of the beautiful Florabella,' she added, 'not even for her prospective rewards.' "

In his analysis of the artistry of *The Bostonians*, Professor Martin theorizes that

A large part of our response to the novel is our wonder at the fact that two things as dissimilar as the novel and the "tale" should be so similar. Then again, the obvious differences between them make us realize that life is a strange, complex and paradoxical affair, because *this complexity is seen in contrast with the naively neat symmetry of the fairy tale. Here, for instance, are the closing sentences of the novel:* "But though she was glad, he presently discovered that, beneath her hood, she was in tears. It is to be feared that with the union, so far from brilliant, into which she was about to enter, these were not the last she was destined to shed." *They did not live (absolutely) happily ever after.*[29]

Similarly, in the remarks of Claire's cited above, James has foreshadowed the realistic ending of a story that Newman himself understandably thinks of as one that he has taken down from the shelf rather than that he has played an important part in. Has he played a part in a fairy tale, in truth? To a remarkable extent, he has. Just which, we get a clue to in the climactic scene of *The American*, the ball at the Bellegardes'. Here, as the marquis takes him about, James tells us of the favorable impression this outlandish foreigner makes on French society: "Everyone gave Newman extreme attention, every one smiled. . . . If the marquis was going about as a bear-leader, if the fiction of Beauty and the Beast was supposed to have found its companion-piece, the general impression appeared to be that the bear was a very fair imitation of humanity." Let us expand this fairy tale in terms of *The American*, as James is inviting us to do here. For his financially needy father of the family, the marquis, read the Bankrupted Merchant; for his loyal daughter, read Claire; and for the Beast, read Newman. On a realistic level, of course, Claire ends up not by marrying the Beast but by breaking his heart; and she does this submissively at the autocratic command of the Father, rather than acting at the brave dictate of her heart. Yet in a way, as James has indicated, the very prospect of winning Beauty has made a handsome Prince out of the mighty but uncouth Beast from across the ocean and the continent.

Thus has James again used the fairy tale as an artistic device to heighten his effect, as a magic colored light that intermittently and persistently plays over story and person alike, thereby shuttling us between pedestrian actuality and fabulous possibility. The American is not Midas, nor Sardanapalus, nor a giant with seven-league boots, nor Beast; and Claire is not a princess; but suggesting that they are, as James does, is to enrich the imaginative possibilities for his readers.*

Time and again the French wonder at Newman's charm, at the incredible success of his courting. " 'What is the witchcraft you have used?' Valentin asked." And the duchess: " 'Your success is a miracle. What is your secret?' " Newman cannot answer, of course; but whatever his miracle or witchcraft was, it was enough to move cynical French aristocracy to an act of acceptance that later, as a result of deliberations not susceptible to his magic, they would cruelly repudiate. Thirty years later, the implausibility of the motivation of this about-face bothered James enough for him to revise it practically out of existence. Yet the original white magic of Christopher Newman and of his conquest of his lady fair, he allowed to let stand, almost every word.

* By heaping up these allusions to fable, James invests his story with a wide range of fabulousness, but with no one fable sustained. He would not consciously have produced a palimpsest-like effect for the duration of a book, feeling as he did that the writer could invoke the world of the fairy-tale much more successfully in the "short and sharp and single" anecdotal form than "when we go in . . . for great lengths and breadths." (*The Novels and Tales of Henry James*, XII, Preface.)

V. THE MASTER LENDS

A. JAMES THURBER'S "FOUR PIECES"

*The filaments of individual sensibility are seldom more
sharply wrought, or more constantly manifest, than in his
work. The psychological nuance is rarely more intricately
drawn, even in those tidy sketches in which he is reducing
it to absurdity. . . .*

*[I]n all of the instances in which I felt like a Thurber
drawing, there were women around—behind me, in front
of me, and, most of all, above me. What contemporary
disquiet has he caught here? . . . [T]he women
lampooned in Thurber are alive and operating . . . , at
their worst when they are a little too much like the
preoccupied men . . . , at their best possessing a certain
virility lacking in the male. . . . The male is on the wane,
corroded with introspection, deflated by all his own
inefficient efficiency. . . .*

(P.D., "James Thurber: The Comic Prufrock," *Poetry*,
LXIII [December, 1943], 151, 154.)

From beyond the grave, in what must be the most feline and yet
complimentary thrust at an author ever entered in the ledger of literary chit-chat, Ellen Glasgow quotes James Branch Cabell as saying that " 'Mrs. Gerould's story is so much like Mr. Henry James
that it might have been written by Mrs. Wharton.' " [1] The remark
dates from some time after 1900, and indicates the extensiveness of
the practice of imitating James that Howells had begun calling
attention to as far back as 1882, when he wrote that it was James
"who is shaping and directing American fiction. . . . It is the ambition of the younger contributors to write like him; he has his following more distinctly recognizable than that of any other English-
writing novelist." [2] Accordingly, Ellen Glasgow quotes Cabell, so far
from ridiculing the James Way, actually for the purpose of illus-

trating the inevitability, at least for any beginning writer, of following That Way:

*I . . . wanted an art. . . . I needed a philosophy of fiction, I
needed a technique of working. Above all, I felt the supreme necessity of a prose style so pure and flexible that it could bend without
breaking.*

*Where could I find this by seeking? Who could direct me?
Others were imitating, or at least serving a successful apprenticeship, under Henry James. . . . No, I did not wish to be like anyone, not even like Henry James, whom I admired with fervor. . . .
Still, I read Henry James from beginning to end . . .*[3]

The names of the "others" have long been well known: Willa
Cather, Dorothy Canfield Fisher, Katherine Fullerton Gerould,
Anne Douglas Sedgwick, Edith Wharton, Constance Fenimore
Woolson, and who knows how many other granddaughters of the
Damned Mob of Scribbling Women that James's own master, Nathaniel Hawthorne, had railed against. What is perhaps not so well
known is the influence that Henry James had on certain male practitioners of the craft of writing in this country as the 1900's yielded
to the 1920's. I have in mind at present two of them. Curiously
enough, neither was primarily a novelist. The first was one of the
most widely acclaimed satirists—both literary and graphic—of this
century; the other, the obscure author of one of the century's most
successful stage plays.

: :

That the late humorist Thurber (James) knew his way through
darkest James (Henry), no one who read "The Beast in the Dingle"
in the late 1940's could doubt. But the actual extent of his familiarity with this progressively impenetrable jungle Thurber waited
until 1959 to demonstrate formally. This he did in "The Wings of
Henry James," a striking performance on several counts, and not
all of them predictable. "The Wings" is a long piece that starts out

as a study of James's *The Wings of the Dove* and, as it meanders in its inimitably mazy motion, courses through the vast James continent and reveals not only an acquaintance with James's *Wings* dating back to World War I, when he took a course in the modern novel in his University Days at Ohio State, but a bibliophilic and bibliographic—not to speak of psychoanalytic—knowledge of Henry James as impressive as that of his plots and effects.

How much else—I found myself, for all the world like one of James's own fictional devotees, wondering—had he done with James? Possibly enough to warrant a collection for the entertainment and edification of us Jamesians? I asked him in a letter in the summer of 1961 (the last of his life). He put me off with characteristic modesty, confessing that although he was grateful for my interest, he had written only "four pieces" about Henry James: "One was an early casual in *The New Yorker*, and another, probably the best known in academic circles [such as my letterhead betrayed mine to be], a pastiche called 'The Beast in the Dingle.' I don't believe that it adds up to a collectable group. . . ."

That "early casual," I supposed, a search of *New Yorker* files might turn up. Then (subtracting the obvious and recent "Wings" article that had prompted my inquiry) what was the fourth, that Thurber couldn't identify even as casually as he did that "early casual"? I was just challenged enough to try to find out, and in the intervening two years and more have done enough leg (as well as seat-of-the-pants) work to find out that although his contributions to Jamesiana *don't* add up to a collectable group, Thurber's memory was fallible: that count of "four" was far short. Exactly *how* far, I leave to what Thurber called "some strong young literary executor" to determine.* For the present I would like merely to report on a few excavations of my own. They are not the familiar, recognizable, and accessible Thurber-on-James pieces.[4] Rather, they

---

* As for me, I am no longer young or strong; moreover, like Thoreau—and *un*like James's own over-curious searchers—I believe that two years are enough for any one pursuit; and I have other, if less fascinating, literary lives to lead before retirement.

are five or six still other, fairly unfamiliar ones (not to speak of at least that many fragments, odds and ends—one or two of which I have already made use of in Chapter One, above, that Thurber did not see fit to reprint—could not, it would appear, even remember). From these alone it is possible to draw at least two conclusions: One is that Henry James figures far more prominently in James Thurber's own works than the modest disclaimer of his letter first gave me to believe; another, that James Thurber is a far more sensitive admirer of the indefinable qualities which people admire in Henry James fiction as well as a devastating satirist (that is, critic) of the qualities we regret in it, than he has yet been given credit for.

: :

The Wings of the Dove may have been the James that Thurber recalled in *his* "Wings" from that course in the modern English novel, but the truly lasting effects of Professor Joseph Russell Taylor's patient evangelizing, Thurber had disclosed parenthetically earlier in "The First Time I Saw Paris." For here we discover that it was through no less original a window than James's *Ambassadors* that young Thurber did his seeing in anticipation when, in November, 1918, he debarked at Saint-Nazaire in his first trip abroad. (The third of the late James trio, *The Golden Bowl*, was quite another story, as we shall see.) His youthful excitement revives for us in this thirty-year-old reminiscence of his approach to the fabulous city to which, Thurber possibly already knew—from James's "International Episode," if not from its original source—all good Americans ordinarily went only when they died: "The train trip down to Paris was a night to remember. . . . I lay awake a long time thinking of the only Paris I knew, the tranquil, almost somnolent city of Henry James's turn-of-the-century novels, in which there was no hint of war, past or present, except that of the sexes." [5]

This reminiscence I find noteworthy in several ways. First, considering that—as Thurber himself pointed out in his "Wings"—it was not until the 1940's that the Henry James Revival took place; that, at the time Thurber is recalling, James had been dead only two years and had died unread, unmourned, and—partly because of the state of the world in 1916—practically unnoticed; * that at this time if romantic young Americans envisioned Paris through the window of art, it was Du Maurier's Paris, or Dumas's, or Hugo's, or Puccini's or Zola's; in view of all these factors, this 1918 conversion to Henry James must be one of the earliest on record of the many following James's death.

Secondly, there is the phrase "war . . . of the sexes." I think that it would be worth the while of some other ponderer of literary relationships to determine the extent to which the massive, menacing, tyrannical females of line drawing and short story in James Thurber's long and voluminous career are inspired by The Henry James Female. "*She* is of the strenuous pattern"—could not James Thurber have described, say, Miss Ulgine Barrows of "The Catbird Seat" as exactly by the phrase that The Master had used in his Notebooks in projecting Mrs. Newsome of *The Ambassadors?* Or Kate Croy in *The Wings of the Dove?* Austin Warren has called to our notice the metaphors with which James's male characters frequently conceive such females: † Mrs. Lowder, as seen through Merton Densher's eyes in *The Golden Bowl,* is encased in armor; is a steamboat steering an imperious course; is "a projectile, of great size, loaded and ready for use." Even the barely seen Mrs. Midmore of *The Sense of the Past* and the completely unseen Mrs. Newsome of *The Ambassadors* are, Professor Warren continues, "women as

---

* Around this time, too, Heywood Broun recalled, in response to his order from Switzerland for James's *The Better Sort* (1903), "One [London] bookshop replied that Mr. James had never written a book of that title, another that it was then in the process of being published—[while in truth] it had been out some five or six years. . . ." (*The Turn of the Screw,* Modern Library [1930], Introduction.)

† Actually, even the James females are capable of looking upon other females with this trepidation. Witness the repeated metaphors of *enormousness,* of immensity, and their companion of *might* in which the morbidly fearful Adela Chart of "The Marriages" conceives Mrs. Churchley: when the maid announces " 'a lady,' " Adela, mistakenly thinking it Mrs. Churchley, asks " 'Is she big and dreadful?' "

massive as, ultimately, menacing. . . ." [6] Correspondingly, Thurber's Mr. Mittys and Mr. Martins and the "poor sensitive gentlemen" of James's "attested predilection" seem to beg for a similar identification.

Pending the appearance of the ponderer called for, I offer for his starting point a volume of Thurber's entitled, beckoningly enough—in view of his association of James's novels of the Major Phase with "war . . . of the sexes"—*The War Between Men and Women.**

I should also offer the reminder, however, that that sex-war-oriented commentary on *The Ambassadors* is as misleading as it is thought-provoking; for no matter what his later contemplations or readings of that novel may have inspired, James Thurber's first meeting with the Countess was a case of love at first sight. This he declared in various ways and over a long period of time. In the Mood Critical-Autobiographical-Historical, we find his remarks to Mark Van Doren and Lyman Bryson in the symposium "Henry James: *The Ambassadors*." Here he maintains that *The Ambassadors* "isn't tedious . . . if you are on all three or four levels of appreciation when reading it. But for that, I admit, you have to be a Henry James man. I happen to be one, and this is one of my favorite books. I have read it four times in the last thirty-five years." [7] He catches Mr. Van Doren in an error of fact (it was the scenario, not the manuscript, of *The Ambassadors* that the reader for *Harper's* rejected in 1903; and for publication as a serial in *Harper's* magazine, not as a book under the Harper imprint); and anticipating his vast knowledge of Jamesiana in the 1959 "The Wings," goes on to list various James fictions that "became popular in other people's hands," ending with the reminder that *The Ambassadors* had been done twice on television and once on radio.

* "P.D." finds enough challenging parallels (in "James Thurber: The Comic Prufrock") between Eliot's unmanly men and manly women and Thurber's to make us wonder whether we need go back as far as James for influence (if influence there is). Then we recall that Eliot praised James fulsomely, that his title "Portrait of a Lady" was taken from James. Is Thurber then James at one remove?

Next, in the Mood Militant, there is his reminder, in "Magical Lady," to the authors of the recent and wildly successful musical comedy *My Fair Lady* (from Shaw's *Pygmalion*) that in addition to Shaw's plots there are the equally defenseless ones of James, whether the lesser ones or "James's own favorite work, *The Ambassadors*":

This last is about a young American in Paris involved with a charming, but older, Countess de Vionnet. A middle-aged American named Strether comes over to break up the romance, with what could hardly be called the invaluable help of a pretty American girl from Massachusetts. Strether is won over to the side of the countess in the end. I can hear him now singing one of the piece's major themes, "If you haven't had your life, what have you had?" [8]

But more than all else, there is the Mood Mellow and Romantic. Going back to the 1951–1952 symposium, we find Thurber recollecting that Ohio State University professor Joseph Russell Taylor had said that in this same Mme. de Vionnet "Henry James has created a woman of great charm, whose activity in the novel is charm, and charm is a very hard thing to have, or to write about"; and that apropos Strether's final support of the lovers even after he learns that their relationship is carnal, Strether "has this line that Professor Taylor used to print and that I've often used in stories: 'When she touches a thing, the ugliness, God knows how, goes out of it.' * Taylor used to say that that is as fine a definition of charm in a woman as has been written." [9]

Now it is an easy step from here to an episode *not* included in "The Secret Life of James Thurber," and, if reprinted in book form not once but twice,[10] yet under the cover of a title ("A Call on Mrs. Forrester") that will throw off the scent all but the genuine "Henry James man," who will find hidden underneath: "After rereading, in my middle years, Willa Cather's 'A Lost Lady' and

---

* "As she presented things the ugliness—goodness knew why—went out of them. . . ." (*The Ambassadors*, Book Twelfth.)

Henry James's 'The Ambassadors.'" * In this charming 1948 phantasy the narrator is palpably an American Lambert Strether, as all of the blatant mockery, and Walter Mitty-like practicality are powerless to conceal from the reader. Like James's middle-aged hero at the end of *The Ambassadors*, Thurber-Strether, on a call to Marian Forester in Burlington after fifteen years, "wondered, standing there in the rain, how it would all come out." † He thinks of himself as waxing eloquent with brandy and betraying to one lost lady his secret attachment to another: "I would then confess my love for Madame de Vionnet, the lady of the lilacs, of Gloriani's bright Sunday garden, of the stately house in the Boulevard Malesherbes, with its cool parlor and dark medallions." (Yet it closes with the no-nonsense voice of admonishment of an invisible Mrs. Mitty-Newsome: "A man's a fool who walks in the rain. . . . Besides, if you miss the 6:15 . . . , you have to wait till midnight for the next train east. A man could catch his death, dozing there in that cold and lonesome station.")

But to get back. In the above charming bit of whimsy, written well along in Thurber's career, there is a distinguishably Jamesian note. But it is one that Thurber had struck long years before in his relationship with Henry James—in, as a matter of fact, the first serious venture into The Master's jungle that Thurber ever made (so far as either of us has been able to discover). This is one that appeared in the January 11, 1930, issue of *The New Yorker* as apparently merely another in a series of slight satiric sketches featuring one John Monroe. Its title, "The Middle Years," promises a link with James's story of the same name that the story itself fulfills; for Thurber's is in a random sort of way an imitation of James's.

---

* That equally early Henry James Man, Edmund Wilson, had associated *A Lost Lady* with Henry James as soon as she raised her wistful head, but only to identify the technique of the novel with James's "indirect method," the "Jamesian glass" Cather uses to show us her heroine by—namely, the various "limpid and sensitive young men" of her story. (See *The Shores of Light*, p. 42.)

† "He remembered everything, . . . falling back above all on the great interests of [his and Maria's] early time, the curiosity felt by both of them as to where he would 'come out.'" (*The Ambassadors*, Book Twelfth.)

The imitation is not greatly of the style, but of the situation in James's story, which invites it, verging as it does on the merely wishful, the possibly silly. James's central figure, the middle-aged writer Dencombe, is recovering from a serious illness. His latest book, *The Middle Years*, just out, he sees clearly as his best yet. It gives him hope of an "extension" of his lease on both life and his art (about which his illness had caused him to brood). Particularly does this hope revive when Dr. Hugh, a young Dencombe admirer met by chance at the health resort, both praises his new work and assists Dencombe's own doctor in Dencombe's treatment. But Dr. Hugh's employer-patient—a huge, demanding countess—and Miss Vernham—an intriguer for Dr. Hugh's hand and pocket (he is the countess's heir)—do battle with Dencombe for Dr. Hugh's attention. He becomes a shuttlecock—even geographically, toward the end— between his two loyalties. Eventually, Dencombe wins: the countess dies, after disinheriting Dr. Hugh, who returns to the dying Dencombe's side with the final proof of Dencombe's success (an influential review) and his repeated personal assurances of Dencombe's triumph, not in what Dencombe has wanted to do in a second lease on life but in what he has done. Dencombe dies in peace, his despair "altered and transfigured."

What Thurber has done to this story is to transpose its plot into silliness, not stopping short of the broader comic effects which the brittleness of the original invites. His central character, a 35-year old businessman named John Monroe, is submerged in the tepid and enervating (but comfortable) bath of long married years. The inspiration of his hopes of renewed virility is an unnamed married woman (her husband, like Monroe's wife, out of town at the moment) who has leaned back just a little far as he helped her on with her coat. His adversary is the laughing or mocking face of his absent wife and, eventually, his own lack of passion (or even energy). The successes he looks back to are amatory ones uncomfortably far behind now; and there were failures in that line too; even the sight, now of the name of his quarry's husband in the telephone directory seems "like a cold, black barrier." He half-heartedly invokes his past

aggressiveness, then even the spirit of Henry James: sitting down
to read *The Golden Bowl* in an attempt "to fortify himself for this
adventure," (Merton Densher, thou shouldst be living at this
hour!), he finds (like his creator) that it takes, alas, only three minutes of this—drowsed, to be sure, with the fume of an unaccus-
tomed cigar—"to make him undeniably" sleepy. Whereupon he
gives up the idea and goes to sleep.

Was this the projection of an early aversion to *The Golden Bowl*?
As late as 1959, we find Thurber remarking in "The Wings"
apropos H. G. Wells's professed familiarity with that novel: "I
doubt . . . whether he ever got through 'The Golden Bowl,' but
if he did he left me somewhere in the middle of it." Whether or no,
the links in this story with Henry James do not stop with the James
title and the introduction of a James novel into its plot. There is,
in addition, a parody within a parody: the first paragraph, presenting Monroe's uneasy awareness that this woman (a society trollope,
or flirt, at least) and this situation (an invitation to intimacy) are
repeating an experience of his of ten years ago, may easily be a
parody in itself of the beginning of James's "The Beast in the Jungle," which Thurber would single out for parody many years later.*

There is even this thrust at James's usual unwillingness to give
sex a respectable hearing: "He would begin the communion on a
mature, a 'wonderful' plane. . . . [Then] it crossed his mind that
the lady might have other patterns in mind than those of Henry
James." Finally, even verbal echoes of The Master are faintly
audible. Monroe's final, deep sigh could be any one of "poor"
Dencombe's many, and Thurber's description of Monroe's response
to the invitation to intrigue ("He merely favored her with an intense and wonderful glance . . .") sounds like something lifted

* So too Monroe's recollection of his adolescent feats of courtship seems like a
parody of Gretta Conroy's pathetic recollection of a girlhood worshipper in
Joyce's "The Dead": "Mr. Monroe recalled a cold, glittery night of a long-
gone December, when he had stood for hours under a girl's window, throw-
ing pebbles up at it until, for the sake of her reputation, she consented to go
to the Christmas dance his fraternity was giving, instead of to another fellow's. She had been reported engaged to the other fellow, too. . . . Judas it
had been cold standing under that window! It *must* have been."

entire from James's own work. And it is an amused mockery that
runs through Thurber. In the much later piece we find him writing:
"I was upon it in a moment, hastily assuming my best Henry
James garden-party manner. 'How perfectly charming of them both,
dear lady,' I wonderfully cried." [11] Again, in a quite serious manner,
in the symposium on *The Ambassadors*, when commenting on the
phrase "intensely there" from the early Wells lampoon on James,
Thurber pleads: "Well, 'intensely there' is, of course, one of the
finest two words ever written. 'Intensely there' is right, in his purposes and everything else." *

To return: what impressions do we carry away from this bagatelle? First, that it is no longer very entertaining. If, as a study in
ineffectuality and marital subjugation and boredom, trading in
buffoonery ("His heart didn't throb in his throat like a dollar
watch") and Prufrockian self-examination ("It struck him . . .
that a tall thin man looks like an ass in socks and garters"), it fore-
shadows the typical Thurber piece, yet it is still below the level of
"Walter Mitty." But in one important respect it is like "Mitty"
and not only it but James's *Ambassadors*. Mrs. Monroe *is* Mrs.
Newsome: she dominates the chief male (middle-aged) in spite of

---

* This same mixture, or alternation, of annoyance and admiration with respect
to James's style can be found very early in Thurber's *New Yorker* pieces. In
an article (one of a series entitled "Our Own Modern English Usage") on
"Which" appearing on May 4, 1929, Thurber wrote that "Not even Henry
James could have successfully emerged from a sentence with 'which,' 'whom,'
and 'being' in it." And in a much longer piece ("Isn't Life Lovely!") of June
25, 1932, an out-and-out *jeu d'esprit*, Thurber rewrites Ford Madox Ford's
Return to Yesterday as Elsie Janis would have written it. In this imitation
Thurber includes a good deal of reminiscence of Henry James (whom Ford
knew well). The only part of this nonsensical drollery to our point concerns
James's style: "Mr. James was adorably funny. He began in the middle of a
sentence and spoke both ways at once, reaching the beginning and the end
of what he was trying to say at the same time. 'He appears to be getting some
place but he is really going nowhere, with his hat and coat on backwards,'
Crane said."

And in a piece for *Punch* ("The New Vocabularianism," reprinted in *Lanterns and Lances*): "A sensitive gentleman in one of Henry James's novels
exclaims at the end, triumphantly, 'Then there we are!' not because he and
his fair companion have arrived at a solution of anything but because they
have come upon an embraceable impasse."

(because of?) her very absence; indeed, her felt laughter and mock-ery arise from the fact that she knows (and he knows that she knows) that he is tame, harmless, and incapable of intrigue or other manly arts. Finally, in view of the early inaccessibility of James's works in this country,* this sketch must have been a verbal bouquet of rare essence, even to the sophisticated *New Yorker* audience; for even now, in the flood tide of The James Revival, his "Middle Years" is a story seldom found in collections of American short stories, even of James's.

Yet, if this is little to say of a James story these days, even less can be said of the next James story that Thurber drew on for a lampoon, a *New Yorker* profile of July 30, 1932, entitled "Some-thing to Say." Certainly "The Coxon Fund," in whose light it must be seen, is so distended and flaccid a production that, to my knowledge, no one has seen fit to reprint it since its appearance in the New York and London editions of James's works.

Beginning, as James later recalled, with the idea of the brilliant talker Coleridge as Campbell's book suggested it to him, James pre-sented here one Frank Saltram in a parable of the life of the mind. Saltram is an egregious, lovable and infuriating genius-ass. He dresses outlandishly, keeps dinner waiting, comes down as a guest so late for breakfast that cook after cook has quit in protest; "drinks like a fish"; fails to keep speaking engagements that admirers have generously arranged; is indifferent to the fate of his wife and lawful children (not to speak of three bastards sired earlier); and repays his generous and long-suffering sponsors and hosts with the coin of wit and aphorism rather than the written or publicly delivered word. James ends this story suddenly and patently ironically, by having a financial windfall (the Coxon Fund) prove Saltram's actual ruin: "Its magnificence . . . quite quenched him; it was the beginning of his decline. . . . The very day he found himself able to publish he wholly ceased to produce," leaving the narrator to

---

* In "The Wings," Thurber recalls that when he managed to buy a complete set of James in 1932, it was only through a collector and from a private library at that.

reflect mournfully that "we were all happier as well as poorer before. . . ."

It is from this trying person that the central figure of Thurber's "Something to Say" originates, although in an epigraph Thurber identifies his original target as an unconsciously uproarious passage from *Memoirs of a Polyglot* by one William Gerhardi: "Hugh Kingsmill and I stimulated each other to such a pitch that after the first meeting he had a brain storm and I lay sleepless all night and in the morning was on the brink of a nervous breakdown." Thurber's brilliant talker bears the name Elliot Vereker. It happens that the surname of this cad is borrowed from an equally difficult man of letters from yet another James story (included in the same volume of the New York and London editions that contains "The Coxon Fund"), "The Figure in the Carpet." Its Hugh Vereker is an equally trying (but prolific) writer. Still other parallels with "The Figure in the Carpet" can be cited, as curious as they are individually inconsequential. One is James's Drayton Deane, a literary critic who reappears in a minor passage as Thurber's literary critic Marvin Deane. In an even less important context there are James's Miss Poyle, identified as "the vicar's sister," and Thurber's talker's penchant for using four-letter words "when he was talking to a little child or the sister of a vicar." *

But it is "The Coxon Fund" that is Thurber's main model, beyond any doubt. His Elliot Vereker is not so much a travesty of Frank Saltram as he is a consistent and logical extension of him. Now, in the original, James's narrator is generally able to maintain an objectivity toward Saltram—a moral distaste and esthetic delight simultaneously existing—that permits Saltram's boorishness and charm to vie with one another (a method of characterization that Austin Warren terms "dialectic"—that is, definition by thesis, antithesis, and synthesis). Thus, he records that the night he

---

* Could it be that Miss Poyle could not help reappearing, even if anonymously, because Thurber had remembered James's characterization of her as "a robust unmodulated person" who is capable of "thrust[ing] her chin half[way] across the cloth" of the dinner table?

first met Saltram he "came back from Wimbledon so agitated with a new sense of life that, in London, for the very thrill of it, I could only walk home . . ." (a passage, it should be noted, that matches exactly the Gerhardi one that Thurber actually cited), and later describes him as "the greatest of talkers"; yet his discriminating friend George Gravener thinks of Saltram as a mere "chatterbox" and "windbag." The narrator actually concedes that he is ashamed of Saltram; that Saltram "was like jelly *minus* its mould"; that he "doesn't seem to have much force of character"; and finally and repeatedly that Saltram has no dignity (wherefore the narrator's disbelief at hearing that Saltram is being considered for the first award from the Coxon Fund). And yet . . . If Saltram is "an absorbent," he is "no parasite"; if he is offensive personally, he yet shines to advantage beside his relentless wife; and after the narrator's feeling of shame, he has to return to Saltram, by now a presence indispensable to him. In short, for each unlovely quality, the narrator provides a compensatory one in Saltram. Yet James's very idea is subject to a double jeopardy in the working out. For not only is it not really possible to convey the effect of Saltram's presence— an ineffable combination of charm and luminousness—merely, as James tries to do, by repeating his assertion that it exists and works: it is, conversely, all too easy to convey the sense of Saltram's oafishness simply by citing instances from his personal actions. And the quality of the man that remains imprinted in the reader's awareness is, unfortunately, this very oafishness, for it is demonstrated at the story's every turn.

Now it is precisely this quality that Thurber not only restricts himself to but, appositely enough, develops by copious illustration. His Elliot Vereker is a thoroughgoing poseur. He effects outlandish traits. He has "no reverence and no solicitude," is a wantonly destructive houseguest. His literary work is all of the abortive variety ("His entire output . . . consisted of only twenty or thirty pages, most of them bearing the round stain of liquor glasses. . . ."), but "His was the true, artistic fire, the rare gesture of genius . . . ," and all of his friends feel that he is "one of the great original minds of our generation. That he had 'something to say' was obvious in everything he did."

He converses brilliantly on literary subjects whether he really knows them or not, and tries everyone's patience badly; yet "he was always stimulating." Eventually, his friends "make up a fund" to enable Vereker to go to Europe to write. To everyone's surprise, he accepts the $1500 without tantrum or tirade. Yet he gets drunk that night, spending wildly and brawling indiscriminately. Three nights later, at a party given in honor of his sailing, he gets very drunk, denounces recent novelists one and all (including Henry James) and slips out of sight. Later his murdered body is found on the roof. A sympathetic bystander murmurs, " 'The world's loss . . . is Hell's gain.' " To which Thurber adds the closing sentiment, "I think we all felt that way."

The most interesting aspect of Thurber's travesty is the way in which it develops—while it outrages—one of James's themes without actually even intruding on the other. That is, the farcical antics and outrageous diatribes of Vereker stem naturally from the outlines that James had himself provided. Where his Saltram was The Talker in the abstract, Vereker is The Talker made flesh; and if none of the numerous dicta that flow from Vereker's drunken brain are better than silly, James has intimated that a large part of what Saltram himself actually said might be construed as silly when in truth it did not simply mirror the man's innate charm itself. Indeed, for all that James's narrator himself early declares worshipfully that Saltram "yielded lessons as the sea yields fish," the sea that is "The Coxon Fund" indeed yields its fish grudgingly: during the entire course of a much-too-long story James cites only one possible instance, and even this (as related to the narrator, it is "that a man was never to suffer his relation to money to become a spiritual relation") is one that the narrator himself has to confess that he doesn't understand. No wonder, then, that although he insists that Saltram's "incomparable gift . . . dazzles me still," he adds that "It dazzles me even more in remembrance than in fact."

From this the descent to Thurber's Vereker's silliness is easy and natural.

Yet even if one contends that Vereker is simply a parody, a violation, of the James original, Thurber still must be seen as barely, if at all, concerning himself with the aspect of the Saltram story that gives James's story what little claim it has to a reader's attention. I refer to the complexity of the relationships that form and re-form among the various Saltram admirers, dependents, and sponsors, victims and champions, as a result of the talker's capricious antics. These are as implausibly complex and motivated as those that result from the original Vereker's equally mystifying conduct in James's companion piece, "The Figure in the Carpet." And this, Thurber never touches, restricting himself to the more naturally burlesqueable antics of Saltram himself. This was, inherently, the weak part of James's story, and Thurber demolished it hilariously.

: :

But seventeen years later, as though returning to business left unfinished, Thurber wrote a piece whose subtitle announces its composition as resulting from ". . . Reading Two or Three Literary Memorials, To This or That Lamented Talent, Written By One Critic or Another," and whose title is "A Final Note on Chanda Bell," [12] but whose substance is a burlesque of Henry James's "The Figure in the Carpet," for all that. There James had implausibly set in motion a group of characters who put aside all other concerns in life in order to discover the meaning underlying the clever but ostensibly superficial novels of Hugh Vereker. George Corvick does find this elusive figure in the carpet (to Vereker's own satisfaction), but he does not tell it to the narrator, nor even to his fiancée Gwendolyn—until they marry. Then he dies, and the widowed Gwendolyn refuses to tell the secret of the "figure" in Vereker's "carpet" to the again-thwarted narrator. When, years later Gwendolyn, remarried, dies, the narrator hopes to learn the figure at long last from her second husband. Alas! he finds to his dismay that Gwendolyn had never confided it to him. At the end of the story the two men are left "fellow victims of unappeased desire" to find out what the secret of Vereker's fiction was.

Never had Henry James written anything to such an airy thinness beat, had he carried to such absurd extremes the sacrifices to which a basically silly proposition would carry people, even the hypercurious. For the reader, the fatal weakness of the story is that if its Vereker has not made his underlying theme apparent even to the initiate after twenty volumes, it is not possible that the theme is an idea at all; whereas if, on the other hand, the underlying theme is not an idea but simply a device or trick,—that is, literally a *figure*,—then it is not possible for any person of normal character to concern himself about it for any great length of time. But, as becomes clear at once, James's people are not normal beings at all, none of them. The narrator himself tells us that "For the few persons, . . . abnormal or not, with whom my anecdote is concerned, literature was a game of skill, and skill meant courage, and courage meant honour, and honour meant life." To Gwendolyn the discovered trick is, she insists, just that, her life; and to divulge it, even to a member of the faithful like the narrator, is to lose her life. The narrator himself spends the years of his life pursuing, first the figure, then its blessed possessor. And so far from being sobered at the start by the possibility that the figure in question is not " 'some idea *about* life, some sort of philosophy,' " the very likelihood that it is *no idea* at all encourages him!

"Unless it be," I added with the eagerness of a thought still happier, "some kind of game you're up to with your style, something you're after in the language. Perhaps it's a preference for the letter P! Papa, potatoes, prunes—that sort of thing?" [Vereker] was suitably indulgent: he only said I hadn't got the right letter.

Thurber explodes this concatenation of absurdities with an instrument perfect for the provocation—silliness. His cryptic author is an aging woman who, like Vereker, both invites the narrator *

---

* In both James's and Thurber's stories, the narrator is someone who has written an understanding review of the author for the public press.

and teases him to guess the meaning of her fiction: " 'You have found the figure, . . .' she told me one afternoon, 'but have you found the carpet?' "

A year of my friendship with the gifted lady had passed . . . before I could be sure that I knew what she was trying not to say. . . . Her use of the triple negative, in such expressions as "not unmeaningless," and her habit of starting sentences in the middle bewildered [Vayne], and so did her fondness for surrogate words with ambiguous meanings, like the words in dreams: "rupture" for "rapture," "centaur" for "sender," "pressure" for "pleasure," and "scorpio" for "scrofula." She enjoyed frustrating him, and she made the most of his discomfiture.

Thurber's narrator is also incredibly curious, indefatigable, and worshipful. It is true that as time passes he suffers disenchantment, but this is only fitful. His suspicion that Chanda is not so much a mystery as a hoax does not keep him from such valiant efforts at deciphering her as reading one of her books backward and upside down—an undertaking that leaves him unable to tell "whether it was beauty or balderdash." After her death, he confronts her one intimate, the butler Hadley, with a demand for the meaning of her mystery (" 'What is the carpet?' I shouted"), only to be told, " 'I do not know what you mean.' " (" 'I don't know what you're talking about,' " Gwendolyn's second husband had told James's equally outraged narrator.) And whereas, unlike him, Thurber's critic lives in mortal fear that in some posthumous manuscript Chanda Bell will expose "her stuff as the merest junk" (and his own "penetrating analysis" of it, therefore, "as a monument to a fatuous gullibility"), still he ends his narration with a renewed demonstration of that gullibility (possibly, of dawning common sense?): "Meanwhile, I have hit on a new approach to the works of Chanda Bell. I am trying to read them sideways."

: :

The excessive speed with which time was, even in the 1930's, making up for its neglect of Henry James is the provocation for Thurber's "early casual," which I herewith identify as his "Recollections of Henry James" of the *New Yorker* for June 17, 1933. This begins as an expression of annoyance that "In almost every autobiography that I have picked up in the past four or five years, there has been a chapter devoted to reminiscences and impressions of Henry James." He lists those not only by such plausibles as Gertrude Atherton, W. H. Hudson, Ezra Pound, and Hugh Walpole, but others by Ambrose Bierce, Gene Tunney, and *um Gotteswillen!* "Doug and Mary Fairbanks." This kind of tomfoolery distinguishes the *jeu d'esprit* that is the greater part of Thurber's piece, in which he imagines an afternoon in the past when Henry James was telling—actually *not* telling—the plot of a current hit, "The Bat," (in the presence, not only of "all these raconteurs" *and* of Joseph Conrad and "Stevie" Crane but of Mrs. Thurber's own son Jimmy) to the counterpoint of a narrow-gauge but still hilarious negro dialect about New Orleans by a rival raconteur, one Joseph H. Choate.

I would not affront the memory of either of these story-tellers (nor Thurber's, for that matter) by attempting to paraphrase this delightfully silly performance; instead I would single out two passages that together stand for all Thurber's life-long grasp and treatment of Henry James. One, which will have a familiar ring to "Beast in the Dingle" initiates, is his marvellous ability to compose in the later James manner, to imitate his "magic use of words," as he does in having "the Old Man" drone on in this wise:

"She had been, as I have said, made, first of all, to I might almost say 'feel,' as indeed so had we all, an incapacity for that way of pleasurable residence within the halls of a house for which my companion had—oh, so rightly!—the word 'contentment,' this incapacity beautifully growing out of what I shall describe as a 'warning' which the poor dear lady had 'received,' all in a by no means restrained flutter, if I may say flutter; I rather thought that the dear

lady, to put, for its effect on me, a slightly more 'wingish' word,
flapped—"

But more impressive (since imitating such native stylists as James
and Hemingway—who, meanwhile, was busily imitating Sherwood
Anderson, who, etc.—was even then becoming literary industry big
enough to figure in the Gross National Product of America) is the
other passage. It is one in which Thurber defines the essence of a
Henry James fiction with a Jamesian expertness and felicity that no
serious critic has to this day surpassed:

> We had watched him [James] create for us, on the point of a
> needle, a gleaming and gracious hour, peopled richly with the most
> sensitive and aware characters, whose evanishment into thin air left
> us somehow with the feeling that we had become inextricably en-
> tangled forever with a group of persons who, while they had never
> for a moment existed, nevertheless left us, in their departure, with
> an emptiness that nothing ever again in this world could quite
> "make up for."

 : :

But James Thurber could write yet another form of criticism of
Henry James than the one that subtle limitations or sentimental or
ludicrous farces constitute. He was capable on occasion of formal
insights worthy of serious consideration. Evidence of this aspect of
Thurber's relationship to James is less frequent and less striking but
is in its way possibly the most impressive of all, intellectually speaking, for it reveals the true range of Thurber's mind. It appears unexpectedly in the context of a review of Eugene O'Neill's *Days Without End* that Thurber wrote for *The New Yorker* of January 20,
1934, entitled "One Man in His Time." Here Thurber relates the
technical virtuosity of the dramatist to the innovation of the earlier
novelist:

> One of my speculations has been about a certain similarity be-
> tween Mr. O'Neill's devices in the drama and Henry James's strate-

gies in his later novels. They have at least one thing in common —an "indirectness of narrative technique," as Ludwig Lewisohn has called it. Had Mr. James lived another ten years, he might conceivably have got so far away from direct narration that instead of simply telling what occurred when two persons came together, he would have presented it through the consciousness of a Worcester, Massachusetts, lawyer who got it from the proprietor of a café who had overheard two people at a table piecing together a story they had listened in on at a large and crowded party. The difference between the indirectness of James and that of O'Neill lies in the fact that whereas James got farther and farther away from his central character by filtering that central character through the perceptions of other people, O'Neill achieves his remoteness of contact by having his central character get farther and farther away from himself through splitting up into various phases of viewpoint and behavior.

But Thurber's most sustained venture into criticism of James (which also resulted from his duties as a play reviewer), to my knowledge, is also one of his most unfamiliar pieces of writing. He gave an ever-so-faint clue to his low membership number in the James Club in his review, cited earlier, only a few years ago, of the Broadway musical *My Fair Lady*. Here, in his "Magical Lady," Thurber invited its composers to make musical capital of still other unexploited, non-Shavian, turn-of-the-century fictions. For example, one of Henry James's (this at the end of a list of already exploited James plots). Actually, if not Messrs. Lerner and Loewe, at least another team of popularizer-pillagers had long before (in fact, only ten years after James's death) begun the digging into Henry James's buried treasure; and no one in New York City knew this better—or had reason to have known it longer—than James Thurber himself.

Of this fact, evidence of two sorts exists. For one, Thurber included in his above list the first of James's books to be reclaimed for popular acceptance, even rapture. For another, *not* included in it (nor among the "four pieces" of his letter to me) is Thurber's own valuable critical reaction to that act of exhumation. The occasion was the New York opening of the play by John L. Balderston,* *Berkeley Square;* almost the first of Thurber's ventures into James was his brief but knowing review of that play entitled "A Popular Hit and Its Debt to a Novelist." This is to be found in the *New York Tribune* for February 2, 1930.

Notwithstanding "the brief acknowledgement printed in the program of the play" ("The plot suggested by Henry James's posthumous fragment 'The Sense of the Past' ") practically inviting comparison of texts, we find Thurber complaining, "Not many critics of the play seem to have made this comparison—in fact, not any." As a matter of fact, he declared, "What the play actually takes from his book is many of the characters and much of its plot." And it was down on the tantalizing flesh of the plot of this play (a time-travel phantasy to be examined in detail in the next section of this chapter) that Thurber, talons eagle-sharp and sight eagle-clear, swooped.

First, a paragraph or two of acknowledgments. The play having been modeled on a ghost story of James's, Thurber went unerringly to James's own pronouncement on this genre in his preface to the *Altar of the Dead* volume:

> The peril of the unmeasured strange, in fiction, [is] the silly, just as its strength . . . is charming. . . . The ideal . . . is the straight fairy tale. . . . It may seem odd, in search of the amusing, to try to steer wide of the silly by hugging close to the 'supernatural'; but . . . 'the ghost story' . . . has ever been for me the most possible form of the fairy tale.

The Master, Thurber reminded his readers, was a story-teller, not a Thinker: "The notion seems to exist that the authors merely borrowed James's 'general idea of metaphysics'—I heard it so described one night at the play—between acts. Henry James, of course, didn't give a hang about metaphysics as such." James, he insisted, "saw no danger in being 'wrong' in any scientific sense—but only in

---

* With the "invaluable assistance of J. C. Squire."

being 'silly.' " Fortunately for the play, however, it had borrowed James's "method of dealing with 'strange encounters' and 'odd matters' "—namely, "to come at them through someone's normal relation to them," as opposed to Edgar Allan Poe's "way of dealing starkly and outright with supernatural phenomena. Poe tried to make them as horrific as possible, James as charming as possible." If Balderston's play had a "unique quality among plays of the sort," Thurber maintained, he had Henry James to thank.

In all other regards, the play was a falling off from James's original. There had been "much beautiful writing" in *that*. To be sure, there had been some bad writing in it, too ("drops in interest, long moments when the illusion threatens to crash of its own preposterous magnificence, particularly when James slows it down perilously close to a safe minimum flying speed with his intensely preoccupied refinements of gestures and dissections of emotions"). And, unlike the play, *The Sense of the Past* lacked humor. Still, Thurber maintained, the original "also lacks anything as bald as the World-War-vision scene, which comes so close to being silly." An anachronism of this sort (in which the hero, a young man of the 1920's, presents to the London people of the 1780's, of whom he has become one, a vision of the horrors of twentieth-century warfare) would, Thurber went on, have been considered simply unreasonable by the history-minded writer of the original story, who left in his notes for the novel a jotting "of the fact that the young man, there in the past, must naturally have excited surprise and suspicion because of his '*soignées teeth*.' "

Now, although Henry James had no interest in metaphysics—in ideas in the philosophical sense of that word, as Thurber (and T. S. Eliot before him) had pointed out, what he personally had at all times and what interpenetrated his entire literary production was a love of the past beyond telling. And here in just this regard was *Berkeley Square's* chief offense against the spirit of Henry James. For James to send his young man from 1910 back into 1820 was one thing; for Balderston, back 140 years or more, quite another, actu-

ally.* For, as Thurber pointed out—again going for his evidence
to a James preface, this time to the *Aspern Papers* volume—to
James the only past to be visited, whether in phantasy or reality,
was the *just vanishing* past: this alone could actually be experienced.

*I delight in a palpable imaginable visitable past—in the nearer
distances and the clearer mysteries, the . . . world we may reach
over to as by making a long arm we grasp an object at the other end
of our own table. . . . That, to my imagination, is the past fragrant
of all, or almost all, the poetry of the thing outlived and lost and
gone. . . . With more moves back the element of the appreciable
shrinks. . . . —the view is mainly a view of barriers. . . . It would
take me too far . . . to tell why the particular afternoon light that
I thus call intense rests clearer to my sense on the Byronic age . . .
than on the periods more protected by the "dignity" of history.
With the times beyond, intrinsically more "strange," the tender
grace, for the backward vision, has faded, the afternoon darkened;
for any time nearer to us the special effect hasn't begun.*

In that passage, cited at a time when, except as the author of
Daisy Miller and of that *earlier* ghost story, "The Turn of the
Screw," Henry James was largely unknown to the American public,
Thurber had singled out what is now generally taken as possibly
James's most valuable insight into his person and his art. Adding
this insight of Thurber's to the one that concludes his "Recollections of Henry James," and these, in turn, to his numerous other,
far-ranging comments, we realize that, prank-playing, mockery and
all, one of the earliest and always one of the most reliable of the
many guides to the solemn, formidable Master in this country was
James Thurber.

---

* It is true that the England that James's Clement Searle (in "The Passionate
Pilgrim," 1871) wants to be carried back to is precisely the England of Sir
Joshua Reynolds, Tobias Smollett, and Queen Caroline that Balderston sent
his young man back into; but Searle's "almost morbid appetite for any over-
scoring of time"—I quote some of his rant in the next chapter—betrays a
delusion that eventually becomes an actual derangement; whereas Ralph
Pendrel's characterization was meant to be thought of as nothing of the kind.

B. JOHN BALDERSTON AND "THE SENSE OF THE PAST"

If, as James Thurber revealed, the theatre critics of the 1929–1930 season did not know their *Sense of the Past*, this was hardly to be wondered at. One of the chief reasons why John Balderston did not dramatize it as soon as it came out in 1917 was that James's phantasy, published posthumously during the Great War, had done so little for the reputation of the man who had once described himself as "eminently unsaleable." During the early 1920's in London, "people had literally never *heard* of 'The Sense of the Past,' " the late playwright recalled to me.*

The intervening forty years—*including* those of the Revival—have done nothing to repair this particular neglect, and understandably: *The Sense of the Past*, which had so curious a posthumous celebrity, is in itself one of the most curious of all James's productions. It is a brooding bit of time travel that James laid aside back in 1900, then resumed work on a year or two before his death in 1916. Like the Hawthornes, the Jameses had come home to America just before the outbreak of civil war. The war itself—that "hurricane that is sweeping us along with it"—would render the aging Hawthorne unable to continue with a certain "work of fiction," and as he confided to Franklin Pierce in his dedication to *Our Old Home* (1863), "the Present, the Immediate, the Actual has proved too potent for me." So now half a century later the aging James, distressed by the outbreak of the Great War, found it difficult to proceed with the serious *Ivory Tower*. But even now, augment *The Sense of the Past* as he might, James did not live to complete it; and although the notes he left for its completion (printed

---

* In the pages that follow I am referring to letters written to me by the late John L. Balderston during June-August, 1948.

with the text) are as eloquent as they are copious, even Jamesians have considered it a somewhat lame or baffling work of art. T. S. Eliot, to be sure, at once admired its "genuineness," and his praise of its "deeper psychology" eventually requires him to add the disclaimer that *The Sense of the Past* is not "his best"; and a few years later Professor Phelps called it "far and away the best novel of his late years," adding that "it must be reckoned among the masterpieces of fiction"; but these reactions are far from typical. Its fragmentary form (a defect aggravated by the prolixity of the scenario for the action to have followed) has more or less disqualified it from serious criticism, of whatever bias. Even so, Yvor Winters has damned it roundly and the admiring Ezra Pound found in it evidence of weariness in James's old age.[1]

There is for that reason an irony in the fact that this was the story for which James received his first—if mere credit-line—posthumous recognition. And there are other ironies, too; for the medium of this recognition—the theatre—was one in which James himself had failed badly; and this recognition was in great part ascribable to the widespread popularity of a concept of which James must have been completely unaware (or, if aware, completely indifferent to). For the concept was no less than Professor Albert Einstein's theory of the Relativity of Time. Just how this violent yoking of opposite talents * was effected proves a memorable example of what Whitehead has called "the adventures of ideas."

: :

The Sense of the Past relates the successful attempt of Ralph Pendrel, an excessively intellectual and imaginative young American of thirty, to escape into the past, and his ensuing disenchant-

---

* Balderston himself disagreed: "I incline . . . to think," he wrote to me "that James in this plot . . . picked Einstein out of the air before there *was* an Einstein. That would be genius. He was a genius. That any other theories about other time dimensions were present in his conscious mind can scarcely be true: but I feel rather the same way about James here and what Henry Adams was playing with, but didn't *quite* bring off, in his shuttling between the twelfth and twentieth centuries in *Chartres* and the *Education*."

ment. His "natural passion for everything old," his fiancée tells us, "is as calculable as tomorrow's dawn." To him comes this windfall, the unexpected inheritance of the early-eighteenth-century Pendrel mansion, at No. 9 Mansfield Square in London, at the death of a distant English relative. The latter had been attracted to Ralph's *Essay in Aid of the Reading of History*, having "nowhere seen the love of old things, of the scrutably palpable past, nowhere felt an ear for stilled voices, as precious as they are faint, as seizable . . . as they are fine, affirm a more remarkable power than in the pages that had moved him to gratitude."

Well acquainted with those pages and with Ralph himself, his fiancée is certain that once Ralph has gone to England, he will not care to return: if even the barren native soil has wafted so rich a scent to the sensitive young man, she wonders, what hope is there that his head will ever clear once he sets foot in Europe, that fragrant field of the past? She herself stubbornly refuses to return to Europe (which she knows well from experience); but her other reason for rejecting Ralph's proposal is that the man she marries must be an adventurer—something of a modern Jason. (The irony of the plot as it will unfold is already apparent.)

It is in this connection that James plotted his story to document his favorite thesis—one that he had stated formally in print and had put to use in a lifetime of writing: that the only true "adventures" are those of the mind. For what Ralph Pendrel wants to discover is not El Dorado but the *real* buried treasure, is

the very smell of that simpler mixture of things that had so long served; . . . the very tick of the old stopped clocks . . . the hour of the day at which this and that had happened, and the temperature and the weather and the sound, and yet more the stillness, from the street, and the exact look-out, with the corresponding look-in through the window and the slant on the walls of the light of afternoons that had been. . . . Recovering the lost was at all events . . . much like entering the enemy's lines to get back one's dead for burial; and to that extent was he not, by his deepening penetration, contemporaneous and present? "Present" was a word used by him in a sense of his own, and meaning as regards most things about him markedly absent. It was for the old ghosts to take him for one of themselves.

First, of course, one must make an overture to the past, to conjure its spirit, however readily it awaits one's approach; and in his *Essay* Ralph had intimated: "There are particular places where things have happened, places enclosed and ordered and subject to the continuity of life mostly, that seem to put us into communication, and the spell is sometimes made to work by the imposition of hands, if it be patient enough, on an old subject or an old surface." It was to a pass such as this that he had been brought by his sense of the past, by his desire "to remount the stream of time,* really to bathe in its upper and more natural waters, to risk even . . . drinking of them."

Ralph's first step in his voyage up the stream of time is to embark for England and to inspect the house on Mansfield Square. He is enchanted by the wainscoting, the stone floors, and the paintings, particularly the portrait of a young Pendrel of 1820 caught in a surprisingly capricious, unconventional, almost animated pose. "As the house was his house, so the time, as it sank into him, was his time." This explains the double meaning of his remark to the American ambassador † that he is not himself; instead of "losing" he feels that he has actually *found* himself; and while on the one hand he tells the ambassador that the latter must surely think him raving mad, he asserts that " 'I strike myself as of a sanity I've never enjoyed before.' " He is about to embark on his voyage; the creature "that *had* been" is none other than the young man of the portrait, who has the sense of the future, Ralph insists, and who is at the very moment on his way from 1820 into the twentieth century. The ambassador sees his guest to the door, conscientiously accompanies

---

* Trying to recall the source of "The Beast in the Jungle," James confessed: ". . . I remount the stream of time" futilely. (*The Novels and Tales of Henry James*, XVII, Preface.)

† His only confidant, the real-life model for whom was James Russell Lowell, as no-nonsense a diplomat as James could have invented.

him to Mansfield Square, then stays long enough to watch Ralph lift the knocker and disappear into the year 1820.

He had, we know, been on his way there for almost half a century, ever since 1871, when Hubert Lawrence of *Watch and Ward* had confided to Nora his infatuation with the history-"empurpled air" of Rome, when Clement Searle of "A Passionate Pilgrim" had told the elderly English lady of Lackley Park: " 'You've some history among you all, you have some poetry, you've some accumulation of legend. I've been famished all my days for these things. Don't you understand?. . . . To see it all called up there before me, if the Devil alone could do it, I'd make a bargain with the Devil! . . .' "

Much of what happens thereafter during the six months Ralph remains (or was to have remained) proves fascinating, if difficult, reading, particularly the gradual change that comes over him after his successful intuitive initiation into the past. For the malaise responsible for Ralph's attitude toward his own age now appears petty compared with the horror he begins to feel as it dawns on him that he may not be able to return from what he had planned as a mere "excursion"—that he may have *condemned* himself to remain in the past. And with this note beginning to sound, the novel breaks off (although James's notes make plain the course the remaining action was to have taken).

Now time-travel of this sort will be recognized as a poetic device familiar even in James's day. In addition, modern scholarship has taken note of how much writers of the post-World War I era owe to philosophical or theological speculation: Proust, Eliot, and Stein, for examples, to Bergson and Bradley; Mann, to Locke and Kant; Priestley, to J. W. Dunne; Joyce, to Vico; and Aldous Huxley, to Christian and oriental mysticism. In fact, one has only to go back to Wyndham Lewis's *Time and Western Man* (1928) to marvel at the extent to which mental time-tripping pervaded the works of the above writers, not to mention others forgotten or discarded in the generation that has elapsed. Nevertheless, the license that James's own phantasy displayed in its resurrection in play form some few years after his death was neither religious, poetic, nor philosophical:

as Balderston recalled clearly, it was *scientific*, from the time he first conceived *Berkeley Square*.

"I was very much excited by the Einstein Theory which broke in the lay press in 1919," he wrote to me, "and by its verification through those eclipse expeditions. No one I knew in London seemed to talk of anything else at the time." And just what *was* it they were talking about?

Indeed, even today one's reaction to an explanation of this theory must remind one of the elderly Anatole France's to Einstein's explanation, as Edmund Wilson reports it: " 'When he told me light was matter, my head began to swim and I took my leave,' " * And in truth one cannot approach Einstein's work intelligently without an understanding of the findings of the geometricians and physicists who anticipated or made his possible. At the risk of over-simplification, nevertheless, one can sum up that part of Einstein's theories which relates to this discussion as follows: he not only rendered optional Euclid's concept of space but disproved the concept of absolute time which had been accepted by and large since the days of Newton. The "revolution" he started is dated 1905, when he published a short paper, his "Special Theory." Until then "no one had thought that there would be any ambiguity in the statement that two events in different places happened at the same time," or that the time order of events is "not always and altogether an intrinsic relation between the events themselves" but depends partly upon the observer. With the publication of this paper, as Jeans put it, "the study of the inner workings of nature passed from the engineer scientist to the mathematician."

Einstein explained his Special Theory, the "Relativity of Simultaneity," with an engaging simplicity. He supposes a train in motion, an observer on the train, and an observer on the embankment, and asks: "Are two events (e.g. . . . two strokes of lightning . . .)

---

* *Axel's Castle*, New York, 1936, p. 90. In the following pages I have relied heavily on (and quoted copiously from) Einstein's own explanations and from those of Darrow, Eddington, Frank, Manning, Barbedian, Jeans, Lodge, Nurnberg, Reichinstein, Reiser, and Russell.

which are simultaneous *with reference to the railway embankment* also simultaneous relatively to the train?" Not at all, he declares, and so demonstrates, concluding his demonstration with this summary:

Events which are simultaneous with reference to the embank-ment are not simultaneous with respect to the train, and vice versa (relativity of simultaneity). Every reference-body . . . has its own particular time; unless we are told the reference-body to which the statement of time refers, there is no meaning in a statement of the time of an event.

Now before the advent of the theory of relativity it had always tacitly been assumed in physics that the statement of time had an absolute significance, i.e., that it is independent of the state of mo-tion of the body of reference. But we have just seen that this as-sumption is incompatible with the most natural definition of simul-taneity; if we discard this assumption, then the conflict between the law of the propagation of light in vacuo and the principle of rela-tivity . . . disappears.

The implications of Einstein's first findings were extended by the publication of his General Theory in 1915, which admittedly owed much to the work of the geometrician Minkowski, whose contribu-tion was to link time and space into one dimension to be added to the conventional three of Newton's world. Thus it was that in 1908 space-time, the Fourth Dimension, came into scientific parlance.

Now just what space-time is, none of the learned explicators has been able to convey graphically, however valiant his attempt; how can the ordinary human being accustomed to dealing only with a two- or three-dimensional geometry grasp the principle of an added invisible, inconceivable fourth dimension? Russell's explana-tion insisted on the inadequacy of a three-dimensional continuum to represent the arrangement of objects in rapid motion, but how to relate this knowledge to the layman's point of view? Russell him-self admitted that the philosophical consequences of relativity "are neither so great nor so startling as is sometimes thought," and Jeans much later confessed that "the progress of science has itself shown that there can be no pictorial representation of the workings of nature of a kind which would be intelligible to our limited minds." And yet it is highly probable that had it not been for one pictorial representation in particular, Einstein and Relativity would have remained the exclusive property of physicists and mathematicians. Not that the implications of that representation were generally understood, but that it was sufficient to give immediate world-wide celebrity to a man of whom comparatively little had been heard for almost fifteen years.

In 1905 Einstein had postulated that the velocity of light *in vacuo* is constant. In his General Theory he had advanced to the assertion that *"in general, rays of light are propagated curvilinearly in gravitational fields."* Not only had he predicted that a ray of light travelling from a star to the earth past the sun would deviate slightly toward the sun because of gravitational attraction: he had even calculated the extent of the deflection. But how to test this theory? A star's light cannot be photographed under ordinary circumstances because the light of those stars in the comparative vicinity of the sun is visible by human observers only when the moon screens the sun's glare. But it happened that a solar eclipse was to occur in the vicinity of the equator on May 29, 1919. Two British expeditions which took photographs of the eclipse returned to England with indisputable evidence that Einstein's prediction had been correct, even to the amount of the deflection of light calculated. These photographs seem to have been as newsworthy as— and certainly more sensational than—the signed draft of the Treaty of Versailles which the British delegation brought back to London almost at the same time. Here was the amazing proof that stars apparently in one position when the sun is in a distant part of the sky perceptibly shift position when the sun is in their vicinity! No matter that the theory which the photographs corroborated (the curvature of space) is unimaginable: the photographs, at least, spoke for themselves. "The results of the eclipse expeditions kindled a popular as well as a scientific interest . . . unprecedented in the history of science. . . . Until the English astronomers returned to London, Einstein was almost unknown outside the domain of science—thereafter his name was on everyone's lips and he belonged to the world." Einstein's rise to fame was accordingly assured. In 1919 the *Berliner Illustrierte Zeitung* carried a picture of him on the front page; in 1921 he received the Nobel Prize for physics; and in 1922 he was introduced to a King's College audience by Lord Haldane as "the Newton of the twentieth century, a man who has called forth a greater revolution of thought than even Copernicus, Galileo, or Newton himself." Einstein's own explanation of his theories, selling at ten shillings, was soon in its tenth edition.

But what is truly remarkable to the present-day reader (at least to one who, forgetful of the overwhelming popular acceptance of such intellectual endeavors as Wells's *Outline of History* and Durant's *Story of Philosophy* during the post-War years, associates those years only with the apathy and spiritual desiccation of The Waste Land and the Lost Generation) is the extent to which so incorrigibly abstract a theory reached the Main Street level of interest. For within ten years no less than five thousand "popular" explanations of Relativity made their appearance. Dingle's two-shilling *Relativity for All* was soon in a third edition, and Sir Oliver Lodge's "very elementary exposition" at one shilling was soon in a fourth. By 1923 (along, to be sure, with their "fireless cookers, the Russian Ballet, Charlie Chaplin, *The Little Review*, the tango, Marcel Proust, Dadaism, glands, mah jong, and Coué") the people in this country were talking about Professor Einstein, Irene and Allen Cleaton remind us, "and would have become able to discourse brilliantly on Pasteur, Shaw, Monet, Aristotle, Why Rome Fell, or Relativity, if the information had not been assimilated in shockingly muddled form." [3] On Einstein's triumphant arrival in New York in 1921, when asked to explain the mass enthusiasm for his abstract theory, he jokingly suggested that "it was a problem for psychopathological investigation to determine why people . . . otherwise quite uninterested in scientific problems should suddenly become madly enthusiastic over the relativity theory." Yet he was helpless to counteract popular interest in him and the theory he had expounded. Parents began naming children after him; and at the time of his 1931 trip to the United States, advertising agencies here offered him from $50,000 to $100,000 for endorsements.*

For whatever reason, then, the words Einstein and Relativity had become shibboleths within a breathlessly short time. But how —we go back to this—did it come about that the scientific revolution begun so quietly in 1905 would within twenty years infiltrate the jargon of the ordinary man when its doctrines were actually still as incomprehensible to him as ever? When the shilling pamphlet one imagines him as buying to repair his ignorance offered him the admission of its author (a famous scientist, at that) that the Fourth Dimension defied exposition? "I cannot draw it, and I cannot tell you what it is doing, because it is an imaginary figure and it may be changing in time,"—what wonder, then, Aldous Huxley's exasperated barb in 1923: "Coleman exploded with delight. . . . 'The laws of gravity, first formulated by Newton, now re-codified by the immortal Einstein. God said, Let Newstein be and there was Light. And God said, Let there be light; and there was darkness o'er the face of the earth.' He roared with laughter." [4] No less wonder that another Byron did not arise to taunt these latter-day Coleridges with an invitation to explain their explanation!

And such explanations! For in their attempts to explain Relativity and the Fourth Dimension, the theorists employed illustrations that, although understandably having the initial effect of arousing wonder and fascination, came to be interpreted literally, and then ended with becoming bewildering. What leads to such a deduction is that the patently phantastic illustrations offered by the initiates began to be reproduced on a wide scale by pseudo-scientific writers of fiction, and even, in one way or another, to make their appearance in the province of serious literary creation.

* Including, inevitably, one for a laxative. But then—as a musical comedy of the time (Of Thee I Sing, 1932) reminds us—had no less than royalty (Marie, of Roumania) not endorsed a brand of hand soap?

It was noted above that the accounts both of Einstein and of other interpreters, presented without their mathematical and scientific apparatus, stressed these facts: (1) There is no such thing as absolute simultaneity. (2) To a body in extremely rapid motion, events happen at a different time from that at which a stationary body sees them happen. The first of these principles is one that the human intelligence can understand with little difficulty. To illustrate it, Sir Oliver Lodge used a certain new star in the constellation of Perseus. Exactly when, he asked, would you say that it first appeared? "1901"? Not at all: the year was 1603, and the twentieth-century witness who exclaimed "There is a new star now" would have been using the word *now* only in a relative sense. "You see it now. The messenger which brought the news of the new star was light, and we know of no quicker messenger. Had it been any other messenger, such as sound, we could not have heard of it yet." So far, so lucid. There is nothing here more startling than the realization that our system of measuring universal time from a terrestrial standpoint is purely arbitrary. Thus the semblance of initiation in the remark that Malcolm Cowley reports: when one of two acquaintances (who had been drinking for three days) asked what day it was, the other—a man sixty-three years old—replied deliberately: " 'Time is relative. . . . Time in the abstract doesn't exist. On Mars it may be Wednesday, on Venus Thursday, on Jupiter Friday. I live in a world beyond time, that embraces all time. On the earth, I think it is Tuesday morning.' " [5]

However, as Bertrand Russell admits, "Our definition is no longer satisfactory when we have two sets of observers in rapid motion relatively to each other"; and on the basis of his General Theory, Einstein had predicted that "the mass of a body, that is, its inertia, increases with velocity, reaching infinity at the velocity of light." Now once the non-scientific (or the pseudo-scientific) mind had been given license to imagine the possibilities inherent in this abstract equation, what breath-taking examples might it not conjure up!

Yet it remained for the scientists themselves unwittingly to furnish a basis for fictional spectacles as incredible as they were readable. "Suppose that a man would be able to fly with the velocity of light and would leave our earth to return a million years later, he would come back as young as he left," Einstein himself dazzlingly proposed; and Eddington offered the example of the youthful adventurer travelling at the speed of light to Arcturus in a trip that took hundreds of years yet returning to earth not a day older. Now these are patently suppositious premises—hypotheses which the trained scientist would recognize as footnotes designed to illustrate via exaggeration: for if the speed of light equals infinity (being so great that no fraction of it has duration worthy of measurement in terms of terrestrial speeds), then *no* human body *can* move with its speed. But the language, the images, and the analogies of these illustrations did their work; their manifold duplication and elaboration can easily be imagined. Once the supposedly possible travels cited above had been set forth, pseudo-science began to extend them from the amazing to the absurd: if by travelling at the speed of light a man would never grow older, would he not grow *younger* by travelling *faster* than that speed? Might he not thus travel both into the future and the past?!

As far back as the 1890's at least two writers with scientific backgrounds had an affirmative answer. H. G. Wells had been guilty of this fallacy in having his *Time Machine* traveller insist that inasmuch as "a civilized man . . . can go up against gravitation in a balloon, . . . why should we not hope that ultimately he may be able to stop or accelerate his drift along the Time Dimension; or even to turn about and travel the other way?" [6] To gratify that hope, Wells had enabled him to perfect a machine which carried him millions of years into the future by far exceeding the speed of light. And only a few years before, the French astronomer Flammarion had written a phantasy (*Lumen*) in which a man flew backward into history and not only witnessed the Battle of Waterloo but saw the events happen in reverse. And in a far less solemn vein:

There was a young lady named Bright
Whose speed was far faster than light;
She set out one day
In a relative way
And returned home the previous night!

Such instances are indicative of what was to happen when Relativity began to reach lower levels during the 1920's. Of course, Time travel, as noted above, had long been a device of literature, as witness the travels of Barrie, Bellamy, Irving, Morris, Newbolt, Twain, and Wells, to mention examples familiar to James's time. Of these, only Wells's, however, had pretended to be scientific; the others employed time phantasy only as a springboard for comedy or edification, or both.* But during the Twenties the theme of "scientific" escape into Time began to appear in literature as Relativity became the dominant theme in physics.

The most influential medium for the dissemination of literature of this kind was the new "scientifiction" magazine. The first, *Amazing Stories* (1926), was a medium for the republication of stories by Wells and others; and a study of this fiction includes such variations on Wells and Flammarion as Cummings's *The Man Who Mastered Time* (1924); Hunting's *The Vicarion* (1926), whose inventor is perfecting an instrument "based on the impressions events make upon the ether" which "reproduces scenes from any point in the past, present or future . . . in three dimensions, with color, sound, scent, and even heat"; † Wright's *The World Below* (1929)—all time-travel stories in most of which the serious purpose of the tra-

* It was Bernard De Voto's opinion that "Since 1889, before footlights and between covers, a good many persons have traveled back and forth in time-space who would never have made their journeys if, after a fight, the [Connecticut] Yankee had not waked to 'a far-away town sleeping in a valley by a winding river,' and casually asked, 'Bridgeport?' " (*Mark Twain's America*, p. 277.)
† And Wyndham Lewis prophesied: "A quite credible domestic scene of the future is this. Mr. Citizen and his wife are at the fireside; they release a spring and their selves of long ago fly on to a screen supplied in the Wells-like . . . Future to all suburban villas. It is a phono-film; it fills the room at once with the cheery laughter of any epoch required." (*Time and Western Man*, p. 258.)

ditional phantasy, while still apparent, is now subordinated to the "popular thriller" element.[7]

But further study of Einstein's influence on the 1920's would also have to take notice of the emergence of his theory in the work of serious writers. Here it might be merely fleeting, as in Robert Frost's "Desert Places," with its disclaimer of fear of talk about "empty spaces / Between the stars, where no space is"; or in the morning reverie James Joyce attributes to his Dublin Everyman, Leopold Bloom, in 1922: "Somewhere in the east: early morning; set off at dawn, travel round in front of the sun, steal a day's march on him. Keep it up forever never grow a day older technically." [8] Or in the "Proclamation" contained in the June, 1929, issue of *transition* reading: "Time is a tyranny to be abolished." [9] The effect intended might be amusement, as in Huxley's *Crome Yellow:* " 'Tell me, Mr. Barbecue-Smith,' " Priscilla Wimbush, who "dallies" with "New Thought and the Occult," asks, " 'you know all about science, I know. . . . This Einstein Theory. It . . . makes me so worried about my horoscopes.' " [10] And, eventually, attack, as in *Point Counter Point*, with its accusation that "By torturing their brains [scientists] can [merely] get a faint notion of the universe as it would seem if looked at through non-human eyes"; [11] or in Thomas Mann's Jesuit Leo Naphta, who denounces "the doctrine of the illimitability of time and space" as "astronomical quackery," "windbaggery," "blasphemous rubbish," and "hollow, preposterous overweening drivel." [12]

But now and then Relativity might appear merged with the traditional desire of the artist for actual escape from the confines of time. Dali's painting of limp watches, "The Persistence of Memory," bore the legend that the painter was suggesting "that the flexible watches symbolize both the relativity of time and the artist's control over reality through art by bending even time to his will." [13] Herman Hesse's *Steppenwolf*, Harry Haller, looks toward the day "when . . . we should hear King Solomon speaking, or Walter von der Vogelweide"; and by the end of the novel "had encountered Mozart and Goethe, and made sundry holes in the web of time . . . , though it held him a prisoner still." [14] The dying poet whom the twentieth-century narrator of Thornton Wilder's *The Cabala* visits near the Spanish Steps in Rome is obviously John Keats, whose fame spreads around the civilized world from the time of his death only a short while after the story opens.[15] Thomas Wolfe, whose *Of Time and the River* would include a page-long entry from his 1924 journal revealing a man fascinated and bewitched by the different explanations of Time from Zeno to Einstein,[16] has the Eugene Gant of *Look Homeward, Angel*, "ring bells" in North Carolina towns during 1916–1920 with an air of timid inquiry, saying "Is this number 26? My name is Thomas Chatterton. I am looking for a gentleman by the name of Coleridge —Mr. Samuel T. Coleridge. Does he live here? . . . No? I'm sorry. . . . Yes, 26 is the number I have, I'm sure . . . Thank you. . . . I've made a mistake. . . . I'll look it up in the telephone directory.

"But what, thought Eugene, if one day, in the million streets of life, I should really find him?" [17] But most frequently the literary medium used for escape was the drama. Of dozens of examples of this type, John Balderston's *Berkeley Square* was possibly the most successful.

We have seen that Balderston's starting point was science and that he was greatly excited by the publication of the Einstein Theory in the lay press in 1919. At the Savile, in private homes where Bertrand Russell and A. N. Whitehead spoke, and in some of the many "explanations" appearing in print he learned in metaphor and ordinary language "what Relativity was about." This was followed by several years of writing and re-writing *Berkeley Square*, which opened in the St. Martin's Theatre in October, 1926. The play ran nearly all season, during which time Balderston was writing "a very considerably different version . . . in which I tried to correct obvious technical mistakes I had made." He adds that there was "a great deal too much about Time and metaphysics in general" in this version, that he found that "the closer I got back to human relations, comedy and heartbreak, the better the whole thing became."

Unfortunately, the original "working" version of the play as presented during 1926–1927, full of the "abstractedly expository . . . 'time' angle" as it was, has not survived. Doubtless it would indicate the full extent to which its author was influenced by his intense interest in Relativity. Yet even the considerably revised text of 1928 bears the imprint of the theory, particularly in the early climactic scene which prepares the audience for the hero's flight into the past.

Up to this point, Balderston's adaptation had indeed borrowed heavily from the James original. Its Peter Standish has inherited an eighteenth-century house in London's Berkeley Square from a remote English cousin impressed by an essay Peter wrote. Standish too is a sensitive, brooding young American more attracted to the atmosphere of the Queen Anne house than to his sweetheart. He too is taken with his own resemblance to his eighteenth-century ancestor, Peter Standish, whose portrait hangs in the morning room. To him too there is an overpowering impulse to project himself back in to Time—specifically, into the time when the original Peter Standish whose grandfather built the house first arrived in England from America. Like James, Balderston has Standish's interview with the American ambassador serve as the dividing point between present and past. But whereas Pendrel has his ineffable intuition and the mutely eloquent invitation of the figure in the portrait to make his journey into Time inevitable, Standish has a knowledge of the limitless possibilities opened up to the mind by the Theory of Relativity. He harangues the Ambassador with this illustration in the first act:

"Now look here. Here's an idea. Suppose you are in a boat, sailing down a winding stream. You watch the banks as they pass you. You went by a grove of maple trees, up-stream. But you can't see them now, so you saw them in the past, didn't you? You're watching a field of clover now; it's before your eyes at this moment, in the present. But you don't know yet what's around the bend in the stream there ahead of you. There may be wonderful things, but you can't see them until you get around the bend in the future, can you? Now remember, you're in the boat. But I'm in the sky above you, in a plane. I'm looking down on it all. I can see all at once! So the past, present, and future to the man in the boat are all one to the man in the plane. Doesn't that show how all time must really be one? Real Time—real Time is nothing but an idea in the mind of God!"

In this speech Balderston's original "serious" and "foolish" attempt to explain Relativity on the stage of a theatre has obviously been softened into a vague and essentially romantic metaphor. Actually, however, during the first week or two of the play's London run Standish originally explained relativity of time for the Ambassador by using a tape measure, calling his attention to the inch marks as representing units which might be of Time, and then folding the tape measure up and driving a pen through it—an idea Balderston may have picked up from one of the eminent expositors of Relativity he had listened to. At this point, Balderston wrote to me,

There was a debate . . . on the stage of the St. Martin's . . . about the meaning of the play, in which G. K. Chesterton in a friendly way took the line that it was all nonsense, and Sir Oliver Lodge defended the main thesis as possible and indeed probably representing actual occurrences in life (or lives)—people being dead in one layer of Time and alive in another. He took issue with the play only on the very solid ground that it did not recognize the validity of sequence, as something which could not be set aside or tampered with in the spiritual or any other world of any dimension.*

In the course of his speech from the stage he improvised the River of Time image to illustrate his own belief. I saw at once that this was much better than my tape measure analogy, and asked him at once if I might give it to Standish, incorporate it in the play. He was very pleased. So was I. So while the words as they now appear are mine, the image is that of Oliver Lodge. . . .

* A weakness in Berkeley Square that was wittily exposed in a New Yorker jeu d'esprit shortly after the play opened in New York.

From here on, the play continues to borrow from and to take liberties with the novel. But it is with respect to Standish's two touchstones to the Past that *Berkeley Square* essentially parts company with *The Sense of the Past*. To give his hero's journey a kind of sanction, Balderston, as we have seen, has endowed him with a quasi-scientific authority which Standish expounds to his auditor in the Present; and to make for a plausible reception when he has reached his destination, the playwright has provided him a complete, detailed diary in which the original Peter Standish has recorded not only all the facts of his arrival at Berkeley Square in 1784 but an account of the later history of all the characters.

To the first of these improvisations, James's reaction would doubtless have been much like that of Anatole France to Einstein: bewilderment mingled with impatience. That he was not interested in ideas, his voluminous notebooks (cram-full with webs spun about ideas for incidents or people to "dramatise") would have demonstrated long before Eliot or Thurber. In fact, his only reference to the animated controversy about chronology at the turning point of the twentieth century is an irritated parenthesis in a letter to Charles Eliot Norton begun on November 24, 1899, postscript dated January 13, 1900:

This should be a prescript rather than a postscript . . . to prepare you properly for the monstrosity of my having dictated a letter to you so long ago and then kept it over unposted into the next century—if next century it be! (They are fighting like cats and dogs here as to where in our speck of time we are.) [18]

But both man and literary creation were deeply interpenetrated, if not by any recognizable categorical *idea* of Time, yet most profoundly by the *look*, the *feeling*, the *tone* of Time. If Henry James's universe was a severely limited one to modern eyes, it revolved in a curious orbit, for the Past was its circumambient. This is why T. S. Eliot, coupling him with Hawthorne, has written that they "have a kind of sense, a receptive medium, which is not of sight. Not that they fail to make you *see*, . . . but sight is not the essential sense. They perceive by antennae. . . ." It is also why Eliot would have it that in *The Sense of the Past* "James has taken Hawthorne's ghost-sense and given it substance," that in it "we may by a legitimately cognate fancy seem to detect Hawthorne coming to a mediumistic existence again. . . ." [19]

In other words, his attraction to the past would never have permitted him to write a work of mere infatuation. He would never have thought it possible for himself (or, therefore, for Ralph Pendrel) to establish true rapport with any age more remote than the "palpable imaginable *visitable* past," as we have seen Thurber insist on in his review of Balderston's play—for him, the Byronic age; for Pendrel, the Midmores of the Regency period. For that reason, as Thurber had also insisted, to move the past of James's novel back into the age of Samuel Johnson, as Balderston did, was to violate the integrity of James's esthetic principle.

And as for the second Balderston improvisation—Standish's diary—Henry James would himself have rejected it as both too little and too much: to any time-traveler inherently deficient in James's ineffable sense of the past, even such credentials would have been sadly inadequate; and to a man such as Ralph Pendrel or Henry James—a man whose most valuable sense was not that of sight, who could "perceive by antenna"—simply unnecessary.

APPENDIX A.

HAWTHORNE'S AND JAMES'S "DEEPER PSYCHOLOGY"

There is a passage in *What Maisie Knew* (1897) that is likely to linger in the memory with an insistence greater than the situation seems to warrant. I have in mind the passage referring to the child and her father in which James informs us that "while they sat together, there was an extraordinary mute passage between her vision of this vision of his, his vision of her vision, and her vision of his vision." This Laocoön-coil point of view is momentarily bewildering, but not markedly more complex than various other passages in James's fiction, all of them reminders of the addiction to "the intellectual adventure" that governed his, as well as his Gabriel Nash's, career. Parallel visions and cross-visions, in fact, abound in James. Earlier, in *The Tragic Muse* (1890), we are told that "Biddy abstained from looking round the corner of the [portrait of Miriam Rooth] as she held it; she only watched, in Peter's eyes, for this gentleman's impression of it. That she easily caught, and he measured her impression—her impression of his impression." And, of course, speaking in his own person much later about "The Pupil," he pointed out that all that he had given of the Moreen family was "little Morgan's troubled vision of them as reflected in the vision . . . of his devoted friend." He was, he confessed, "[a]ddicted to seeing 'through'—one thing through another, accordingly, and still other things through *that*. . . ." He insisted on his "love . . . of anything that makes for proportions and perspective, that contributes to a view of *all* the dimensions." [1]

Now it was this very addiction to the vision of another vision, to the view of *all* the dimensions, that had reflected itself quite early in his career in a piece of criticism about one of his earliest and most enduring of masters, Nathaniel Hawthorne; that had caused him to say that "the fine thing in Hawthorne is that he cared for the deeper psychology. . . ." [2] In turn, only two years after James's death still another critic, an admirer of the two writers, recognized this kinship between them. Citing James's admiration for Hawthorne's "deeper psychology," T. S. Eliot wrote in 1918 that "Hawthorne and James have a kind of sense . . . which is not of sight. . . . They perceive by antennae; and the 'deeper psychology' is here." After which Eliot goes on to a most perceptive definition of his term, concluding that "Hawthorne was acutely sensitive to . . . situation; he [grasped] character through the relation of two or more persons to each other; and this is what no one else, except James, has done." [3]

If Eliot's was a point about Hawthorne worth making (and, today particularly, during the high noon of James idolization, worth remembering), it was after all one that had been made in Hawthorne's own life-time, and dates back to Hawthorne's eventual appearance on the literary scene as a writer of book-length fiction. In the Duyckincks' *Cyclopaedia* (1855), for example, the Preface to *The House of the Seven Gables* is referred to as "an apology, in fact, for the preference of character to action"; and it is recorded, apropos

The Scarlet Letter, that "Few as are these main incidents, the action of the story, or its passion, is 'long, obscure, and infinite.' It is a drama in which thoughts are acts." (A generation later, James would ask in "The Art of Fiction": "What is character but the determination of incident? What is incident but the illustration of character?") E. P. Whipple, of course, had made this very point about *The Scarlet Letter* in his review: he wrote that "from the peculiar method of the story, [the principal characters] are developed more in the way of logical analysis than by events."

If we needed an example from Hawthorne to match those of his pupil, which would we cite? Let us accept for this occasion only the one Eliot invites us to consider—"the situation which Hawthorne sets up in the relation of Dimmesdale and Chillingworth." In so doing, let us fill in the outlines that James and Eliot have provided. In this extended situation one "incident" stands out prominently; one which James surely would have insisted on as "an expression of character" as much as those that he dwelled upon so lovingly in his own prefaces. I refer to the last pages of Chapter XX in *The Scarlet Letter*. Arthur has returned to his study in a state of excitement bordering on derangement from his meeting with Hester in the forest, from learning there that his close companion, house-mate, and physician for all these years is wicked and sinister, and from planning his and Hester's flight. Roger has just sought Arthur out in the study. He is solicitous, suspecting that Arthur is in a condition of exhaustion. Arthur, in turn, refuses his ministrations firmly, if courteously:

All this time, Roger Chillingworth was looking at the minister with the grave and intent regard of a physician towards his patient. But, in spite of this outward show, the latter was almost convinced of the old man's knowledge, or, at least, his confident suspicion, with respect to his own interview with Hester Prynne. The physician knew, then, that, in the minister's regard, he was no longer a trusted friend, but his bitterest enemy. So much being known, it would appear natural that a part of it should be expressed.

They do indeed "perceive by antennae." These are the antennae which Isabel Archer would perceive by, as James would later point out:

. . . Isabel, coming into the drawing-room at Gardencourt, coming in from a wet walk or whatever, that rainy afternoon, finds Madame Merle in possession of the place, Madame Merle seated, all absorbed but all serene, at the piano, and deeply recognises, in the striking of such an hour, in the presence there, among the gathering shades, of this personage, of whom a moment before she had never so much as heard, a turning-point in her life.[4]

Just like Isabel's are the deep recognitions, the antennae, of the Roger-Arthur situation. For the two men, from the mere act of "motionlessly *seeing*," have made momentous discoveries about each other. We know, of course, that at the time this interview begins, Arthur knows of Roger's treachery. But now from Arthur's look and tone, Roger perceives that Arthur knows of his treachery. And Arthur knows that Roger knows that he (Arthur) knows of his treachery, and accordingly that Roger must know that Arthur henceforward looks upon him as an enemy. Arthur's walk has then had as decisive an outcome as Isabel's. Just such a turning-point has been reached, Hawthorne's shrewd villain realizes, as he watches Arthur now and, we may be sure, searches for causes and consequences. That his victim is probably planning escape, we deduce he suspects from the *double-entendre* of his next remark to the "lost and desperate" minister; and that he acts to forestall this escape with a characteristic deviltry, we learn in the very next chapter.

If James was thus one of the founders of the new novel of psychological realism, he would appear to have owed as much to Nathaniel Hawthorne as to Alphonse Daudet. And as to Howells' doubts (in his 1882 article) whether the reader of the future would "be content to accept a novel which is an analytic study rather than a story" (and which left *him* "arbiter" of the characters' "destiny"!), history has certainly dispelled them.

APPENDIX B.

HAWTHORNE'S AND JAMES'S
"THIRD PERSON"

At about the time the nineteenth century was turning into the twentieth and certain souls in England were, to Henry James's annoyance, "fighting like cats and dogs . . . as to where in our speck of time we are," he, concerning himself—like his idol Balzac—with the realities of so momentous an occasion rather than its phantasmal aspects, was publishing a volume of short fiction containing a ghost story entitled "The Third Person." In the two-thirds of the new century that have since elapsed (whenever in truth it began) both dispute and story have long been forgotten: Einstein effectually substituted a far more fascinating dispute about Time only a few years later; and "The Third Person" incurred the double jeopardy of coming midway between James's most popular ghost story (the 1898 "Turn of the Screw") and his most important group of novels (the three of his Major Phase, 1903–1905) and of being discarded by its own author.*

This is a pity of sorts, for the story is a little gem: a bagatelle, to be sure, but flawless; and, more important than that (for James could be structurally impeccable and yet inert) thoroughly charming. Moreover, it has an added interest to us if it is read in still another light—that of its origin.

The first two persons in James's story are the Misses Susan and Amy Frush, English spinsters who inherit an ancient home in the town of Marr, on the English coast, and discover in a recess of one of its walls a small chest containing various relics from olden times including several packets of letters in an antique, "scarce decipherable" script; the third person is Cuthbert, an eighteenth century Frush ancestor stirred into ghostly existence by the discovery of the chest and its evidence that he had been hanged long ago for smuggling. The substance of this story is the failure, then the success, of the frightened yet fascinated maiden ladies to set Cuthbert's soul at peace again.

Professor Leon Edel has recreated in detail the circumstances of the writing of this tale.† James had at last left behind London, the scene of his failure as a playwright, and moved to Rye, a very old channel-coast town, like Marr in his story originally of importance in shipping but now completely withdrawn from it. Within a few months after "The Third Person" appeared he would publish an essay about the place, "Winchelsea, Rye and 'Denis Duval' "; and it would appear that "Tale and essay illuminate each other; both were derived from James's saturation with the history and aspect of Rye, and the stimulus of a re-reading of Thackeray's *Denis Duval*

---

* And ignored by almost everyone else. It has been reprinted only in the London (1923–1925) collected edition and in Leon Edel (ed.), *The Ghostly Tales of Henry James*, New Brunswick, 1948.

† *The Ghostly Tales of Henry James*, xxiii–xxiv, pp. 630–632.

James himself left not a single clue. He excluded "The Third Person" from the New York edition, which contained recollections of varying length (and reliability) about the stories included; and this story is one of only half a dozen of all James wrote that are not even mentioned in his *Notebooks* (at least, during the years he kept them regularly).

[in which the title character's grandfather is a smuggler]." Now that he had made Rye his home, James "steeped himself in its past, read old books, pored over old maps, listened to old tales and legends. . . ." What he described in a letter as his "red-roofed town, on the summit of its mildly pyramidical top" reappears in "The Third Person" as the "huddled, red-roofed, historic south-coast town," and his reference in his 1901 article to the "cunning" practices of its forefathers, to "nightly plots and snares and flurries, a hurrying, shuffling, hiding, that might at any time have put a noose about most necks," reminds us of the prominence of the only gruesome aspect of the story, Cuthbert's noose-broken neck. And Lamb House, which James now owned, had ancient roots: "There was a room in which two kings had slept; there was even a story that the house had its special ghost. Here Henry James could find rest and peace; here he could cultivate to the full his sense of the past." It is easy to imagine what fascination Lamb House held for this lifelong worshipper of the charm of ancient houses; and that, warmed by his new surroundings, nothing would have been more natural for him than to weave its threads into a fiction such as "The Third Person." Yet of all the ghost stories James had written, none before this one—nor any after it—had the droll tone of "The Third Person." Then there is the curious relationship between the three persons that it develops. These considerations lead us at least to wonder whether this story can owe some part of its rare flavor to a part of Henry James's experience in addition to the domiciliary. I am thinking of certain passages in the celebrated preface to Nathaniel Hawthorne's *The Scarlet Letter*.

: :

If James's method of dealing with "strange encounters" and "odd matters" was, James Thurber believed, "to come at them through some one's normal relation to them," to make supernatural phenomena "as charming as possible," would he not have been able to say the same about Hawthorne? Hawthorne's concern with ghosts could be deep-seated as well as professional, resulting from affinity as much as from detachment. Certainly in his *American Notebooks* there are at least two ghosts that reappear with enough insistence to cause Hawthorne some actual anxiety. Mentioned three times is "Old Bab" of the island, the pirate haunting the space between hotel and cove, dressed in a frock, wearing a dreadful countenance— a luminous ghost, silent, and with a ring around his neck. Mentioned four times and at some length is Dr. Ripley, former occupant of the Concord Manse, whom Hawthorne hears crumpling sermons in his bedroom and whose ineluctability he confesses to even in Salem: "stalking" Hawthorne through the gallery, and down the staircase, and "peeping into the parlor" of the Manse, the old Doctor seems to be "*tête-à-tête*" with him there even miles away. But particularly pertinent to us in the present context is Hawthorne's imagined reaction of this old ghost to the new appearance of his ground-floor sleeping quarters in the Manse, after Nathaniel and Sophia had converted the Manse's dismal, dusty, disarrayed, unpainted interior into "a comfortable modern residence" and had transformed the sleeping-apartment in particular "by the aid of cheerful paint and paper, a gladsome carpet, pictures and engravings, new furniture, *bijouterie*, and a daily supply of flowers," into "one of the prettiest and pleasantest rooms in the whole world." Confronting this now unrecognizably cheerful room, Hawthorne supposes, (in a passage that James would quote in his book [1]) "the ghost gave one peep into it, uttered a groan, and vanished forever." (And anyway, he tells us in an entry of some months' later date, his apprehension that the old Doctor's ghost would visit him was needless: "I rather think his former visitations have not been intended for me, and that I am not sufficiently spiritual for ghostly communication.")

Now I think that Hawthorne's relationship to his ghosts here exactly fits Thurber's description of James's. They are the more frightening as ghosts because they are domesticated; the context is characteristically casual, even social. We can believe that Hawthorne almost believes them to be real. For the above examples were not taken from the ghosts of New England history that Hawthorne invokes in his tales so objectively (to use James's words for Hawthorne's method): these ghosts were personal.

But might there be a better reason for believing in them than that they were people who had inhabited places he was visiting or even living in? Surely, it would be that they were people whose blood he had in his own veins. For this reason, the old Reverend Ripley, while convincing to Hawthorne as a ghost, is not as convincing as the ghosts of his own family as he invokes them in "The Custom House" sketch. Let us review some passages early in that sketch in which Hawthorne stands back from and looks at his native town, for in a number of ways they remind us of details and effects of James's story. This is particularly interesting in view of the fact that in James's own book on Hawthorne he had paid a good deal of attention to them, citing them verbatim at length in one place and referring to them meaningfully in another.[2]

Like the Misses Frush's Marr, Hawthorne's Salem was at one time a busy port but now is in discard. Hawthorne speaks of its once "bustling wharf" as being now "dilapidated" and "burdened with decayed wooden warehouses." In his book James paraphrased this into: "Salem is a sea-port, but . . . deserted and decayed. It belongs to that rather melancholy group of old coast-towns . . . of New England, . . . superannuated centers of the traffic with foreign lands . . ."; and later, in his story, he would describe Marr as "a little old . . . historic south-coast town which had once been in a manner mistress, as the [Frush ladies] reminded each other, of the 'Channel'. . . ." As Hawthorne's sullen, mournful adjectives proliferate, James's keep step. Salem's Custom-House is "cob-webbed," "dingy," slovenly, with "decrepit and infirm chairs," and the town itself has a dull look, "its irregularity" being "neither picturesque nor quaint, but only tame. . . ." Now Marr is certainly picturesque yet it too appears as having a "big, bleak, blank, melancholy square," and what its vicar calls "a shabby little shrunken present."

Yet with this relic of a town Hawthorne has ties of blood and affinity. The first Hathorne came here from England in the seventeenth century and "here his descendants have been born and died, and have mingled their earthy substance with the soil; until no small portion of it must necessarily be akin to the mortal frame wherewith . . . I walk the streets." Now the Misses Frush came to Marr late in life (although like them, Hawthorne has "dwelt much away from" Salem), but they too have their origin there: "They were still here in the presence . . . of their common ancestors. . . ."

Even stronger, Hawthorne confesses, is the moral bond of Puritanism. And summoning up his first ancestor and his son from the shades in a long passage that James found worth quoting in the entire, Hawthorne proceeds to a serio-comic colloquy with them. He imagines Major Hathorne and Colonel Hathorne looking at him, talking about him to each other in the presence of him,—the third person. Did they repent of their cruelties (Quaker whipping, witch hanging), he wonders, "or [are] they now groaning under the heavy consequences of them, in another state of being"? In James's story the two ladies find that they have "let in the light on old buried and sheltered things, old sorrows and shames," and when they accidentally invoke their third person by their own curiousness about the family's history, they find their ancestor in torment too.

What possible way is there to put these ghosts to rest? Both Hawthorne and James play with two opposing ones. Hawthorne's first is to acquiesce in their guilt. He solemnly volunteers to take unto himself their penalty: ". . . I, . . . as their representative, hereby take shame upon myself for their sakes, and pray that any curse incurred by them . . . may be now and henceforth removed." So does Miss Susan. In keeping with what she feels to be a family responsibility, she sends to the Chancellor of the Exchequer a sum of twenty pounds as "conscience-money." This, she tells the wondering Miss Amy, becomes what the vicar calls Cuthbert's "atonement by deputy."

" 'But' "—the shrewd Miss Amy asks her—" 'what if it isn't re-morse?' " Apparently it isn't, in Hawthorne's any more than in James's ghostly drollery. Hawthorne quickly retrieves his first pro-posal. With a wry playfulness he imagines the first and second per-sons of his triangle considering themselves actually absolved of their guilt by their discovering the overtowering guilt of their third-person descendant's occupation:

"What is he?" murmurs one gray shadow of my forefathers to the other. "A writer of story-books! What kind of a business in life . . . may that be? Why, the degenerate fellow might as well have been a fiddler!" Such are the compliments bandied between my great-grandsires and myself, across the gulf of time!

Such is the state of his affairs, then, that the two ancestors may find it "quite a sufficient retribution" for their sins. This it is, Haw-thorne suggests, that will remove the curse on them and put an end to their groans beyond the grave.

Correspondingly, in James's story we learn that, despite Miss Susan's act of atonement, the third Frush is still in torment. Whereupon, the second approach, Miss Amy's. Now Hawthorne had viewed the departure of his two ghostly ancestral conversers with the confession that, "scorn me as they will, strong traits of their nature have intertwined themselves with mine." Yet as it turns out, it is Miss Amy who succeeds in giving her and Susan's ghostly third person's soul eternal rest for this reason: because "strong traits" of Cuthbert's nature "have intertwined themselves" with hers, so to speak. It's not remorse that causes Cuthbert's ghost to walk, she tells Miss Susan: it's *bravado.* And after her success in "appeasing" him, she explains. " 'He wanted no "conscience-money" spent for him . . . ; it was quite the other way about—he wanted some bold deed done, of the old wild kind; he wanted some big risk taken. And I took it.' " The risk? An act of smuggling of her own (this time, successful). For, as Amy insists, " 'It was the *spirit* of the deed that told.' " In matching, rather than counteracting, the family's ancient transgressions in this way, James parts company with Hawthorne.*

As he does, to be sure, in one important aspect of the situation with regard to their ghost that he places the Misses Frush in. For even if we concede that it was Hawthorne's preliminary brush stroke or two that James has here expanded into a full-length portrait, still the individuality of his achievement is a complexity of relationships within "The Third Person" not attempted in the Custom House sketch. His two Misses Frush are as finely characterized as the two Hathornes are vague. When these two spinsters first meet, in the act of taking possession, they react distantly to each other. Then they manifest actual old-maidish jealousy about the hanged man: although his neck is horribly broken, still he's young and otherwise handsome, and each woman alternates between feelings of horror and jealousy at the particular direction—and bedroom "intimacy"!—of his nightly wanderings. And the close of the story finds the two ladies where they were before the one, ghostly romance of their lives began—with the widely traveled Miss Susan thinking of the actual details of the stay-at-home Miss Amy's successful act of smuggling and musing "a little ruefully as they went—'you got at last your week in Paris!'"

For Hawthorne, to mix romance with personal ghosts would have been unheard of. But in the light, amused touch of his story, James does not depart very noticeably from Hawthorne's passages. For both, these ghostly fictions were a strikingly rare occurrence. Professor Edel speaks of "the mellow *Third Person*" as "Henry

---

* Unless (a) (as is strongly suggested), it was simply a forbidden book (a Tauchnitz edition) that Miss Amy smuggled in and (as is nowhere suggested) Cuthbert disappeared, like the two ancient Hathornes, out of sheer mortification; or

(b) the very act of their descendant's writing the ultra-Puritanic pages that follow the Custom House sketch may be imagined as striking the two ancient Hathornes as—in James's words—"a chip of the old block." As James himself declared: "To him as to them, the consciousness of *sin* was the most important fact of life, and if they had undertaken to write little tales, this baleful substantive, with its attendant adjective, could hardly have been more frequent in their pages than in those of their fanciful descendant." But this too seems like critical procrusteanism.

James's one venture into ghostly gaiety," as "the lightest," "the sunniest of James's ghostly tales"; and where was what James called Hawthorne's "duskily-sportive imagination" more memorably displayed than in these and other pages from this most sportive piece of prose ever written by our moping writer of melancholy romances? Worried about the possible effect on his readers of his main, "hell-fired" narrative, he would counteract its balefulness with a prefatory piece of contemporary satire and ghostly jollity wholly untypical of the author of the *Tales* and the *Mosses*. For once, at least—as Henry James may have recalled—he had piped a tune fit to dance to.

NOTES

CHAPTER I

1 *Henry James and the Jacobites*, Boston and New York, 1963.
2 W. H. Auden, "At the Grave of Henry James," 1943. Reprinted in F. W. Dupee (ed.) *The Question of Henry James*, New York, 1945.
3 *Nation*, I (November 16, 1865), 625–626.
4 Edith Wharton, *A Backward Glance*, New York, 1934, pp. 323–325.
5 "Honoré de Balzac," *The Galaxy*, XX (December, 1875). Reprinted in *French Poets and Novelists*, London, 1878.
6 Theodora Bosanquet, *Henry James at Work*, London, 1927, p. 27.
7 *Return to Yesterday*, New York, 1932, p. 209.
8 Various, *The Whole Family*, New York, 1908, p. 155.
9 *Henry James: The Major Phase*, New York, 1944, p. 90.
10 *Maule's Curse*, Norfolk (Conn.), 1938, p. 186.
11 *Days of the Phoenix*, p. 50.
12 Joseph Warren Beach, *The Method of Henry James*, New Haven, 1918, p. 149.
13 "The Aesthetic Idealism of Henry James," *On Contemporary Literature*, New York, 1917, p. 229.
14 *A Little Tour in France*, Boston, 1884, p. 238.
15 *Italian Hours*, London, 1909, p. 44.
16 *Ibid.*, pp. 136–137.
17 *Nation*, VI (February 6, 1868), 114.
18 Various, *In After Days*, New York, 1910, pp. 199–233.
19 *Henry James at Work*, p. 27.
20 *North American Review*, CII (April, 1866), 599–606. Reprinted in Pierre de Chaignon La Rose (ed.), *Notes and Reviews*, Cambridge (Mass.), 1921, Preface; pp. 173–187.
21 *French Poets and Novelists*, pp. 80–81.
22 *Henry James: The Major Phase*, p. 143.
23 *Italian Hours*, p. 92.
24 *The Thought and Character of William James*, Boston, 1934; II, p. 429.
25 Percy Lubbock (ed.), *The Letters of Henry James*, New York, 1920; II, p. 21.
26 Simon Nowell-Smith (ed.), *The Legend of the Master*, New York, 1948, pp. 35–36.
27 Logan Pearsall Smith, "Notes on Henry James," *Atlantic Monthly*, CLXII (August, 1943), 76.
28 *French Poets and Novelists*, p. 82.
29 *Letters of Henry James*, I, pp. 310–311.
30 *North American Review*, CI (July, 1865), 276–281. Reprinted in *Notes and Reviews*; *Hawthorne*, Ch. II; *The Odd Number: Thirteen Tales by Guy de Maupassant*, New York, 1889, Introduction, xv.
31 *Atlantic Monthly*, XXVIII (August, 1871), 248–251.
32 *Nation*, XX (June 3, 1875), 381.
33 *The Novels and Tales of Henry James*, New York, 1907–1909, XV, Preface.
34 *The Parisian* (Paris), No. 48 (February 26, 1880), 9. Reprinted in Leon Edel (ed.), *The Future of the Novel*, New York, 1956.

35 *Notes and Reviews*, p. 58.

36 *Nation*, XXIII (July 27, 1876), 61.

37 "Culture and Progress," *Scribner's Monthly Illustrated Magazine*, XXI (March, 1881), 796.

38 *On Contemporary Literature*, pp. 249, 232.

39 *The Spirit of American Literature*, New York, 1913, p. 338.

40 From a letter. Reprinted in *The Question of Henry James*.

41 *On Contemporary Literature*, p. 240.

42 "The Ambiguity of Henry James," *Hound and Horn*, VII (April-June, 1934). Reprinted in *The Triple Thinkers*, New York, 1948, and *The Shores of Light*, New York, 1952.

43 *On Contemporary Literature*, pp. 234-235.

44 "A Sentimental Contribution," *Hound and Horn*, VII (April-June, 1934), 523-525.

45 *On Contemporary Literature*, p. 235.

46 "A Prize for Ezra Pound," *Partisan Review*, XVI (April, 1949). Reprinted in William Van O'Connor and Edward Stone (eds.), *A Casebook on Ezra Pound*, New York, 1959, pp. 49-53.

47 Various, "The Question of the Pound Award," *Partisan Review*, XVI (May, 1949). Reprinted in *A Casebook on Ezra Pound*, pp. 54-66.

48 *Letters of Henry James*, II, pp. 488-489.

49 *On Contemporary Literature*, p. 246.

50 Anna R. Burr, *Weir Mitchell: His Life and Letters*, New York, 1930, pp. 322-324. (Letter of 1905 to Mitchell.) I am indebted for this interpretation to Dr. Saul Rosenzweig.

51 "The Pilgrimage of Henry James," *The New Republic*, XLII (May 6, 1925). Reprinted in *The Shores of Light*.

52 *The Great Tradition* [1948], New York, 1954, pp. 16, 21.

53 *Image and Idea*, New York, 1957, pp. x, 83.

54 *American Literature and Christian Doctrine*, Baton Rouge, 1958, pp. 15, 106.

55 "The Technique of Fiction," *Collected Essays*, Denver, 1959, pp. 136-137.

56 "Myth and Dialectic in the Later Novels," *Kenyon Review*, V (Summer, 1943), 568. Reprinted (in revised form) in *Rage For Order*, Ann Arbor, 1948.

57 C. Hartley Grattan, *The Three Jameses*, New York, 1932, p. 365.

58 *Maule's Curse*, p. 214.

59 *The Short Stories of Henry James*, New York, 1945, pp. 598, 599.

60 "Three Commentaries: Poe, James, and Joyce," *The Sewanee Review*, LVIII (Winter, 1950), 5.

61 "A Note on 'The Beast in the Jungle,' " *The University of Kansas City Review*, XVII (Winter, 1950), 117.

62 "The Beast in Henry James," *The American Imago*, XIII (Winter, 1956), 437. Also, see Mary Ellen Herx, "The Monomyth in 'The Great Good Place,' " *College English*, XXIV (March, 1963), 439-443.

63 Mary L. Aswell (ed.), *The World Within*, New York, 1947, p. 105.

64 *Henry James: The Major Phase*, p. 73.

65 Ilse Dusoir Lind, "The Inadequate Vulgarity of Henry James," *PMLA*, LXVI (December, 1951), 886-910.

66 Leon Edel (ed.), *The Complete Tales of Henry James*, I (1864-1868), Philadelphia and New York, 1962, Introduction, p. 11.

67 "Culture and Progress," *Scribner's Monthly Illustrated Magazine*, XXI (March, 1881), 796.

68 "Myth and Dialectic in the Later Novels," 567–568.

69 See the long bibliography of memoirs appended to Simon Nowell-Smith, *The Legend of the Master.*

70 "A Brief Note," *The Little Review*, August, 1918. Reprinted in *The Literary Essays of Ezra Pound* and in Leon Edel (ed.), *Henry James: A Collection of Critical Essays*, New York, 1963.

71 Thomas Beer, *Stephen Crane*, New York, 1923, p. 170.

72 *Howells, James, etc.*, New York, 1924, p. 138.

73 *The Woman Within*, New York, 1954, pp. 206–207.

74 H. M. Fielding, "Henry James, the Lion," *The Reader Magazine*, V (February, 1905), 366.

75 Austin Warren, "Myth and Dialectic in the Later Novels," 566.

76 Logan Pearsall Smith, *Unforgotten Years*, Boston, 1939, p. 220.

77 "The Interview," *The New Yorker*, XXVI (February 25, 1950). Reprinted in *Thurber Country*, New York, 1953.

78 H. M. Fielding, "Henry James, the Lion," 365.

79 Owen Seaman, *Borrowed Plumes*, London, 1906. All the imitations had appeared in *Punch.*

80 Fred L. Pattee, *The New American Literature*, New York, 1930, pp. 409–410. See Van Wyck Brooks, *New England: Indian Summer*, New York, 1940, *passim*, e.g., pp. 140–148; also Howard Mumford Jones, *The Theory of American Literature*, Ithaca, 1948, p. 127.

81 *Days of the Phoenix*, pp. 81, 159, 180–181.

82 *America's Coming-Of-Age*, New York, 1915, p. 15.

83 *The Pilgrimage of Henry James*, New York, 1925, pp. 141, 138.

84 Norman Foerster (ed.), *The Reinterpretation of American Literature*, New York, 1928, p. 144.

85 *The Beginnings of Critical Realism in America*, New York, 1930, pp. 240–241.

86 *The Spirit of American Literature*, p. 325.

87 "The Ambiguity of Henry James," 400–401.

88 *America's Coming-of-Age*, pp. 4–5.

89 Stuart P. Sherman in the *New York Evening Post* ("Literary Review") of December 31, 1921. Quoted by Fred L. Pattee, *The New American Literature*, pp. 400–401.

90 *Image and Idea*, p. 2.

91 *The American Mercury*, I (January, 1924), 52.

92 "A Sentimental Contribution," 523.

93 Leslie A. Fiedler, *Love and Death in the American Novel*, Cleveland and New York, 1962, p. 338.

94 *William Faulkner: Early Prose and Poetry*, Boston, 1962.

95 *The Portable Twain*, New York, 1946, p. 775.

96 Thomas Beer, *Stephen Crane*, pp. 168, 124.

97 "The Historical Interpretation of Literature" (1940), *The Triple Thinkers*, London, 1952, pp. 243–254.

98 *The Letters of Henry James*, II, pp. 487–488. His letter was written in 1915.

99 *Ibid.*

[100] "Wilder: Prophet of the Genteel Christ," *New Republic*, LXIV (October 22, 1930), 267. Quoted in Daniel Aaron, *Writers on the Left*, New York, 1961.

[101] *The Great Tradition*, New York, 1933, pp. 305–306, 105; *The Foreground of American Fiction*, New York, 1934, vii, pp. 341–368.

[102] *Expression in America*, New York, 1932, pp. 255, 266.

[103] "The Literary Class War," *New Republic*, LXVI (May 4, 1932). Reprinted in *The Shores of Light*.

[104] Percy H. Boynton, *America in Contemporary Fiction*, Chicago, 1940, p. 32.

[105] *Literary Blasphemies*, pp. 213, 225.

[106] *Writers in Crisis*, Boston, 1942, Preface, pp. 276, 288–289.

[107] *Henry James and the Jacobites*, p. 5.

[108] *Ibid.*, p. 12.

[109] *Ibid.*, p. 9.

[110] "The Letters of Madame Sabran," *The Galaxy*, XX (October, 1875). See *French Poets and Novelists*, pp. 291–292.

[111] "The King of Poland and Madame Geoffrin," *The Galaxy*, XXI (April, 1876), 549.

[112] *Henry James and the Jacobites*, p. 9.

[113] "Henry James and the Almighty Dollar," *Hound and Horn*, VII (April-June, 1934), 439.

[114] "The Ambiguity of Henry James," 390–393.

[115] *Henry James and the Jacobites*, p. 9.

[116] *Ibid.*, pp. 9–10.

[117] Quoted in *Writers on the Left*, p. 47.

[118] *Ibid.*, p. 26.

[119] *Ibid.*, pp. 180–181.

[120] *Ibid.*, pp. 331, 438.

[121] "The Ambiguity of Henry James," 404–406.

[122] "Henry James and the Almighty Dollar," 442–443.

[123] *Henry James and the Jacobites*, p. 3.

[124] *Image and Idea*, ix.

[125] *Writers on the Left*, pp. 297–299.

[126] *Henry James: The Major Phase*, xvi.

[127] *Writers on the Left*, p. 236.

[128] *The Theory of American Literature*, p. 52.

CHAPTER II

[1] B. R. McElderry, Jr., "Henry James's Revision of *Watch and Ward*," *Modern Language Notes*, LXVII (November, 1952), 457–461.

[2] "The Ambiguity of Henry James," 394.

[3] Oscar Cargill, *The Novels of Henry James*, New York, 1961, p. 26.

[4] *Nation*, XXVII (December 19, 1878), 387.

[5] *Notes on Life and Letters*, p. 18.

[6] *Literary Friends and Acquaintance*, New York, 1901, p. 3.

7 R. S. Mackenzie (ed.), *Noctes Ambrosianae*, New York, [1854], 1863, I, xvi.

8 *The Luck of Roaring Camp and Other Tales*, Boston, 1902; General Introduction, xii.

9 Algernon Tassin, *The Magazine in America*, New York, 1916, p. 241.

10 *The Orpheus C. Kerr Papers*, New York, 1862, pp. 63–73.

11 "The Literary Record," *Harper's New Monthly Magazine*, LIX (July, 1879), 309.

12 *North American Review*, CXIV (April, 1872), 444–445. Reprinted in Cady and Frazier (eds.), *The War of the Critics over William Dean Howells*, Evanston, 1962.

13 Leon Edel (ed.), *The Complete Tales of Henry James*; I, Introduction, p. 20.

14 *Ibid.*, p. 12.

15 "The Hawthorne Aspect," *The Little Review* (August, 1918). Reprinted in Edmund Wilson (ed.), *The Shock of Recognition*, and F. W. Dupee (ed.), *The Question of Henry James*.

16 "Travelling Companions," *Atlantic Monthly*, XXVI (November-December, 1870). Reprinted in Leon Edel (ed.), *The Complete Tales of Henry James*, Philadelphia and New York, 1962, II.

17 "A Roman Holiday," *Atlantic Monthly*, XXXII (July, 1873). Reprinted in *Transatlantic Sketches* (1875).

CHAPTER III

1 Van Wyck Brooks, *The Pilgrimage of Henry James*, p. 21.

2 "The Princess Far Away," *The Saturday Review of Literature*, I (April 25, 1925), 701–702, 707.

3 *Scrutiny*, XVII (Summer, 1950); reprinted in *The Complex Fate*, London, 1952.

4 Leon Edel, *Henry James: The Conquest of London*, New York, 1962, p. 368.

5 *Atlantic Monthly*, XL (November, 1877), 634.

6 *Nation*, XX (June 3, 1875), 381; XV (September 19, 1872), 183.

7 Leon Edel, *Henry James: The Conquest of London*, pp. 218–220.

8 "A Note on the Genesis of *Daisy Miller*," *Philological Quarterly*, XVII (April, 1948), 184–186.

9 *North American Review*, CXVII (October, 1873), 462.

10 "A Note on the Genesis of *Daisy Miller*," 184.

11 *Nation*, XX (June 3, 1875), 381.

12 "Mr. James's Masterpiece," *Harper's Bazaar*, XXVI (January, 1902). Reprinted in Albert Mordell (ed.), *Discovery of a Genius*, New York, 1961.

13 *Anonymous*, Nation, XXVII (December 19, 1878), 387.

14 *The Novels of Henry James*, pp. 182–202.

15 *Nation*, XXVII (December 19, 1878), 387–388.

16 *Ibid.*, 388.

17 Henry James, *The Tragic Muse*, New York, 1960, Harper Torchbooks, Introduction, xiv.

18 "Editor's Study," *Harper's*, LXXXI (September, 1890), 640.

CHAPTER IV (A)

[1] *On Contemporary Literature*, p. 255.
[2] *Hawthorne*, Ch. I.
[3] *The Novels and Tales of Henry James*, Prefaces to Vols. IX, XV, and IV.
[4] "The Architecture of Henry James's 'New York Edition,'" *New England Quarterly*, XXIV (June, 1951), 177.
[5] *Thackeray the Novelist*, Cambridge, 1954, pp. 299–300.
[6] Oscar Cargill, "*The Ambassadors*: A New View," *PMLA*, LXXV (September, 1960), 439–452.
[7] Matthiessen and Murdock (eds.), *The Notebooks of Henry James*, New York, 1947, pp. 406–407.
[8] *The Novels and Tales of Henry James*, XVIII, Preface.
[9] *Atlantic Monthly*, XXXVII (March, 1876), 279; XXIX (January, 1872), 113.
[10] *Henry James at Work*, pp. 13–14.
[11] Ch. V.
[12] *The Three Jameses*, New York, 1932, p. 365.
[13] *New England Quarterly*, XXIV (September, 1951), 292.
[14] *The Novels and Tales of Henry James*, XXI, Preface.
[15] *The Past Recaptured*, concluding paragraph.
[16] *Swann's Way*, "Overture."

CHAPTER IV (B)

[1] *The Novels and Tales of Henry James*, XVII, Preface.
[2] Theodora Bosanquet, *Henry James at Work*, p. 24.
[3] *The Crooked Corridor*, New York, 1949, p. 161.
[4] *Henry James and the Jacobites*, pp. 4, 8.
[5] *The Princess Casamassima*, New York, 1948; I, xiii.
[6] R. W. B. Lewis, *The American Adam*, Chicago, 1955, p. 153.
[7] *English Studies in Africa*, II (1959), 98–109.
[8] *Nation*, XXI (October 14, 1875), 251.
[9] *A Little Tour in France*, Boston [1884], 1900, pp. 56, 206.
[10] *The Princess Casamassima*, New York, 1948; I, xiii.
[11] "Theophile Gautier," *North American Review*, CXIX (October, 1874), 421.
[12] "Myth and Dialectic in the Later Novels," 554 ff.
[13] "Émile Zola," *Atlantic Monthly*, XCII (August, 1903). Reprinted in *Notes on Novelists* and Leon Edel (ed.), *Henry James: The Future of the Novel*, New York, 1956.
[14] "To the United States" (1827).
[15] See Harry Levin, *The Power of Blackness*, New York, 1958, pp. 240–248.
[16] *The American Renaissance*, New York, 1941, pp. 13–14.
[17] An important recent study of this aspect of American fiction in certain selected writers is Daniel G. Hoffman, *Form and Fable in American Fiction*, New York, 1961.

[18] *Notes on Life and Letters*, p. 13.

[19] *The American Adam*, p. 1.

[20] *Our Young Folks*, January, 1865, pp. 10–11.

[21] *The Luck of Roaring Camp*, Boston, 1870, Preface.

[22] "The Use of the Fairy-Tale: A Note on the Structure of *The Bostonians*," 108–109.

[23] Ferner Nuhn, *The Wind Blew From the East*, New York, 1942, p. 139.

[24] *Henry James: The Major Phase*, p. 93.

[25] *The Novels and Tales of Henry James*, XII, Preface.

[26] *Henry James: The Major Phase*, pp. 59–60.

[27] *The Portrait of a Lady*, Boston, 1956, Riverside Edition, ix.

[28] *A History of American Literature Since 1870*, New York, 1915, p. 193.

[29] "The Use of the Fairy-Tale," 109.

CHAPTER V (A)

[1] Ellen Glasgow, *The Woman Within*, p. 124.

[2] "Henry James, Jr.," *The Century Magazine*, XXV (November, 1882). Reprinted in Albert Mordell (ed.), *Discovery of a Genius*.

[3] *The Woman Within*, pp. 123–124.

[4] "The Beast in the Dingle" is reprinted in *The Beast in Me and Other Animals*, New York, 1948; "The Wings of Henry James," in *Lanterns and Lances*, New York, 1961.

[5] "The First Time I Saw Paris," *Holiday*, XXI (April, 1957). Reprinted in *Alarms and Diversions*, New York, 1957.

[6] "Myth and Dialectic in the Later Novels," 560.

[7] *Invitation to Learning*, I (Winter, 1952), 365–366.

[8] "Magical Lady," *New York Times*, Aug. 12, 1956. Reprinted in *Lanterns and Lances*.

[9] *Invitation to Learning*, I, 367.

[10] In *The Beast in Me and Other Animals*, and *Alarms and Diversions*.

[11] "Party of One: Such a Phrase as Drifts Through Dreams," *Holiday*, XXVIII (Dec., 1960). Reprinted in *Lanterns and Lances*.

[12] *The New Yorker*, XXV (October 15, 1949). Reprinted in *Thurber Country*, New York, 1953.

CHAPTER V (B)

[1] "The Hawthorne Aspect"; *Howells, James, etc.*, pp. 145–146; *Maule's Curse*, p. 193; *Instigations*, New York, 1920, p. 159.

[3] *Books and Battles: American Literature, 1920–1930*, Boston and New York, 1937, pp. 147–149.

[4] *Antic Hay*, New York, The Modern Library, p. 90.

5 *Exile's Return*, New York, 1934, p. 209.
6 *The Time Machine*, New York, 1895, p. 13.
7 J. O. Bailey, *Pilgrims Through Space and Time*, New York, 1947.
8 *Ulysses*, New York, The Modern Library, p. 57.
9 *Exile's Return*, pp. 275–276.
10 *In Retrospect: An Omnibus of Aldous Huxley's Books*, New York, 1933, p. 96.
11 *Point Counter Point*, New York, n.d., p. 153.
12 *The Magic Mountain* [1924], New York, 1930; II, pp. 869–870.
13 *Art in Our Time*, New York, Museum of Modern Art, 1939, Plate 189.
14 *Steppenwolf*, New York, 1929, pp. 108, 144–145.
15 "First Encounters," *The Cabala*, New York, 1926.
16 *Of Time and the River*, New York, 1935, pp. 670–671.
17 *Look Homeward, Angel*, New York, The Modern Library, pp. 597–598.
18 *Letters of Henry James*, I, pp. 337, 343.
19 "The Hawthorne Aspect."

APPENDIX A

1 *The Novels and Tales of Henry James*, XI, Preface.
2 *Hawthorne*, Ch. III.
3 "The Hawthorne Aspect."
4 *The Novels and Tales of Henry James*, III, Preface.

APPENDIX B

1 *Hawthorne*, Ch. IV.
2 *Ibid.*, Chs. I, III.

INDEX